On Murder 2

On Murder 2

True Crime Writing in Australia

Edited by Kerry Greenwood

Black Inc.

Published by Black Inc.
An imprint of Schwartz Publishing
Level 5, 289 Flinders Lane
Melbourne Victoria 3000
Australia
email: enquiries@blackincbooks.com

National Library of Australia Cataloguing-in-Publication entry

On Murder 2: True Crime Writing in Australia

ISBN 1 86395 378 7

1. Crime - Australia - Case studies. 2. Murder - Australia - Fiction. 3. Crime - Australia - History. I. Greenwood, Kerry.

364.994

Kerry Greenwood is a Melbourne-based legal aid solicitor who has written more than twenty books, ranging from crime and mystery novels through to historical fiction, young adult novels and two books of non-fiction. Her twelfth Phryne Fisher book, *Murder in Montparnasse*, will be published in 2002.

Table of contents

Introduction Kerry Greenwood 1

No Ordinary Neighbourhood Craig Sherborne 3

'Two and Two Don't Make Four with That Bloke' John R. Carroll 13

'He Wasn't Afraid of Death' Richard Hall 27

The Windsor Murder Rachael Weaver 33

Murder Ballads Nick Cave 43

The Glass Coffin Richard Evans 53

Pure Evil Andrew Rule & John Silvester 73

Serial Killers Are Losers Vikki Petraitis & Terrence Gardiner 85

One Kind of Bad Lindy Cameron 99

The Policeman's Wife Shirley Hardy-Rix 117

The Trial of Annette Myers Martin Wiener 125

Jean Lee Kerry Greenwood & Ashley Halpern 133

Another's Shoes Richard Bourke 141

Hit and Run Shelley Robertson 151

Room for Disquiet Mark Whittaker 159

'Go Hang Yourself' Tom Austen 173

Keitho and Davo Steve Dow 189

Lady's Day Andrew Rule & John Silvester 197

Jockey Smith's Last Stand Peter Haddow 209

The Triggerman Pippa Kay 227

Atonement Lucy Sussex 247

Notes on contributors 267

Publication details 271

Introduction

Kerry Greenwood

TRUE CRIME BOOKS are a great underground success, because no respectable person will admit to reading them (but someone out there is buying them). As with pornography, another underground success, this has led, in some cases, to shoddy production, sloppy editing, sensationalised writing and covers with bloodstained knives on them, because if no one will admit to reading the books, who cares about how they are produced?

We care. This book is a collection of essays which would stand with any comparable writing in the literary field. This is not death-porn but a genuine attempt to analyse and sympathise with the victims of serious crime, not murder alone. We were aiming for fresh, interesting, compassionate writing with something new to say, and we have found it. Inside this book you will find new light shed on historical crimes and analyses from the professionals in the field who ordinarily have no voice in True Crime: a barrister, a forensic pathologist, social historians and a policeman's wife. Plus a few crime writers and a duty solicitor or three.

And for people who read introductions, here is a new theory on why we are so fascinated with murder. We can ask a soldier about war, we can ask a rock climber how it feels to fall off a cliff, we can ask a battered wife how it feels to be beaten up every day. But we can't ask a murder victim how it feels to be murdered. Murder remains a puzzle which always has the most important piece missing.

No Ordinary Neighbourhood

Craig Sherborne

IN THE GHETTOS OF THE BUSH the children have children. At sixteen or seventeen they have their first; twenty years old is old. They become boy-dads with spindly goatees who wear check-flannel shirts and tracksuit pants; and girl-mums with lank hair and boab-shaped bodies in leggings. They quit school, don't have jobs and push prams to the local shops, strolling in the midday sun like it's an outing. They are the ones the middle-class call 'bogans'. Relationships break up, they make new ones, have another child. On it goes through their twenties. They create brittle step-homes, greenhouses for violence and child abuse, according to the experts. Sometimes they live in small, dying towns, caravan parks or low-rent homes with sagging verandahs and overgrown lawns. Sometimes they live in a place like Ashmont on the outskirts of Wagga Wagga, a brick-veneer queue of modern houses. It's a place where people have a protective layer against outsiders: eyes stare in challenge at a stranger's passing car, and mouths shut if a stranger asks too many questions. Particularly since 'it' happened. Backs are turned on non-locals with a sudden flick of rejection; lips twist to a hostile sneer.

The 'it' is the torture and murder of a seven-month-old baby named Jordan Anderson-Smith in Ashmont on 25 February. The infant's death was a slow one; his body was systematically smashed. So far no one has been charged with the crime and the case is drifting. The police have two 'persons of interest' on their books: Jordan's mother, Louise Anderson – and her de-facto at the time, Chris Hoerler, twenty-three. Both say they didn't do it. In Ashmont, those protective layers have hardened. The police cannot penetrate the locals' code of silence, a resolve not to give up vital clues in the case. This was a brutal crime against a baby, a defenceless innocent. Surely there is somebody prepared to break the code for Jordan's sake?

'A lot of people are frightened,' says Kerrie Lewis, the detective heading the investigation. 'People are afraid of repercussions.' But Lewis clams up when asked to explain exactly what she means by 'repercussions'. She will not put a name to the fear, real or imagined, that the people of Ashmont are experiencing. She says answering the question could harm the prosecution's case should someone be charged over Jordan's death. Those few Ashmontians willing to provide an answer refuse to give their names, even their Christian names.

'I live four streets from where the murder happened,' one woman says over her shoulder, changing her shopping to the other hand and hurrying off. 'It's had a huge effect.' This code of silence compounds the usual parochialism that permeates such communities: answering relatively tourist-like questions such as, 'What's the area like?' is an ordeal for some. The postmaster, a thin old man in grey uniform, shakes his cheeks and utters: 'I don't want to divulge what goes on around here.' Outside the Ashmont hotel, a teen father peeling back a lolly wrapper for his toddler avoids eye contact. He silently taps his finger on a line of graffiti on the wall. 'FUCK you, fuck me, fuck the world.' To the left of the angry scrawl, someone named Leonie declares heart-shaped love for Hoerler, dated 1996.

The local high school is Mount Austin. Its acting principal, Col Feather, a rumpled, weary figure in baggy jumper, refuses to discuss the area's teenage pregnancy problem – 13.5 per cent of all mothers who gave birth at the Wagga Base Hospital last year were under nineteen. That's double the New South Wales average. Feather presses his palms to the air and attempts a bit of bush-PR: 'We like to concentrate on the positive things.'

Wagga Wagga is a big, pretty town, population nearing 60,000. It has fine old stony homes with bull-nose fronts, knobbly vines and woody green gardens. There is a strip of shops it takes an hour to walk through. Ashmont is divided from the town centre by an industrial quarter – exhaust and windscreen repairers, wheel aligners, panel beaters, car dealers and barbeque suppliers, all in a row off the highway. Between the industrial estate and Ashmont's houses is a moat of grass – a treeless wasteland with a bike path. There are two sides to Ashmont: there is the better-off side where homes are owned, with shrubby, well-watered front yards. Late model cars decorate neat drives. Then there is the rest: the housing commission homes boxy, low-roofed, fenceless and without flowers; brown outdoor blinds are drawn even on cloudy days. Wagga Wagga lies in a productive farming region, but there are precious few jobs in town, especially for those at the bottom of the social heap. In Ashmont the main industry is unemployment; men poke about under the hoods of clapped-out Camiras and Falcon GLs parked three or four to a driveway. On front doorsteps kids giggle at their children just learning to walk. They smoke, chat across lawns, swig a lunchtime beer. This is the land of the idle poor, of break-and-enters and vandalism, of hanging around, being bored. This is the bleak, listless world into which Jordan Dean Leon Anderson-Smith was born.

His father, Cecil Smith was a seventeen-year-old schoolboy who paired off with Louise Anderson at a party. Anderson was already heavily pregnant to another man and gave birth to a son, Brody, a week after the party. She was already the mother of a two-year-old boy named Jason whose father lived in Werribee in outer Melbourne, a friend of Brody's father. The relationship between Anderson and Smith started as a love-lust fling, but three months after their meeting it was still steaming along. Smith left home and moved a few blocks away to live with Anderson in a tiny house in Blakemore Avenue, a stone's throw from Ashmont's shopping centre. Taking on step-children must have been a big challenge at seventeen, but Smith says he was unfazed. He was used to kids, came from an eight sibling step-family, and besides, it was a way for him to stand on his own two feet, become independent, he thought. 'I think I moved in with Louise because I just wanted out of the house, something a bit different, a bit more freer,' says Smith. 'I wanted a bit more of a life of my own.' That life became little more than parties and sex. His interest in things outside began to wane. He dropped out of school, midway through Year 10 – 'Most of the kids in Ashmont leave in Year 10,' he shrugs. And he stopped concentrating on the one thing that could get him out of there – rugby league. Smith can play rugby league. He's burly, strong and a gifted user of a football. His cousin is St George-Illawarra halfback Wes Patten. Patten and Smith are close. Smith wanted to do what Patten did, make it into the NRL big time, but his life took a new course. Then Anderson became pregnant with his child, with Jordan. 'It was an accident really. A sort of accident, but young people love kids and want one of their own,' says Smith. 'You use condoms, and the girls use pills, but yeah it still happens, she gets pregnant.' But the affair was souring. 'We were fighting all the time. She never cleaned up, in the kitchen and stuff. She never cleaned up anything. I'd have to do it.' Seven months before Jordan was born, Smith moved back home.

Anderson and Smith kept in touch after Jordan was born. She would take the baby around to see her father. But both parents quickly moved on to other relationships. Smith became a parent again, with a new girlfriend, Tamara. Their daughter, Tahlia, was born a month after Jordan's birth. She was a sickly child, twelve weeks premature. Meanwhile, Anderson became involved with Hoerler, a squat, muscular Papua New Guinean, who had settled as a child in Young, north of Wagga Wagga. He moved in with Anderson at Blakemore Avenue.

Anderson and Hoerler hosted a party for six guests on the night of 24–25 February. The party ended sometime around midnight and the guests went home. A little after 3 a.m. a series of 000 calls for an ambulance were made from the house. Police will not confirm who made the calls. When ambulance officers arrived they found Jordan dead with Anderson trying to resuscitate him. They took over, but it was useless. Jordan was gone. Sudden Infant Death Syndrome, they thought. There was a small bruise on his left cheek, but nothing at first glance to suggest injury. Then, literally before the officers' eyes, the bruising started to come out. When police looked in the baby's bedroom they saw blood on the wall and in the bedding. Yet there was no blood on the baby. It made no sense. Anderson and Hoerler said that after the party they had gone to sleep on a mattress in the living room, with Jordan beside them. They told police they woke around 3 a.m. and found him dead.

Jordan's body was sent to the Institute of Forensic Medicine in Sydney for post-mortem examination. It took four days for a pathologist to analyse Jordan's injuries – there were so many. His face had swollen to a mask of purple bruising; his ribs were fractured; his liver ruptured. Some of the injuries were bizarre – Wagga Wagga coroner, Sev Hill, had seen nothing like them in thirty years of coronial work: 'The toes, it's as if they were clamped, as if put in a vice, or pair of pliers, crimped,' he says, pulling the pink ribbon from the files containing Jordan's records. He is sitting in his book-lined office in the town's courthouse. He studies the files in silence a moment, eyebrows arched in concentration over his spectacles. The arch collapses into a frown, a grimace. 'Yes,' he murmurs. 'That was one of the reasons why there was a delay in the (post-mortem) process, because they had to work out the injuries on the toes. The baby appears to have been tortured. It didn't happen in five minutes. It happened over a period of time. I would put it at an hour minimum.' Jordan must have been screaming at the top of his lungs, piercing the night silence. Neighbours must have heard something. Lewis finds this hard to stomach: 'When we went around and knocked on the doors, when we said to people, "You must have heard the baby crying," they said, "Some babies cry all the time. It's nothing unusual."'

The Department of Community Services removed Anderson's two other children from her care after that night. A written statement by DoCS for this story reads: 'Alternative care arrangements have been made for the other children in the family to ensure their safety and wellbeing.' DoCS will not comment on whether its staff had ever been aware of any child abuse in the Anderson-Hoerler home.

Coroner Hill thumbs to a remembered page in the files and gives a summary of its paragraphs: 'The baby had an immunisation needle on the 24th (the day before he died). It appeared to be a well cared-for baby. The doctor who gave the needle didn't notice anything amiss.' Hill turns to another page, a post-mortem document. 'The baby may have had some injuries prior to the injuries on the night because there seems to be some bruising on the scrotum which seems to be an older injury, but …' his voice trails off. He closes the files and ties the ribbon in a bow.

Three hundred and sixteen children were murdered in Australia between 1989 and 1999 – 8.6 per cent of all homicides committed. According to a new report by Canberra's Institute of Criminology, 71.8 per cent of the killers identified were male, most of them were the victim's parent, and 34.7 per cent of them the step-parent. The last figure, however, is deceptive. The report's author, Jenny Mouzos, explains: 'Statistically, children are in fact at much greater risk in a step-family than a biological family because there are fewer step-families in the population than there are biological ones.' The report moots a 'Darwinian view of child homicide' where step-parents are involved, a sort of genetic competing. It says people devote less time to children who are not theirs biologically, exposing them to potential neglect. It contends that step-parents are likely to be less patient and more aggressive towards the children.

Professor Ken Polk, a University of Melbourne criminologist and child homicide expert, hones the profile – an archetypal killer emerges: 'These crimes are class crimes,' he says. 'Nearly always, the family units are under exceptional economic stress, generally the two individuals are unemployed. They tend to have histories of drug use. They are young, very inexperienced individuals and parents, and the young male, the new de facto, is totally unprepared for dealing with a situation where they are in competition with the child for the woman's attention … If the individual has learned a repertory of violence then the violence gets played out.'

But haven't most of us known someone who would fit that mould? And they haven't gone bashing kids to death.

'I think what they [child abusers] see themselves doing is disciplining the child.'

Even to the point of torture?

'Yeah,' he drawls, unequivocal. 'They rarely see it as torture. They see it as discipline. Their interpretation is they are bringing the child into line.' Polk then loops back to where he started, the poverty trap argument: 'At the boundaries of mainstream society you are going to see more and more of these extreme kinds of responses [to poverty], of loss, alienation, lack of connectedness, anger, frustration, all this violence, then it replicates itself.'

Perhaps there's a sense something is missing from the explanation. Any reasonable person can accept that a theft-crime can be a poverty-crime, but it takes a long leap from there to infanticide. Brutality against children is our society's most enduring taboo, it repulses us morally; criminology's explanation of why it happens seems like a lame excuse. We turn to our imaginations or religions for answers and find the word 'evil' to describe and understand the criminal.

Writer Helen Garner felt the murder of toddler Daniel Valerio was a case in point. The boy's step-father, Paul Aiton, was eventually convicted of the crime. Garner covered Aiton's trial for *Time Australia* and wrote: 'I don't see how it is possible to contemplate

Daniel's story without acknowledging the existence of evil; of something savage that persists in people despite all our enlightenment and our social engineering and our safety nets.' 'Evil' is a loaded term, we're used to associating it with tabloid sensationalism or pulpit theatricality. 'Savage' is much the same. But these words are all we have to express our horror. We speculate: at the core of the child killer, does a malign impulse exist that needs hateful, violent expression? An impulse criminologists haven't identified yet, put a proper name to?

No one will be charged with Jordan's murder; not from the current police investigation anyway, that's what coroner Hill predicts. The code of silence is holding. Police impetus is petering out. Initially there was a team of seventeen on the case; now there is only Lewis, with one or two officers available if she needs them. Then there was the Olympics factor – police officers from rural New South Wales, including Wagga Wagga, were commandeered to beef up Olympic Games' security in Sydney. Hill believes Jordan's case was shunted down the list of police priorities in the process. Speaking in the lead-up to the Games, Hill claimed: 'Police will have limited involvement until after the Olympics. I think that it's a sad thing to say.' Lewis backed his claim, to a point: 'It [the Olympics] has had some impact. Some.' But Wagga Police's crime manager, Grahame Winson, rejected it. He admitted that thirty-eight officers from the area's 120-plus squad were assigned to the Olympics, but he claimed this hadn't hurt the investigation. Though he did offer this piece of doublespeak: 'We would like to have more [people on the case]. We have a full commitment to it with limited resources.'

If no one is charged over the murder soon, Hill plans to stand the matter down for a hearing – everyone who has given evidence so far would be made to appear before him and tell what they know all over again, and be questioned. Not that he's confident the process will reveal the murderer. 'I think there will be an open finding once I've had the hearing, and then after that I would hope the police would post a reward.'

But hearings can turn up surprises. In the late 1980s, Hill conducted a hearing into the murder of Sally Ann Jones, a teenager found floating in river shoals at Wagga Wagga. One of those appearing was a local mechanic named Kenneth Cannon. He claimed he discovered the body while going for a training run along the muddy banks of the river. His wife had given him an alibi. But at the hearing, his story suddenly didn't ring true to Hill, himself a keen jogger. 'He was wearing a pair of Dunlop K26s. If you are a serious runner you don't wear those. You get something better than that. And you don't run in mud.' Hill hassled the New South Wales commissioner to order DNA testing on Cannon. It was done. Cannon was convicted of the murder.

If there is music in Ashmont, a lightness of step, it's found in the pub on Friday night. In the lounge bar a one-man band strums his guitar. At smoky tables, hands clap in time and mouths sing along to the chorus of 'I Heard it Through the Grapevine'. In the public bar girlfriends sip on straws watching the boys play pool. The talk and swearing are loud and happy. Outside, it's a quiet evening with tall necks of smoke coming from the chimneys, and bats diving in silhouette through the air, their wings making a squelching sound; no work yet for police cruising the streets. Just some yelling and fighting, the usual kind of drunken thing. In the morning, the birds move in, skittering up through paperbarks, and then the kids who have kids start coming out, hunched behind strollers, scuffing their feet as if they've got the weight of the world on their shoulders.

A new family has moved into the house where Jordan was murdered; baby clothes are pegged on the line in the backyard where his clothes would have hung; a pram is parked near the front door where his pram would have been. The backyard is very small; the whole house appears pushed up tight against its neighbour. The neighbour is in her front garden. She has long gingery hair and wears a greying white T-shirt and short pants. The neighbour is Louise Anderson. 'The police say I can't say anything to anyone,' she insists, though this is news to them. Anderson untangles a hose and waters the few plants. Doesn't she find it difficult living so close to her old house? 'No.' Is she going to stay here? Stay in Wagga? 'I'm probably staying here. It's an alright town.' When she speaks she tilts her head back, then narrows one eye and purses her mouth, a look of timid defiance. According to one source in Wagga Wagga, Anderson is applying for a $50,000 victim's compensation payment through the NSW Victims' Compensation Scheme. Is that rumour true? 'Maybe,' she says, cocking her head the other way.

Smith reckons he's going to leave Ashmont. He has broken up with Tahlia's mother and plans to scrape some cash together and move to Shell Harbour with his new girlfriend, a 22-year-old who lives in the block of flats next door to him. She has a three-year-old child to another man. He wants a fresh start, by the ocean, and hopes for a better chance at a job. He might even go to back to school and get his Year 12. And he wants to play rugby league, have another shot at the NRL. If it works out between him and his new girl, maybe they'll have a baby together, he says. But only after the relationship is established. At least that's the plan. In the meantime he's in counselling. He says: 'They've got me drawing pictures. When Jordan died, I'd dream I was down a hole, and my family was up top. At the start I stayed in my flat, and then I'd snap at people. And I was swearing at my mother, which I would never do because I have so much respect for her. I don't do none of that no more.'

By midday in Ashmont people move onto their steps to sit; cars get tinkered with; weekends or weekdays, the timetable is the same. Or they head into Wagga central, hang around, then go home. When they get home, some will find Lewis's calling card under the door. She has left one many times. On it will be a note for them to call her to talk about 'it'. But of course they won't. They'll tear up the card like always and throw it in the bin, determined to keep their nose out of such business, obey the local lore.

'Two and Two Don't Make Four with That Bloke'

John R. Carroll

IN JULY 1998, Paul Higgins junior was on his way home to Melbourne after a holiday in the United States, where he had gone to escape the seemingly never-ending, gut-wrenching, living hell that had tormented his whole family for more than three years. The holiday had provided some respite, but when he arrived in the Qantas lounge at Hawaii airport it all suddenly hit him again, right between the eyes, as if he had never been away. Emblazoned across the front page of a newspaper was a photo of a prisoner in handcuffs, being led away by guards. The prisoner's name was Edwin Andrew Lewis, and he had just been convicted of manslaughter and murder. The victims in the long-running case were Paul Higgins's father and stepmother, who had both been savagely stabbed to death in their own home on 21 April 1995 – their twenty-fifth wedding anniversary.

Paul Higgins had wanted to avoid the trial's endgame because he knew all the evidence and arguments inside out and just couldn't take it any more. He'd been put through the wringer again and again, heard every word of it both in court and repeated endlessly inside his head every night as he tried vainly to sleep. His life, both personal and professional, was in a state of paralysis. It was tearing at him, dragging him down. After five hearings – including two that were aborted – it felt as if the Higgins family was on trial, not Edwin Lewis. Now at long last there came some relief: the killer was going down. But why did it have to be such an agonisingly drawn-out ordeal?

Eddie Lewis, aged thirty-two at the time of the killings, was something of a pulp fiction cliché: a superficially attractive, extroverted man with grandiose plans, in whom fantasy and reality had a tendency to become confused. A part-Maori from a poor New Zealand background, Lewis was the co-owner of a gym where he worked as an instructor. He was a fit, sleek, smooth-talking individual with well-contoured muscles – a classically narcissistic, body-worshipping gym head, possessing the sleazy charm that some women find seductive. It was even said by some that he had a 'magnetic personality'.

Edwin Lewis's stated ambition was to drive a prestigious car and become a millionaire by the time he was thirty-three. The problem was, his business pursuits had not gone well – in 1994 he had been bankrupted, owing around $70,000. He was behind the eight ball, and the clock was running down fast – his self-imposed schedule left less than a year to make it big. People like Eddie Lewis, however, are ever-resourceful: always on the look-out for the main chance, they can instinctively switch on charm and sexual magnetism to turn their fortunes around. And for Eddie – though he probably didn't know it at the time – his main chance presented itself in January 1995, in the form of Amanda Higgins.

At the heart of Lewis's get-rich-quick scheme was a move to Noosa Heads in Queensland, where he would be able to put the past behind him and build up a successful business enterprise, probably in the fitness or tourism area. How he planned to do this while bankrupt and in debt up to his ears is not clear, but when Amanda appeared at his gym one day with her mother it wasn't long before he saw an opportunity and seized it with both strong hands. If he were to make a fresh start, he needed to get a stake, and a red-hot relationship soon developed.

But Eddie Lewis wanted more than Amanda's sexual favours. He had to insinuate himself into her family, to tap into the money supply. No one can be sure exactly when this idea became fixed in his mind – probably not long after he discovered that Amanda Higgins's father was Paul Higgins senior, a well-known former motoring writer who drove a Mercedes and lived in a superior home, complete with swimming pool, in the leafy, affluent eastern suburb of Forest Hill. On top of that his wife, Carmel, drove a gleaming, nearly new Porsche 911.

Edwin Lewis was envious – Paul Higgins was successful and, by Lewis's standards, rich. Lewis wanted a piece of that action.

He met the family just once, at a restaurant where they all had dinner. Lewis was keen to ingratiate himself, but the evening was not a raging success. Present were Amanda, Paul Higgins senior, Carmel and Paul Higgins's two sons from a previous marriage, Paul and Mark. Lewis failed to impress the two sons, who thought he was a self-absorbed big-noter without much substance. There was also something off-kilter about this outgoing, flashily dressed character: he was evasive and contradictory about his past, but full of grand plans about his future. In short, they thought him a flake. Not taking him too seriously, Paul junior said afterwards, 'Where's the harm in a bit of bullshit?' Mark's opinion was more ominous: 'Two and two don't make four with that bloke.'

Aged sixty-three, Paul Higgins senior was a strong-minded person and a tough judge who did not suffer fools, charlatans or con men. He was anything but easygoing. Family members have described him as intolerant and sometimes overbearing. He held forceful opinions on many subjects and was, to a degree, inflexible. And like any father – perhaps excessively so – he was particular about who went out with his daughter.

He did not need long to decide he didn't have much time for Eddie Lewis. When he gave Amanda a Magna car in March for her twenty-fifth birthday, he made it clear she was not to allow Lewis to drive it. This would not have pleased Eddie. In contrast, Carmel Higgins was more favourably disposed to her daughter's new boyfriend. Although devoted to her husband, Carmel was quite capable of forming independent opinions of people, rightly or otherwise. She had been with Amanda when the couple first met, and was evidently susceptible to the young man's good looks and roguish appeal, despite Mr Higgins's misgivings. That would have made Lewis happy, and doubtless he played on her fondness. He was later to claim that he got on well with both parents, but this was a fiction.

By April, the romance between Eddie and Amanda was on shaky ground. After barely three months, raw physical passion was giving way to mutual bickering, then rancorous disagreement. The causes of this rapid deterioration are unclear, but the history and personality of Amanda played some part, a fact that was to have significant ramifications in the aftermath of the double homicide.

Amanda was the only child of Paul and Carmel Higgins (Paul's sons were from his previous marriage), and there is no reason to believe they did anything but dote on her from the day she was born.

But Amanda was no conventional suburban child. She had a troubled, secretive side – the last thing her parents would have expected, given her comfortable background and stable domestic circumstances. She had a history of running away from home, perhaps in rebellion against the strictness and over-protectiveness of her father. She began injecting heroin, became a habitual user, then a full-scale addict. And – as is so often the case with young women in this situation – she turned to prostitution to support her habit.

Paul and Carmel would have been devastated to learn of Amanda's activities during her times away from home. Like parents the world over, they would have wondered – how could she have turned out like this? What had they done wrong? They offered what help and support they could, but it wasn't enough.

As for Edwin Lewis, it was quite possible that he had no knowledge of Amanda's drug habit until the relationship was underway. With his concern for fitness, he may have challenged her about it, creating bad blood. The strain of being in a relationship with an addict – seeing the worst of her – was an ongoing one. Perhaps, too, she received glimpses of *his* real character – the grasping, calculating one beneath the charmingly sleazy exterior. Maybe he made his intentions plain and wanted her to collude in a scheme to rip off her father. Amanda was no saint – possibly she had stolen from her parents in the past to buy drugs – but such a suggestion would have pulled her up. There could have been a range of factors: this was not a union blessed by the angels.

In the days leading up to the killings, several important new factors entered the equation. Firstly, on 13 April, Amanda informed Eddie that she was pregnant to him and intended to keep the child. Life had now become more of a tangled web than Lewis had bargained for, and it's difficult to assess how he might have responded initially to the news – especially now that the relationship was failing fast. Possibly he was thrown, confused – or maybe, just maybe, he really wanted to marry her and make a go of it.

Secondly, on 18 April, he allegedly discussed with a confederate in Sydney, a man named Michael Woodbine, the possibility of selling a Porsche through some sort of insurance scam.

Thirdly, on 19 April, he bought a diver's knife. Now Edwin Lewis, sports-oriented and fun-loving guy that he was, may have planned to go diving, or maybe not, but whatever the case the timing of that purchase was most unfortunate.

Knowing that the relationship was on the rocks, Lewis had to shift the Queensland plan into a higher gear. Speculating on the situation from his point of view, maybe he thought Amanda's pregnancy could work in his favour – if he was going to father her child, surely that made him a legitimate beneficiary of the Higgins wealth. She was his ticket to success. But if so, he needed to apprise Paul Higgins of this fact. They needed to have a man-to-man talk, which would not have been easy because the old man was a tightwad and had a set against him. To have any chance, he needed Amanda to stick with him, at least until he was on Noosa time. His affair with Amanda was still immature, so there were no firm foundations nor any reason to believe it was guaranteed a solid future. Like countless such dalliances, it was probably doomed to collapse under its own weight. Lewis was undoubtedly aware of this, and had to make hay while he could. The pressure was on. But if all else failed, he would just go in and take what he wanted.

On 21 April, two days after Lewis had bought his diver's knife, Paul and Carmel Higgins were murdered inside their Melbourne home. Their bodies were then buried in shallow graves alongside the pool in their yard. That much is incontrovertibly factual concerning the events of that day. Certain items – including Carmel's midnight-blue Porsche 911, valued at $200,000 – were missing from the house.

The bodies were not discovered until four days later, when Mark Higgins went to the address. He and his brother had been concerned all weekend because they had been unable to contact their father and stepmother. Paul Higgins junior even joked at the time that it 'sounds like foul play'. When Mark telephoned Paul with the news, he had collapsed on his kitchen floor, crying, in a state of numbed shock and disbelief, while his four-year-old son tried to offer comfort.

The day after that, 26 April, Edwin Lewis was picked up by police on the Gold Coast. He had made it to Queensland at last. It wasn't quite panning out the way he had planned, however.

Why were the police able to find him so expeditiously? One might have expected something of a manhunt, with Lewis eluding his would-be captors here and there before finally being cornered. But no, they got him straightaway.

It's clear that Edwin Lewis was not the cleverest of criminals. If he put any real thought into covering his tracks, it didn't show.

When arrested, he was in possession of Mr Higgins's gold cigarette lighter, some of his clothes and credit cards, and the strap from the sheath that held the diver's knife. And he was trying to off-load the Porsche for $20,000 – a fraction of its value.

En route to the Gold Coast, he had stopped in Sydney and spent some time with Michael Woodbine, the man to whom he had offered to sell the Porsche three days before the killings. The two men lived it up, staying in hotels and engaging the services of prostitutes. Mr Woodbine also used Paul Higgins's credit card to buy clothes. It's hard to fathom that level of stupidity. Lewis had confessed to Mr Woodbine, telling him that Higgins was a tight old man who hated him. Did they not think that police would be searching for the perpetrator? And did it not occur to either of them that using the victim's credit card to live it up while Lewis was on the lam might perhaps create a paper trail, pinpointing their whereabouts? Did the thought ever come to Lewis that the thing to do in these circumstances was to lie low rather than splash money around and draw attention to oneself? Evidently not. And once he had reached the Gold Coast, did he really imagine that he could sell such a distinctive, expensive car in the stolen car racket and get away with it?

But of course, all these questions are rhetorical. Edwin Lewis wasn't *thinking* at all in the normal sense of the word. He wasn't even thinking when he confessed to the killings to police in initial interviews on the Gold Coast, saying Mr Higgins had enraged him and provoked him into doing it. When Mrs Higgins appeared on the scene, he killed her too, from panic, to eliminate the only witness. He told similar stories to criminal associates and to an undercover cop in the slammer. It was confession and big-noting time all round, to anyone who would listen. In his jail cell – where prostitutes were thin on the ground – he had little else to do but reflect on what had happened and think about his defence. The best option seemed to be the 'provocation defence'. When extradited to Victoria and interviewed by homicide detectives there, Lewis had his story pretty much in place. Using the provocation scenario, he could say that he had gone to the Higgins home in good faith to inform Mr Higgins that Amanda was pregnant, that he intended to take good care of her in Queensland, get her off the drugs and set up a nice home together. But Mr Higgins took the news very badly. Rather than embrace his future son-in-law, he turned nasty and vicious. He told Lewis he was not good enough for his daughter, that he didn't want a 'black baby' in the family; he accused him of being a drug user and a bad influence on Amanda; he ordered him out of the house; he pushed and shoved him and even threatened to kill him. He went right off his head, practically frothing at the mouth. Upset and angered by the racial abuse and accusations being hurled at him, Lewis then lost the plot. He pulled out his diver's knife, grappled with Mr Higgins and stabbed him numerous times, until he lay dead.

Still in a state of shock, Lewis then paused to collect himself, to come to grips with what had happened. *My God, he had killed a man*! And then, with tragic timing, Mrs Higgins walked in the door and saw the bloody scene. She became hysterical and went for the phone to call the cops. Lewis didn't know what to do, he was still out of it, so in a sort of dazed reflex action he attacked her too, stabbing her in the arms as she tried to defend herself, then killing her with one stab to the chest.

If he were to get this version of events to stick, Lewis saw that his best hope involved playing the race card. In an age of political correctness, there was every chance it would have an effect on the jury, regardless of whether his claims were true. If he were to cry racial vilification, who would argue with him? The only other witnesses were corpses. Added to which, the race card had a successful track record in murder trials, most notably in the O.J. Simpson case. Not that Edwin Lewis was in O.J. Simpson's league, although there are some striking similarities – male and female victims, both stabbed to death, blood and other forensic evidence at the scene; suspect flees in car; strong circumstantial case; certain police evidence deemed inadmissible; racial prejudice factor influencing jury.

O.J. Simpson was acquitted. Why not Eddie Lewis?

The problem was, he had owned up to the killings, which Simpson never did. Never.

So, reviewing his options so far … possibly, with the provocation defence, maybe a manslaughter rap instead of murder for the old man. That could bring his prison time down to a manageable length. The wife, however, was a totally different story. He had just killed her cold because she was there – end of story. No provocation. That would definitely be murder – and she being a helpless 56-year-old woman and all, while he was practically Mr Universe in comparison, would go down horribly with the judge when sentencing time came around.

Maybe Lewis thought some of these things, maybe not. But he definitely thought things through after his interviews with the Victorian homicide detectives and during the early part of his first Supreme Court trial in Melbourne. Either alone or with a little help from legal friends, Edwin Lewis experienced a major brainwave.

He would retract all previous admissions.

A suspect can do that, even in the course of a trial. You just change everything around. And some of the police evidence was dodgy – sneaky, surreptitious prison tape-recordings of his confessions to other convicts and even to an undercover policeman. They were ruled inadmissible on technical grounds. That was a big win for Lewis.

Edwin Lewis would plead not guilty to both murders. He simply didn't do them.

One can almost see the light bulb flashing in his brain at the brilliance of this manoeuvre.

He didn't murder them – *Amanda* did.

Amanda. The spiteful, angry, drug-addicted little whore – she hated the old man.

She killed them both, then forced Eddie to help clean up and cover for her. He wanted no part of it. He was appalled by what she had done. But she threatened to give him up to the cops if he didn't shape up.

The details began to fall into place, one by one. And as they did, Edwin Lewis moved into full sewer rat mode.

His band of lawyers believed this crock – if 'believed' is not too strong a word. What lawyers actually 'believe' deep in their hearts is, of course, one of the great imponderable mysteries, but clearly they were happy to run with it, and to beef it up to such a degree that two Supreme Court juries went cross-eyed in the face of it, and the murderer came within an ace of getting off.

So the whole thing was shifted onto Amanda.

It really was an excellent strategy, because Amanda was so visibly tainted – shocking history as a teenage runaway, hooked on drugs, prostitute: the unholy trinity.

Liar, abuser, thief – killer. Why not? It was an easy transition when considered coolly. Amanda was so out of control, so full of vitriol. So lacking in credibility. She was the perfect patsy.

Eddie Lewis simply didn't know how violent she could be before that terrible day. And his earlier 'confessions' could be explained away as chivalrous attempts to cover for the poor, disturbed creature. Now, however, in the cool light of day, he was exercising his better judgment.

It would be a case of his word against hers, so he was going to have to present the jury with a seamless chain of events that was consistent and credible, leaving her nowhere to go – except to prison, indefinitely.

According to Lewis's version of events, both he and Amanda went to the Forest Hill house on 21 April. There they intended to inform Mr Higgins of Amanda's pregnancy and clear up the situation. Mr Higgins flew into a rage regarding Amanda's heroin addiction, though, saying he was not having a black baby and becoming physically aggressive towards Lewis. The two men grappled. In the middle of this, Amanda, who was fired up after taking drugs that morning, grabbed the knife Lewis had concealed on his person – as you do when you are visiting your prospective father-in-law – and went crazy, repeatedly stabbing her father in a blind fury. When he lay dead on the floor, Lewis took the weapon from her, whereupon she turned on him, saying he was involved now that his prints were on the knife.

Beautiful.

Of course, fingerprints could easily be wiped away then and there, but allowing this to pass (no doubt Lewis wasn't thinking straight in the heat of the moment), the scenario continues to unfold: Lewis fled the scene alone, returning home to his Richmond flat. During his absence, and unknown to him, Amanda also murdered her mother, who had blundered into the place soon after the mayhem. Amanda then went to Lewis's flat and demanded that he come back and help her clean up. Lewis was having none of it, didn't want to know, but Amanda said if he didn't help her, she'd tell the cops he did it. He'd wear the blame. According to Lewis, her words were: 'Who is going to believe you over me, Eddie?'

Poor Eddie's hands were tied. Reluctantly he went back to the scene of her dreadful crimes and spent eleven hours digging graves in the hard ground next to the pool, while she washed up the blood inside and, perhaps, stood over him, taunting him, blood dripping from her hands like some chilling vision of Lady Macbeth: 'My hands are of your colour; but I shame/ To wear a heart so white.'

So poor, browbeaten Eddie Lewis slaved away at his grisly task, after which he took off. In this concoction, it was necessary for Lewis to admit to having buried the bodies, because this was too physically arduous a job for Amanda. Credibility was essential. He was no more than an unwilling accomplice, blackmailed into helping a wicked woman cover her tracks.

As for stealing the Porsche, credit cards and so on – well, he would have to cop that, having been busted *in flagrante*. But that was a small matter. The main thing was to hold fast to the story, hope Amanda's stained character did its work on the jury, and see how well she would stand up to intense interrogation.

Not even Lewis and his lawyers could have anticipated five trials spanning three-and-a-quarter years before a result was achieved. Possibly they imagined that the longer the case dragged on, the better Lewis's chances – his story had shifted the ground enough for genuine doubt to take root and grow. On 3 January 1997, the jury in the first trial was discharged without reaching a verdict, following six days of deliberation. The second and third trials were abandoned – the latter because Amanda could not attend owing to the fact that she'd entered a heroin rehabilitation program. Pressure had been applied during this hearing, and she had seemingly folded by running for cover. No doubt this brought a smile to Edwin Lewis's lips: her credibility was wilting.

The fourth trial ended on 30 October of the same year, when the jury was unable to agree on a verdict after seven days. There seemed to be no way through the thicket to a clear decision – a situation produced in part by the initial ruling that Lewis's secretly taped confessions could not be led as evidence by the prosecution. But this obstacle had been removed by the time the fifth trial began on 8 May 1998. Following an appeal, the High Court had ruled in January that the tapes were admissible.

They were damning for Edwin Lewis. Jury members listened to him boasting to an undercover cop in his prison cell, telling him to get the next day's paper: 'Front page, double murder, that's what I'm in for.'

With the gloves now off, the prosecution was able to reconstruct events in graphic and convincing style. The killing of Mr Higgins was a 'planned assassination', motivated by envy, greed and hatred – and for the buzz of doing it. Lewis had gone to the house with his newly acquired knife specifically to murder Mr Higgins. Following a confrontation that may well have been engineered by Lewis to get Mr Higgins started – the 'black baby' business – Lewis, according to the tapes, 'gave him a couple' in the back, then rolled him over and did the same to his front. Mr Higgins, who was bleeding heavily but clinging tenaciously to life, apparently asked him, 'Why are you doing this?'

Lewis's reply was, 'Because you're a tight old bastard.'

When his victim was dead, Lewis dragged the body into the toilet, leaving a massive blood trail. It was at this time that Carmel Higgins came in the front door. When she moved to enter the toilet, he stabbed her too. Then he spent eleven hours – alone – burying the bodies and cleaning up inside before stealing the Porsche and other items.

The prosecution case was complete.

On 14 July, the jury returned its verdicts: not guilty of the murder of Mr Higgins, but guilty of his manslaughter; guilty of the murder of Mrs Higgins. Justice Bernard Teague had earlier advised the jury that they could find Lewis guilty of manslaughter rather than murder in Mr Higgins's case if they thought there was a degree of provocation involved.

On 6 August, Justice Teague sentenced Lewis to a total of twenty-six years, with a minimum of twenty-one. Considering the time he has already spent behind bars, the sentence effectively means he will be eligible for release in 2016. Is that long enough? Mark Higgins has mixed feelings, but doubts any amount of jail time will improve Edwin Lewis. His relentless, remorseless denials and counter-accusations, without regard for the suffering inflicted on the Higgins family, seem ample indication of that.

Delivering his sentence, Justice Teague made it perfectly clear that Amanda Higgins was in no way involved in the crimes – before, during or after. It was all down to Edwin Lewis. When Carmel Higgins stumbled into the crime scene, Justice Teague said that Lewis faced a choice. 'You could allow her to expose you as the killer of her husband [or] … you could kill her too. You chose the callously expedient choice of killing her.'

It may appear inconsistent that although Paul Higgins was Lewis's primary or sole target, whom he went there specifically to kill, this crime was nonetheless decreed the lesser of the two, because of the so-called provocation argument. If Mr Higgins had sat quietly and allowed Lewis to come at him and stab him, the murder charge would perhaps have stood. Yet because Higgins was said to have responded to Lewis's confrontation, in whatever form, he was deemed partially responsible for his own death.

An issue arises here relating to juries. Having satisfied itself that Lewis, and not Amanda, was responsible, the jury was clear, one would think, to find Lewis guilty of murder on both counts. He did, after all, go to the house armed with a deadly weapon which he clearly intended to use. To an outsider, one not immersed in the intimate details of the proceedings or privy to the performances of the principal players in the witness stand, the jury seems to have been inordinately generous in allowing Lewis the benefit of the doubt after he had been exposed as an out-and-out liar and a brutal killer who had tried to hide behind a woman's skirts, so to speak. Certainly, the jury showed more compassion for him than he displayed for either of his victims. Such apparent leniency may well have been undeserved, but at the end of a long day jurors are only human. Particularly in capital cases, a jury will seriously consider any extenuating circumstance – spurious though it may be – that will appease its conscience and lessen the burden of a hard judgment. So a reduction in the charge at least allowed the jury to feel safer about finding Lewis guilty, which in the eyes of the prosecution was preferable to the alternative of acquittal. In that, Edwin Lewis was lucky. Clearly, the accusations that Mr Higgins had made inflammatory and racist remarks to Lewis played on the jury's collective mind. Paul junior is adamant, however, that his father – despite his flaws – was neither a racist nor an aggressive person.

And what of Amanda Higgins, the tortured soul and invisible victim of the whole sorry saga? Throughout, she'd had to live with pernicious accusations based on no evidence whatsoever. Although not present in court when the verdicts were given, she was 'overcome with emotion' on being informed of them, according to a homicide detective involved in the case. No wonder. As Mark Higgins said outside court, she'd had to put up with a lot more than anyone else in the family.

Mark and Paul junior, who had lived with their mother following the divorce, hadn't seen much of their stepsister during her childhood years, and knew even less about her personal life as an adult. It came as a shock to learn of her waywardness. After the trial, the two sons hoped to have more to do with Amanda and to provide her with whatever support they could. Too late, though –

she decided, apparently, to cut everyone loose and start a new life elsewhere. (She has since married and moved to New Zealand, where she has entered another heroin rehabilitation program.) To start a new life is no easy task – yet, as Mark noted, having braved her way through five trials, Amanda is clearly strong, a lot stronger than Edwin Lewis gave her credit for. When the guilty verdicts were read out, Lewis was apparently seen to mouth the word 'unbelievable'. He was dead right, but not for the reason he meant.

'He Wasn't Afraid of Death'
The Killing of Victor Chang
Richard Hall

IN THEIR CHARACTERISTIC SLIPSHOD STYLE the pair were late, but that morning of all mornings Victor Chang slept in. The Toyota reached Lang Street at about 7.25 and Phillip turned off Military Road for a last survey. Elizabeth Purtell, from around the corner in Melrose Street, had left home a little earlier than usual and was able to set her time by a radio interview with a State politician. She turned into Lang Street on her way to the Military Road bus stop and saw a car driving slowly down the street. 'I noticed it in passing, there are not that many cars using Lang Street at that time of the morning. There were two men in the front seat.' Mrs Purtell got the colour of the car right: dark blue.

The last reconnaissance done, Ah Sung and Phillip went off to bump the Mercedes. Usually Victor Chang woke up in time to leave by 7.10, with the aim of getting to St Vincent's just before eight o'clock. This morning he slept in until 7.00 and hurried to get away by 7.35. The doctor hadn't even tied his tie.

About five minutes after leaving home, probably while pulling up the Spit Hill on the southern side of the bridge, Victor Chang called his wife to discuss a couple of matters missed in his hasty departure. She told police that he appeared to be in excellent spirits. It was the last time they were to speak to each other.

No one would have given the old Toyota a second look, but people remembered Victor Chang's Mercedes Sports coupé, and its personalised number plate – '200' – helped to trigger people's memories. The day before, Ruud van Kruysbergen, a young Dutchman in Australia on a working holiday, travelling as usual with a group of friends in a Kombi, had taken note of the Mercedes because of the numberplate. On the morning of 4 July, he took note of the Mercedes again, as did the driver of the Kombi, Mark Gilbert.

Ian Pickering, an insurance broker, knew his cars well enough to be able to immediately identify the Mercedes coupé as a new model because of its distinctive sloping grille, even though it was a hundred metres behind him. In his rear-vision mirror he saw a car pull out alongside the Mercedes, straddling the lane line, before dropping back. Elizabeth Smith, a medical technologist aged twenty-five driving alone in her car, saw the incident from about fifty metres behind. Although she didn't see the impact, she noted the two cars coming close together, then veering apart.

The explanation for Pickering's and Smith's uncertainty about the collision is explained by the clearest eyewitness testimony, that of Stephen White, a passenger in the Kombi, which was only thirty metres behind. He saw a car almost hit the Mercedes, swerve away, and then swerve back to strike the rear side. So it took two tries before they bumped the car.

Gilbert, the Kombi driver, saw the driver of the car make some signal to the Mercedes driver. Here Victor Chang, the owner of the handsome new car, made his mistake. The offending car was pretty downmarket. The collision, on the evidence later, was relatively minor and Chang, the driver, must have known that it was only a glancing blow. Better perhaps not to waste time getting involved with these people, who, having such an old car, possibly didn't even have insurance to cover the damage. But all that is hindsight. Moving at a fast clip in peak-hour traffic there's not a lot of time for thought. On another level, the fact that the driver was Chinese may have been a factor, tipping the scales towards a confrontation. It is human nature to tend to be harder on the stupidity of one's own people. And, finally, it was a very valuable car.

So when Lim pulled past him into the transit lane flicking his left indicator, Victor Chang followed suit. In the Kombi, Gilbert slowed to let him move to the other lane and said something to the others about the Mercedes from yesterday being in a collision. Van Kruysbergen turned to watch the two cars go into Lang Street. A taxi driver, Geoffrey Parish, had been arguing with his passenger about whether the sports car was a BMW or Mercedes. He didn't see the impact, but saw the Mercedes cut sharply into the transit lane, causing him to slow down. Maria Schneider, who was at the bus stop almost on the corner of Lang Street, saw two cars coming forward close to each other: 'I thought it was unusual for two reasons. The first was that it was a transit lane and very few cars use it. The second being that Lang Street is a very quiet, out-of-the-way street and since catching the buses I have rarely seen cars turn into that street.' The driver of the sports car was behind tinted glass, so Miss Schneider had nothing to say about him, but she was sure that there were two Asians in the sedan. Her bus came within a couple of minutes and she saw nothing more.

The trap was sprung. Ah Sung and Lim now had Dr Chang in their hands. Ah Sung was armed and Lim almost certainly was also, although he denied it later. According to the plan the doctor was to go quietly into their car and they would all go to Clontarf; but it all went wrong.

There are some sixteen witnesses to what happened in the next few minutes, most of them observing events from a distance. Lim made a statement to the police and in court, and Ah Sung made some revealing comments to his fellow Chinese in Melbourne, as well as in a statement before his sentencing. There was also crucial forensic evidence on how Victor Chang died. There are contradictions about things like the colour of the sedan and uncertainties over times, but the outlines are clear enough, as was the fatal outcome.

The cars pulled in on the left-hand side of Lang Street, the Toyota ahead of the Mercedes. Lim said that Dr Chang was very angry and not pacified when Phillip told him that the Mercedes was not severely damaged. Now began the business of trying to get Victor Chang into the car. Ah Sung pushed and pulled at him and at one stage a witness saw him putting his arm around the doctor's neck. All the time they talked in loud voices, and those who overheard them identified it as an Asian language. How long this went on is imprecise. Sifting the witnesses' statements, the probability is somewhere around ten minutes. During the early stages of the argument the parties were standing out on the road, and at that stage guns weren't drawn. How soon Dr Chang knew there were guns can't be known, but he certainly knew before the end. Ah Sung afterwards told people in Melbourne how, 'I held the doctor with my arms around him and I also held his tie. I said to the doctor, "You look at me, you surely know what I want to do." I push him to the car, but he didn't want to go in.' Later Ah Sung told a very frightened Ku Kui Chang, whose farm he was hiding out on,

'I have done so many times in Malaya. Each time they give me money. He wasn't afraid of death. You have son and daughter. Don't you afraid of death? Pointed him with a gun and ask, doctor say, "I don't afraid. I don't afraid."'

The very garbled text of the story had a certain chilling authenticity. There were people around, a stream of traffic a few yards away, and the man who was supposed to go quietly was struggling. The group strayed up the road, level to the back of the Mercedes, and Ah Sung dragged the doctor towards the grass verge. Phillip broke into English and was heard to say, 'Take it easy, take it easy.' Then Ah Sung had Chang pushed against the side of the Mercedes, still holding both his arms, with Lim alongside. As a pedestrian approached, walking along the footpath towards Military Road, Chang tried to break free.

As it happened the pedestrian, David Goff, had his mind on other things. As usual he was listening through his walkman earphones to the radio. But as he drew level with the group, Victor Chang called out loudly enough to penetrate his attention: 'Call the police.' Ah Sung and Lim turned towards Goff, who noted that the man holding the third man against the car had something in his belt on the left side underneath his jacket. Goff turned his head back and kept walking towards Military Road. Chang called again, 'Call the police. They have guns.' For Ah Sung this was trigger-wire. As he said in Victoria: 'Then doctor struggle and there were people passing by. The time is tight.'

Goff's account of the climax is stark in its simplicity: 'I turned and continued to walk north in Lang Street intending to try and find a telephone in Military Road. As I walked towards Military Road I glanced back and saw the man that was against the car step around the man who was standing on his left (northern side) and attempt to follow me. This man grabbed him on the arm with his left hand, held him causing the man to stop suddenly. Then with his right hand this man pulled out a gun from the left-hand side of his belt and put it up against the side of the man's head, in the vicinity of the temple. The man then fired the gun and the man that was shot toppled to the side, and swung around because the man with the gun was still holding his arm. He then fell into the gutter. Then the man with the gun bent down, put the gun to the man's head and fired again. He then straighten [*sic*] up, turned towards me. I put my hands up, backed away and said something like, "It's got nothing to do with me." I began to turn away, ready to run and I saw the man with the gun run to the blue Ford Falcon that was parked in front of the Mercedes (southern side). I think he got in the passenger door because the man that was with him was already in the car.'

That was how Victor Chang died. David Goff was a lucky man that day. If he had run, a rattled Ah Sung would have shot him. He certainly actively considered doing so. In Melbourne he told Stanley Ng: 'There's a witness who saw me. I feel I want to shoot him. To scare him and make lose his memory so he cannot recognise me.'

Across on the other side of Military Road another witness, Owen Wood, was opening up Midas Mufflers for business and had noticed the three men quarrelling in Lang Street a few minutes before he heard two shots. He looked again and saw two men standing over a third crumpling and rolling into the gutter by the verge. Goff looked back as the sedan car pulled out, took a note of the numberplate (MPY 812) and then ran back past the body around the corner to his Melrose Street address and rang the police.

Another witness, Patricia McLaughlin, who lived in the house on the corner of Melrose and Lang Streets, saw a car revving and accelerating as it turned right into Melrose Street, almost mounting the footpath as it did so. In the kitchen at the rear of the house a few minutes before, Miss McLaughlin had become aware of Asian voices raised in argument outside. She had gone out the front door and looked up Lang Street, and saw a man with his back to the sports car, but her view of whoever he was arguing with was blocked by leafy trees. As she was going back through the front door she heard the two shots, separated, she thought, by about three seconds. Running out and back to the corner she saw a man lying in the gutter and a sedan car moving off. She took the number, ran back into the house and called to her fellow tenant, Anna Readshaw, 'Someone's been shot. I've got the rego number. Ring the police.' Anna started to ring 000 and Patricia ran out up the street. She was to be the first to reach Victor Chang's body. She checked his pulse, thought she detected some faint movement, and started desperately talking to him as she knelt beside him. Another tenant from the house, Jin Kheong, followed her, saw the body and ran across Lang Street into Military Road where there was a doctor's surgery next to the liquor store. Wood, the man from Midas Mufflers, was on the scene next, having run through the peak-hour traffic. Next was Dr William Hock, who had responded to Kheong's alarm at the surgery. Patricia McLaughlin was still holding Chang's wrist and had put him into the coma position.

Dr Hock noted afterwards, in the unemotional language of medicine, that he 'saw immediately that the pupils of the eyes were widely dilated. I checked the body's pulse via one of the wrists and I checked the pupil for reaction to light. There were no signs of life.' The oxygen cylinder his nurse had carried from the surgery would be of no use.

'He's dead,' Dr Hock told the group. Doctors know about pagers, so Dr Hock took note of the pager attached to the dead man's belt with the name 'Chang' on it. By now Anna Readshaw, having phoned the police, reached the scene. She noticed that one of Victor Chang's hands was clenched with grass in it.

Immediately she saw a dark wallet about three or four feet from the body. Dr Hock and Kheong had also noticed the wallet. The ambulance arrived at 8.13, eight minutes from the Naremburn station, four kilometres away, a good run against the traffic, but they saw what Dr Hock had seen. No run would have been good enough.

Despite Patricia McLaughlin's desperate hope that she had detected some sign of life, Victor Chang had died instantly from the second shot. If Ah Sung had not fired that second time Chang would have lived. The first bullet had penetrated his right cheek, bored through soft tissue and come out below the right ear. The second shot entered the right temple and went on through the brain to lodge in the top of the skull. No one could have survived.

The first police to arrive were Constable Paul Green and Probationary Constable McFadden, who were on highway patrol duty nearby. The first firm times come from them. The radio message as a result of Anna Readshaw's call went out at 8.02, and two minutes later their car was in Lang Street. To Constable Green, the corpse was 'an Asian male approximately forty to fifty years old'. He noted that the male was wearing 'a grey suit, blue shirt, navy tie with gold colouring, blue socks and slip-on shoes'. The constable took the pulse for himself and as he stood he noticed a black wallet about a metre from the body's feet. As the detectives streamed in, the highway patrol men took the secondary role of securing the scene. There had been a shooting, a murder, but the name of the victim was still unknown, except to Dr Hock, who hadn't made any connection. Chang, after all, is a common enough Chinese name.

The Windsor Murder

Rachael Weaver

THE WEEK BEFORE the public recognition and execration of the name Frederick Deeming (and his various aliases that equally signalled villain, devil, monster in human form) was the week that he was hunted, the crime scene inspected, the clues gathered, the sensation germinated.

It was a story that attracted almost unprecedented popular fascination and media coverage. A naked, decomposed body of a woman had been discovered beneath the hearthstone of an ordinary suburban villa, bound into foetal position with a strong silk cord.

Even on the first day the murder filled columns in every Melbourne daily. You can tell the reporters had coaxed the same witnesses, digested the same police lines. Beneath melodramatic headlines, the uncanny transition from the everyday into the dangerous, the unfamiliar, preoccupied those early reports – the prickling sensation that violence and decay might lie beyond the most innocent suburban facade had been suddenly revived.

*

Number 57, Andrew Street lay in a trim row of terraces, a modest but respectable single-fronted cottage with a garden of boxed hedges, its verandah trailing flowers. 'The only indication that something terrible had occurred', wrote the *Herald*, was the 'crowd of horror-stricken faces', and the line of vehicles now blocking the street.

It started when the owner of the property, John Stamford, had shown a prospective tenant through, attempting to pass off the strange odour that the woman sensed. Late in the afternoon of 3 March 1892, however, further investigations by Stamford and his agent, Charles Connop, produced a more sinister impression, and at 7.30 p.m. the Windsor police were called in.

The sergeant and his two constables began their excavations on the hearthstone of a back room, working solidly for two hours before the masonry came loose and they prised away the slate slab that concealed the thing beneath. Now visible, according to the *Age*, was a solid mass of concrete with 'portions of an adult person' set into it like stone. Here the reports of 4 March are edged with different graphic emphases. The *Argus* saw the policemen wielding picks to dislodge the cement that 'adhered to every portion of the body' before its sex could be told. The *Age* claimed that charring from fires and 'the ravages of time and rats' had effaced all identity, while the *Herald* depicted the form as 'practically a skeleton' though it was 'rapidly decomposing' still. Finally, when the grisly archaeology was complete, the remains were gathered together and shipped in a rough wooden box to the dissecting room of the morgue.

All that was known of the cottage's previous tenants relied on the owner's hazy recollections, and the policemen assigned to the case – Detectives Considine and Cawsey – interviewed him, followed hungrily by the press.

A well-dressed stranger had called at Stamford's High Street butcher shop to lease the Andrew street property before Christmas, leaving no name but paying in advance. 'He was a man of medium height, of fair complexion, with light moustache and beard, the latter being about an inch in length. He seemed mild mannered and of gentlemanly demeanour,' Stamford recalled. When he insisted that 'he could not have associated such a man with so detestable a crime,' a reporter from the *Argus* suggested that his memory had been ruined 'by illness and the horror of the discovery in his house'. 'Upon reflection', Stamford offered, the tenant 'gave the impression of being a man of more than usually developed strength'.

Public interest in the case was continually escalating, and on Saturday 5 March, only two days after the discovery of the body, the *Herald* proclaimed that, 'Through the publicity that has been given to the case, many people have come forward with ready offers by way of testimony.' These testimonies were usually vague and imaginary, but one at least fell within the radius of the crime and that was the evidence of Ernest Büeller, the owner of the Hamburg Laundry in Windsor. Büeller's tale eclipsed Stamford's ramblings, providing an account of the stranger that somehow made him seem a fitting suspect for the murder.

A week before Christmas, the stranger had called at the Charles Street laundry with a large quantity of fine linen, asking for it to be delivered to 57 Andrew Street when done. When the washing was not finished, the man 'was very vexed by the delay.' 'I cannot be continually bothered with you,' the stranger said, but finally completed the transaction, drawing from his pocket 'a large handful of gold'. Also taking out a roll of notes, he bewildered Büeller with a display of wealth that confirmed an initial impression of great affluence: 'He was dressed in a grey tweed sac suit and boxer hat to match, the vest being cut very open to display three fine diamond studs in the shirt front and a flashing diamond pin in the bow tie.' Büeller described the man as 'violent in temper' and 'cutting in his remarks' before concluding his description by noting that 'he sparkled with diamonds, and his vest was loaded with a heavy double gold curb chain and a diamond locket pendant in the centre. I could identify him anywhere and may yet have the pleasure.'

Amongst the others interviewed that Saturday, Charles Connop, architect and agent, was the first to offer a name. Calling at Connop's office several times to extend the lease on the Andrew Street cottage, the stranger – who behaved erratically and continually changed his mind – refused to give a Christian name but referred to himself as 'Drewn'. 'He seemed well educated and bright,' Connop told the *Argus*, 'and he certainly was well dressed, and displayed jewellery with lavishness.' John Woods, the keeper of a High Street hardware store also came forward. Drewn had created a violent scene at the store before Christmas when his order wasn't promptly supplied. Finally, he had waited until a staff member accompanied him to 57 Andrew Street with a spring cart loaded with his retrospectively sinister purchases – a bag of cement, a spade, trowel and broom.

Even more enticingly, two carriers called Harford and Featherstone together added an exotic, international clue. Despite speculation that the couple had arrived on one of the German steamships that docked in mid-December, no 'Drewn' appeared in any of the passenger lists and there was no record of luggage being shipped from the customs house to Windsor. Now it was discovered that two carriers had shipped the couple's luggage in separate legs. On 15 December 1891, Harford had carried it from the customs house in Jolimont to Wrigley's free stores in Queen Street. The next day, Featherstone moved it again to the Federal Coffee Palace in little Collins Street, and finally to 57 Andrew Street in a double handling now suspected to be a ruse. Calling themselves 'Mr and Mrs Williams' the couple travelled with a canary in an ornate cage. When Featherstone worried for its welfare in the open with the luggage, 'Williams' roughly silenced him: 'He has travelled more than you.'

*

On Saturday 5 March, the *Argus* analysed the 'present indications', claiming that the overseas connection was confirmed by fragments of evidence sifted from the crime scene, where papers and letters had been burned in every room. Amongst the discoveries from the ashes were fractions of the *Liverpool Guardian* and London's *Sporting Times*. According to the *Herald*, the dates on these papers revealed the couple had only recently arrived. The debris in the grates also surrendered a Tate's Express baggage label, a smashed phial of raw spirits, fragments of letters, a partially burned invitation and what appeared to be a photograph, its image permanently erased by the flames. All objects, no matter how banal, were regarded as suspect. The writers at the *Argus* speculated about the meanings of torn words – describing 'an "R" (incomplete) "W"'. Another fragment suggested 'such a word as "whiting"'. Such minutiae were described with ritualistic thoroughness.

Also on that Saturday, the *Argus* described the autopsy to its readers, assuring them 'it was a careful and thorough one that extended over several hours.' The reports described the wounds in vivid detail – the heavy blows to the skull from a blunt instrument had divided it in three. The throat was slashed from left to right and the beginning was the deepest point, revealing the work of a right-handed man. The stomach had been despatched to C.R. Blackett, a government analyst, who had not yet reported back.

News of the manner of death brought lurid speculation about its means. The *Age* claimed – supposedly on the advice of the detectives – the murderer had encouraged his victim to take a bath. Then,

> Taking advantage of her helpless condition, Williams rushed into the robing room from a neighbouring apartment armed with a sharp knife or a razor … seized the woman … and putting his left hand upon her mouth and forcing her head back as he did so, slit her throat from ear to ear.

The writer of this scene – forgetting altogether the torn and ruined skull – focuses instead on the force at which blood would pump from a slashed carotid artery. Then, suddenly confounded by the lack of evidence of blood, he or she hastily suggests that 'the scoundrel … killed her in the very centre of the room, thus avoiding the splashing of the walls, which would otherwise have ensued.'

On Sunday the torrents of copy were silenced, but Monday's papers more than compensated for the momentary breach in news. The holiday had brought further crowds of thrill-seekers to witness the homely sounding spectacle of 'Constable Kinniburgh in the process of digging up the garden'. Monday's *Herald* described the Sunday crowds again, commenting that:

> The same excitement was maintained this [Monday] morning, and the large crowds gathered in the street and the ground attached to the house provide positive proof that the discovery of the work of a colonial Jack the Ripper has lost none of its interest or of its sensation.

Around 7 March, too, speculators began to wonder if other crimes could be explained in connection with the murder. As the week progressed, imagined links with the famous and mysterious theft of the Dudley Diamonds, and the great 1889 gold robbery from the Orient steamer the *Iberia*, made front-page news.

By now it was certain that the murderer and his victim had newly arrived in the colony by sea in December 1891. Greedy to participate in the sensation, passengers who had travelled aboard the same ship as the couple, the *Kaiser Wilhelm II*, rushed to offer interviews. The six-week passage from Southampton where they boarded the German mail steamer had provided endless anecdotes about the pair, and over the next few days the passengers' impressions dominated the reports. On 8 March, the *Argus* interviewed Mr Max Hirschfeldt, 'gentleman', in the comfort of the German Club where – 'in excellent English' – he provided a vicious portrait of the murderer as a bragging, delusional man. 'Williams was very talkative and boastful,' Hirschfeldt stated:

> … and delighted to pose as a much-travelled man, who had worked camps of Negroes in Mexico, hunted buffalo in the prairies of the United States, worked the diamond fields or followed the course of the Congo in Africa, and been carried by servants for days together under the burning sun of India.

Williams told these and other stories to anyone who would listen as he strolled upon the deck, but a tendency to lying and exaggeration, according to his acquaintance, was not his only vice. He 'took pride in displaying his jewellery … and his diamonds passed from hand to hand'. Several weeks into the trip, however, he had claimed that one of his treasures – 'a necklace of heavy gold set with precious stones' – had been stolen. According to Hirschfeldt's account, 'Williams worked up a good display of anger and demanded that the commander, Captain L. Stormer, should have the ship searched from hold to masthead or compensate him for the loss.' But the Captain declined, stating he was satisfied of 'the falsity of the report'. Now, in Hirschfeldt's assessment, 'Williams was beside himself with wrath, and adopted many ways of displaying his ill-temper' that the German traveller illustrated at length.

Yet another layer was added to the mystery and excitement surrounding Williams' persona when directly contradictory images were produced. Samuel Bradley, of Petersham, presented a more complex impression of a man whose glamorous and fascinating history was etched – irrefutably – on his body. According to Bradley, 'He had the marks of bullet wounds on the head and a sword wound on the shoulder, and the calf of one leg was partially shot away.' Bradley also described the way Williams' grey eyes twinkled as he entertained the other passengers by singing and relating tales of his travels and adventures in Egypt. His medical knowledge and ministrations of port wine, opium and cognac so benefited the steerage passengers throughout an outbreak of dysentery that Williams saved many lives. Although Williams' taste for jewellery was clearly gauche, his defender averred: 'His on-board conduct was exemplary.'

Mrs Williams, the eager witnesses unanimously agreed, was an example of lovely femininity – in contrast to an *Age* report on 10 March, which described her as a shrew. Almost competitively, the *Kaiser Wilhelm* passengers testified to the likeness between Mrs Williams and the corpse, disclosing to the press the lurid indicators through which the similarities could be discerned. 'Two ladies' who had travelled aboard the ship viewed the body on 7 March – the hottest day in Melbourne for thirty years. As reported in the *Age* of 8 March, 'in spite of the partial decomposition of the face, the ladies recognised the features as those of the unfortunate woman Williams.' Max Hirschfeldt described his visit with fellow passenger Captain Firth, and both confirmed the similarity. But it was the testimony of Dr Robert Scott that seemed the most macabre. He had looked on Mrs Williams with the eye of a physician and now found her personal characteristics 'conspicuously present in the corpse'. Included amongst these attributes 'were the shape of the shoulders which sloped, the prominence of the nasal bone, the immense quantity of hair … and the development of the pelvic arch'.

*

On 8 March at 10.00 a.m., the acting coroner, Dr J.E. Neild, opened the inquest into the murdered woman's death, and the ardent group of witnesses assembled at the morgue. Each earnestly repeated the stories they had offered to the press. In the words of the *Argus*, 'Detective Cawsey quickly presented a chain of evidence sufficient to identify the dead woman as Emily Williams and her murderer as Albert Williams.' Lacking the physical presence of the already publicly condemned man, the inquest was adjourned for a fortnight, in anticipation of his arrest.

The post-mortem examinations and the identification of Emily Williams' body now complete, the corpse was prepared for burial, though the court retained her head. At the funeral on 11 March:

> The sad ceremony was taken advantage of by hundreds of morbidly curious persons to catch a glimpse of something that had a direct relation to the murder. While the coffin – the plain black box of the pauper's funeral – was being

> placed in the hearse the crowd lost all sense of decency and order, and rushed the yard of the Morgue despite the vigorous efforts of the police to restrain them.

Meanwhile the search continued. It seemed certain that Williams had left the colony in January, and all Australasian ports were issued with minute descriptions of his appearance. The *Herald* proudly noted that communications from the general public concerning the case came not only from Victoria but also from 'the very heart of Tasmania', 'remote parts of New South Wales' and other colonies.

Despite such disparate leads, the detectives had been unable to identify anyone resembling Williams in the booking lists of Melbourne shipping agencies for the time when he was believed to have left Victoria. A new line of enquiry arose, however, when a retired sea captain who had travelled on the *Kaiser Wilhelm*, Captain Robert Firth, testified to meeting Williams sight-seeing in late January in the company of a young woman at Sydney's Circular Quay. It emerged that the criminal had booked a first-class passage by telegraph from Sydney before travelling back to Melbourne by train and boarding the S.S. *Albany* – bound for Fremantle – on 23 January.

When interviewed, the *Albany* passengers were certain of the link. Although the name Williams had not appeared, 'Baron Swanston' had made a deep impression. According to the *Age*, Williams had resumed his 'old habits, boasting and complaining' in the manner described by the passengers of the *Kaiser Wilhelm*. More pertinently, however, he had falsely complained of the disappearance of a black Russian dressing case filled with valuables, and had had 'the temerity to place himself in communication with the Adelaide police'. The pattern of behaviour seemed to confirm the physical description – 'Albert Williams' and 'Baron Swanston' were the same.

Swanston had confided his intentions to the other passengers on the steamship: 'He stated his nobility had not shielded him from the pressure of reduced circumstances, and he was anxious to obtain work in an occupation of which he had made himself master in former years,' they told the *Age*. Claiming to be an engineer of great skill and vast experience he had headed for the gold fields at Southern Cross.

On the morning of 11 March a photograph of 'Drewn', 'Williams', 'Swanston' was received from Sydney, provided to the police by a woman who knew him there in the 1880s as Frederick Deeming, plumber and gasfitter. That was the first mention of the name Deeming and the first thrilling revelation that the murderer had lived in the colonies before. The police immediately sent the image to be copied, but by evening its use had been made redundant by a telegram to the Chief Commissioner from the police in Western Australia, announcing that 'Williams alias Swanston [was] arrested today at Southern Cross.' Even as the newspapers celebrated the arrest it was already becoming clear that the Windsor murder was merely one episode in the extraordinary criminal career of Frederick Bailey Deeming.

*

In the weeks that followed, it became clear that the hearthstone murder was merely one episode in the remarkable criminal career of Frederick Bailey Deeming. Deeming was an international jewel thief, swindler, serial bigamist, raconteur, forger and mass murderer, with an array of aliases to accompany his many different trades and proclivities. He quickly became one of the most written-about criminals in Australian history – the *Bulletin* even announced on its front page of 16 April that the lucrative trade in Deeming stories had stalled the planned amalgamation of three significant Melbourne newspapers. Events in Victoria were met with fresh reports by friends, acquaintances and enemies of his nefarious history both internationally and throughout neighbouring colonies. Cluttered with images of great riches, mysterious courtships, jilted brides, ruined virgins, robbery, insanity and murder, such stories sustained the level of public excitement at a fever pitch throughout the months of Deeming's arrest, incarceration, trial and, finally, execution on 23 May 1892 after he was found guilty of Emily Williams' murder.

Murder Ballads

Nick Cave

Henry Lee

Get down, get down, little Henry Lee
And stay all night with me
You won't find a girl in this damn world
That will compare with me
And the wind did howl and the wind did blow
La la la la la
La la la la lee
A little bird lit down on Henry Lee

I can't get down and I won't get down
And stay all night with thee
For the girl I have in that merry green land
I love far better than thee
And the wind did howl and the wind did blow
La la la la la
La la la la lee
A little bird lit down on Henry Lee

She leaned herself against a fence
Just for a kiss or two
And with a little pen-knife held in her hand
She plugged him through and through
And the wind did roar and the wind did moan

La la la la la
La la la la lee
A little bird lit down on Henry Lee

Come take him by his lily-white hands
Come take him by his feet
And throw him in this deep deep well
Which is more than one hundred feet
And the wind did howl and the wind did blow
La la la la la
La la la la lee
A little bird lit down on Henry Lee

Lie there, lie there, little Henry Lee
'Til the flesh drops from your bones
For the girl you have in that merry green land
Can wait for ever for you to come home
And the wind did howl and the wind did moan
La la la la la
La la la la lee
A little bird lit down on Henry Lee

Where the Wild Roses Grow

They call me the Wild Rose
But my name was Elisa Day
Why they call me it I do not know
For my name was Elisa Day

From the first day I saw her I knew that she was the one
As she stared in my eyes and smiled
For her lips were the colour of the roses
That grew down the river, all bloody and wild

When he knocked on my door and entered the room
My trembling subsided in his sure embrace
He would be my first man, and with a careful hand
He wiped at the tears that ran down my face

They call me The Wild Rose
But my name was Elisa Day
Why they call me it I do not know
For my name was Elisa Day

On the second day I brought her a flower
She was more beautiful than any woman I'd seen
I said, 'Do you know where the wild roses grow
So sweet and scarlet and free?'

On the second day he came with a single red rose
Said, 'Will you give me your loss and your sorrow?'
I nodded my head, as I lay on the bed
He said, 'If I show you the roses, will you follow?'

They call me the Wild Rose
But my name was Elisa Day
Why they call me it I do not know
For my name was Elisa Day

On the third day he took me to the river
He showed me the roses and we kissed
And the last thing I heard was a muttered word
As he stood smiling above me with a rock in his fist

On the last day I took her where the wild roses grow
And she lay on the bank, the wind light as a thief
As I kissed her goodbye, I said, 'All beauty must die'
And lent down and planted a rose between her teeth

They call me the Wild Rose
But my name was Elisa Day
Why they call me it I do not know
For my name was Elisa Day

The Kindness of Strangers

They found Mary Bellows ’cuffed to the bed
With a rag in her mouth and a bullet in her head
O poor Mary Bellows

She’d grown up hungry, she’d grown up poor
So she left her home in Arkansas
O poor Mary Bellows

She wanted to see the deep blue sea
She drove across Tennessee
O poor Mary Bellows

She met a man along the way
He introduced himself as Richard Slade
O poor Mary Bellows

Poor Mary thought that she might die
When she saw the ocean for the first time
O poor Mary Bellows

She checked into a cheap little place
Richard Slade carried in her old suitcase
O poor Mary Bellows

‘I’m a good girl, sir,’ she said to him
‘I couldn’t possibly permit you in’
O poor Mary Bellows

Slade tipped his hat and winked his eye
And turned away without goodbye
O poor Mary Bellows

She sat on her bed and thought of home
With the sea breeze whistling, all alone
O poor Mary Bellows

In hope and loneliness she crossed the floor
And undid the latch on the front door
O poor Mary Bellows

They found her the next day ’cuffed to the bed
A rag in her mouth and a bullet in her head
O poor Mary Bellows

So mothers keep your girls at home
Don’t let them journey out alone
Tell them this world is full of danger
And to shun the company of strangers
O poor Mary Bellows
O poor Mary Bellows

Crow Jane

Crow Jane, Crow Jane, Crow Jane
Horrors in my head
That her tongue dare not name
Lived all alone by the river
The rolling rivers of pain
Crow Jane, Crow Jane, Crow Jane, ah hah huh

There is one shining eye on a hard-hat
Company closed down the mine
Winking on the waters they came
Twenty hard-hats, twenty eyes
In her clapboard shack
Just six foot by five
They killed all her whiskey
Poured their pistols dry
Crow Jane, Crow Jane, Crow Jane, ah hah huh

Seems you've remembered
How to sleep, how to sleep
The house dogs are in your turnips
And your yard dogs are running all over the streets
Crow Jane, Crow Jane, Crow Jane, ah hah huh

'O Mr Smith and Mr Wesson
Why you close up shop so late?'
'Just fitted out a girl who looked like a bird
Measured .32, .44, .38
Asked that gal which road she was taking
Said she was walking the road of hate
But she hopped on a coal-trolley up to New Haven
Population: 48
Crow Jane, Crow Jane, Crow Jane, ah hah huh

Your guns are drunk and smoking
They have followed you to the gate
Laughing all the way back from the new town
Population, now: 28
Crow Jane, Crow Jane, Crow Jane, ah hah huh

The Ballad of Robert Moore and Betty Coltraine

There was a thick-set man with frog-eyes who was standing at
the door
And a little bald man with wing-nut ears was waiting in the car
Well, Robert Moore passed the frog-eyed man as he walked into
the bar
And Betty Coltraine she jumped under her table

'What's your pleasure?' asked the barman, he had a face like
boiled meat
'There's a girl called Betty Coltraine that I have come to see'
'But I ain't seen that girl round here for more than a week'
And Betty Coltraine she hid beneath the table

Well, then in came a sailor with mermaids tattooed on his arms
Followed by the man with wing-nut ears who was waiting in
the car
Well, Robert Moore sensed trouble, he'd seen it coming from afar
And Betty Coltraine she gasped beneath the table

Well, the sailor said, 'I'm looking for my wife! They call her
Betty Coltraine'
And the frog-eyed man said, 'That can't be! That's my wife's
maiden name!'
And the man with the wing-nut ears said, 'Hey, I married her
back in Spain'
And Betty Coltraine crossed herself beneath the table

Well, Robert Moore stepped up and said, 'That woman is
my wife'
And he drew a silver pistol and a wicked Bowie knife
And he shot the man with the wing-nut ears straight between
the eyes
And Betty Coltraine she moaned under the table

Well, the frog-eyed man jumped at Robert Moore who stabbed
him in the chest
As Mr Frog-eyes died, he said, 'Betty, you're the girl that I
loved best'

Then the sailor pulled a razor and Robert Moore blasted him
        to bits
And said, 'Betty, I know you're under the table!'

'Well, have no fear' said Robert Moore ' I do not want to hurt you
Never a woman did I love near half as much as you
You are the blessed sun to me, girl, and you are the sacred moon'
And Betty shot his legs out from under the table

Well, Robert Moore went down heavy with a crash upon the floor
And over to his thrashing body Betty Coltraine she did crawl
She put the gun to the back of his head and pulled the trigger
        once more
And blew his brains out all over the table

Well, Betty stood up and shook her head and waved the smoke
        away
Said, 'I'm sorry, Mr Barman, to leave your place this way'
As she emptied out their wallets, she said, 'I'll collect my
        severance pay'
Then she winked and threw a dollar on the table

The Glass Coffin
The Pyjama Girl Murder, Tabloid Crime and Snow White

Richard Evans

'He said unto them, Give place: for the maid is not dead, but sleepeth.'

St Matthew 9:24

AT ABOUT 9 A.M. on the morning of 1 September 1934, the body of a woman was found by Thomas Hunter Griffith, son of a local grazier, about four and a half miles from Albury, New South Wales. Griffith had been leading home a champion bull, the property of his father. Not far from home, he noticed the body. It was partly concealed in the mouth of a culvert which ran under the road, the main highway to Howlong.

Griffith alerted the police, and they arrived later in the morning. The woman had been shockingly battered about the head. An attempt had been made to burn the body, which was clad only in a flimsy jacket and trousers, thought to be pyjamas. The head had been wrapped in a towel, and a hessian bag had also been placed over the top half of the body.

There were no other clues to the woman's identity.

The 'grim find' was immediately treated as a major news story. The larger papers sent reporters to Albury, and their often-breathless copy was prominent all over the country for the next three weeks, even though after the discovery of the body very little happened. This led to paradoxical headlines: 'Still not names', 'Murdered girl still unidentified', 'Albury murder: Still no clues' and stories beating up developments of almost comic triviality.

'A Japanese who was shown the pyjamas in which the body of the murdered girl, found in Albury a fortnight ago, was clad,' gravely intoned the Melbourne *Argus* on 9 September, 'states that the illegible marking on the lower hem of the coat is not in Japanese characters.'

After the body was found, it was examined by the local government medical officer. The most important discovery, made on 4 September, was that the woman had been shot as well as bashed, but this information was suppressed until 1938.

A description was issued. The woman was '18 to 28 years, 5ft 2 or 3 in., slim to medium build, blueish-grey eyes, black-pencilled eyebrows, light brown hair [which may have been bleached], fingernails tinted red and manicured to a point'.

The body was preserved in ice at the Albury morgue, and hundreds of people viewed it. The body's teeth were examined. A cast was taken, and a description of their condition and the dental work in them was issued. A post-mortem photograph, altered to make it more life-like, was distributed to police stations around the country. A sketch of the woman's face was published in the newspapers.

Marks were found on the towel that had been wrapped around the head. These were thought to be a laundry mark and of great significance. However, they could be interpreted in many different ways and led nowhere. Dozens of different women were reported as missing and fitting the dead woman's description. None was found to be the woman in question.

A reward of 250 pounds was offered for information leading to a conviction in the case, and this was later increased to 500 pounds.

On 12 September, embalmers arrived in Albury to preserve the body, which they did successfully. On 12 October, the body was taken to Sydney in a specially made 'jet black coffin', lined with zinc and filled with formalin, and held at the University of Sydney. There the body was viewed by many more people.

The police made a death mask and a painted plaster likeness of the woman's face as it may have been in life. But all efforts at identification failed, and interest gradually subsided.

The case made news sporadically in 1935, then faded from notice almost completely until, in January 1938, an inquest into the death was finally held in Albury. The Coroner found that a woman, identity unknown, had been illegally killed by a person or persons, also unknown. He specifically exonerated Tom Griffith, the man who had found the body, from any involvement in the killing. The police requested, and the Coroner approved, that the body not be buried, but remain in its preserved state.

The inquest revived interest in the 'Pyjama Girl', as she was beginning to be widely known. The reward for information that would solve the crime was increased to 1000 pounds.

In early 1939, the case became front page news again. In March, some women's shoes and cloth from a blouse were found in a deep lagoon near the site where the body was found. The police believed these articles were connected to the case. Not only was a description of them issued, but the New South Wales police commissioned a short film on the case. Despite an alleged death threat to the film's director, Rupert Kathner, the film was released in late July.

The film reconstructs what was known of 'one of the most monstrous crimes ever committed': which, it becomes apparent, was very little. There is an enactment of the police 'theory' of how the body ended up in the culvert. The scene which follows is, at least in the video copies of the film now available, a minute or so of murky blackness. The narrative is pure pulp thriller:

> Under cover of darkness a car crept along the Howlong Road pulling up not far from a lonely culvert. Stealthily the figure of a man emerged carrying a heavy burden, the body of a murdered woman. On he came, and placed the body in the hollow near a drain ... This fiend in human form saturated the body with kerosene, fired it, crept back to the car and drove off into the night.

A model is shown wearing an approximation of the clothing found in the lagoon, and the film concludes with an appeal for anyone with information to come forward: 'Can *you* help?' Nothing came of it, however, and the case was scarcely mentioned in the course of 1940.

On 7 January 1941, it was reported that the body might finally be buried. The room at Sydney University where the body was kept was needed for other purposes, the police told the *Sydney Morning Herald*. In any event, 'The six years of immersion in formalin have caused deterioration of the body, and the police doubt whether any person could now recognise the girl.'

One week later, a law firm announced they were likely to take legal action to obtain possession of the body on behalf of Jeanette Constance Routledge, of Bomaderry, New South Wales, who claimed the murder victim was her daughter.

According to the birth certificate, the father of Routledge's child was John James Morgan, who was at that time Routledge's stepfather. The child's first name was Anne, and she used many surnames during her short and troubled life, but she was usually called by her middle name, Philomena.

Some police had long suspected the Pyjama Girl was Philomena Morgan. Routledge had, she later admitted, deliberately misled the police about her daughter's appearance. She was, she said, worried that she would be accused of the killing.

She changed her mind and came forward after meeting a Sydney doctor, Thomas Alexander Palmer Benbow, who had become interested in the case in 1939 after seeing a magazine article about it.

Benbow had begun making investigations: initially with the co-operation of the police, but later in the teeth of their determined opposition. He had become convinced that the Pyjama Girl was Philomena Morgan, and that she had been killed in Albury, close to where the body was found.

An alcoholic and destitute woman called Lucy Collins had told him that a girl had stayed with her in an isolated shack near Albury in August 1934. After a few days, the girl was visited by a man called Ginger Quin. Collins had believed them to be lovers and left them alone. She had returned to find Ginger Quin savagely beating the girl with a piece of iron bedstead. Quin had fled, leaving the girl battered and bleeding but still alive. Later Quin had returned with his mother, 'snowy-haired Mrs Quin', and had taken Morgan away in a pony trap.

Benbow's theory was that the Quins had then shot the girl, washed the body and dumped it where it was found. He tracked down Jeannette Routledge, won her confidence and launched the legal action on her behalf. While the case was unsuccessful, the judge referred Benbow's inquiries to the Crown Prosecutor. NSW detectives made inquiries in Albury in January 1943, but these did not lead to any action being taken.

In June 1943, Benbow and Routledge appealed to the NSW State Full Court for a new inquest into the death. This too was unsuccessful.

Then, in March 1944, the case took a startling turn. On 4 March, the Commissioner of NSW Police, William John MacKay, called in an Italian man, Antonio Agostini, for an interview at Police Headquarters.

Agostini had recently been released from internment and was now working as a waiter at Romano's, a high-class restaurant where MacKay frequently lunched. The usual explanation for the police interest in Agostini is that a fresh examination of the body's teeth, on 24 February, had found a cavity where a porcelain filling had been dislodged. The discovery of this cavity, along with another filling which had been overlooked, meant the teeth were consistent with those of Agostini's wife, Linda.

During the interview, which lasted three or four hours, Agostini allegedly confessed that the Pyjama Girl was his wife, an Englishwoman whose maiden name was Florence Linda Platt. He had accidentally killed her at their home in Carlton, in inner Melbourne, in late August 1934. She had accidentally been shot while they were struggling for a gun. He had initially intended to go to the police, but had decided to conceal the tragedy because of the scandal it would cause. He had carried the body to his car, driven through the night to Albury, placed the body in the culvert and set fire to it.

This confession was later challenged by Agostini. He said that MacKay had told him the police had already identified the body as that of his wife, and that if he did not confess he might hang for her murder.

Agostini was not arrested but agreed to accompany the police to Albury. There he identified the site where he had placed the body. Next he was taken to the house in Carlton where he showed detectives where the death had occurred. He was charged with murder on 6 March. He was refused bail and was reportedly held in the same cell as that recently occupied by Edward Leonski, the American serviceman convicted of the 'brownout murders' two years earlier.

Because of the new evidence, a new inquest was held, at the City Court in Melbourne. Jeanette Routledge requested, and was granted, permission to call witnesses and produce evidence at the inquest. It commenced on 23 March 1944, and sat for nineteen days, with several adjournments, until 28 April. The inquest quickly developed an adversarial character, with Benbow and Routledge arguing that the dead woman was Philomena Morgan, and the police arguing that she was Linda Agostini. There were sixty-two witnesses called, and a great deal of expert and allegedly-expert evidence was argued over.

The Coroner, Arthur Tingate, gave his decision on 2 May. He found that the dead woman was Linda Agostini and committed Antonio Agostini to stand trial for her murder. (He completely exonerated the Quin family.)

The trial, before Justice Charles Lowe, began in the Victorian Supreme Court on 19 June. It took eight sitting days. The central issue was whether Agostini had deliberately killed his wife, or whether it was an accident as he maintained. His confession had not mentioned the terrible injuries to the woman's head: these were explained later as being caused by him accidentally dropping her body down a flight of stairs.

The trial concluded on 28 June. The jury found Agostini guilty of manslaughter, though not of murder. This verdict was criticised by Lowe, who described it as 'scarcely conceivable' and said the jury had probably been 'merciful': a murder conviction then carried a mandatory death sentence in Victoria. Lowe sentenced Agostini to six years hard labour, well below the possible maximum sentence.

After the trial, Agostini said that the body was not that of his wife, and that he did not take any responsibility for it. The body was buried in the Preston General Cemetery, in northern Melbourne, on 13 July. Five journalists and a taxi driver acted as pallbearers.

Agostini was released from custody on 21 August 1948 and immediately deported. He returned to his native Italy, where he died in 1969.

He was scarcely heard of again, except for a strange report in *Truth* in 1959, suggesting that Agostini wanted to return to Australia, and that he had connections with the underworld which might make this possible.

Philomena Morgan was never accounted for, although police suggested that Jean Morris, who was murdered in Queensland in 1932, may have been Morgan.

*

The body of the woman who came to be known as the Pyjama Girl was found in September 1934. She was buried in July 1944, a month after a man had been convicted of her manslaughter.

The newspapers that reported the long police investigation into the Pyjama Girl's death, the legal battles over her identity and the arrest and trial of her killer, also chronicled ten years which were perhaps the most tragic in human history. In that time, much of the world descended into madness, tyranny and mass slaughter. Tens of millions of people died, often victims of appalling cruelty.

But while the world was experiencing death camps and carpet bombing and a million other horrors, the Pyjama Girl was still big news. The front page of the *Argus* on 17 March 1939 showed pictures of German troops marching through Prague and carried a report on a minor development in the Pyjama Girl case. On 15 December 1942, a NSW parliamentarian called for a fresh investigation into the case; this received three times as much space in the Melbourne *Herald* as the latest news from the battle of Stalingrad. On 29 June 1944, readers of the *Sydney Morning Herald* learned of a break in the enemy line around the Allied beachhead at Normandy. Sharing the front page is the news that Antonio Agostini, accused of killing the Pyjama Girl, has been found guilty of manslaughter.

The fascination of the case endured, too. Apart from hundreds of newspaper articles, the Pyjama Girl has been the subject of one full-length book and chapters in at least nine books on Australian crime. The case featured in a short documentary film, and it was used as a basis for a novel, a short story, a feature film and a comic book.

Barry Humphries painted a picture of her. There was even a popular song written about the case. At parties people would sing, to the cheerful tune of 'Finiculi Finicula':

My name is Antonio Agostini
I killed my wife and now I'm doing life!

The Pyjama Girl case has featured in two television programs, including Peter Luck's *This Fabulous Century*, a piece of performance theatre, and was recently the subject of an experimental short film.

One of the attractions at the Police and Justice Museum, in the old Water Police building near Circular Quay in Sydney, is a display concerning the Pyjama Girl. In what used to be a cell is a glass case. It contains a diorama showing the finding of the body, the woman's death mask, the painted plaster likeness and placards telling the story of the case. Against the opposite wall is the zinc-lined coffin in which the body was kept. The cell walls are of thick sandstone. The room is cold and quiet. It is a little like a side chapel in a cathedral, dedicated to some minor saint.

*

In *This Fabulous Century*, Peter Luck interviewed Tom Griffith, by then an elderly man, who repeated the story which must have become a mantra to him: How I Found the Body. 'It was quite obvious it was a body,' he said, rather blandly. 'It wouldn't have been obvious to anyone from a vehicle, but to me walking along the shoulder of the road, quite obvious.' Peter Luck, off camera, suggested that it must have been 'a gruesome sight'.

'Oh, yes.'

Indeed it was. The report made by Dr Leslie Woods, the government medical officer who first examined the body, said the body was badly burnt. The left side of the body was dry from heat, the feet were badly burnt and the legs were charred and scarred. The left side of the lower back and buttocks were also deeply burned, almost to the bone, exposing the rectum.

The head had suffered eight wounds to the left side, including a gaping wound over the forehead which was so deep that it exposed the brain. The bone in the area of the wounds was smashed and loose. There were also many minor wounds and a puncture wound which turned out to be the hole made by a bullet. He said the death had probably occurred more than twenty-four hours earlier.

In the days after the body was found, police established that a fire had been seen in the culvert at 2.30 a.m. on the previous Wednesday. This led them to believe that the woman had been killed on Tuesday evening, meaning that the body would have been four days old when it was found.

It is no surprise then that, as the *Argus* reported on 6 September 1934: 'Many people who thought they could assist were repulsed when they were shown the photograph [of the corpse], which indicates clearly the ferocity of the murderer's attack.'

Those who later viewed the body preserved in formalin at Sydney University had similar reactions. 'She was partly burnt, she was in a neglected condition,' said one witness at the 1944 inquest. 'The body was filthy, it was dripping with formalin ... it was nasty to look at.'

This was the unknown woman the newspapers immediately called 'a good-looking young woman', 'the pyjama-clad girl with the lacquered finger-nails' and 'pretty'.

While it was perfectly possible that the woman had been beautiful in life, it would surely have been impossible to say this with certainty given the posthumous condition of the body.

But the loveliness of the unknown woman clearly struck a chord with the public. On 4 September, a Coburg garage proprietor said that he had seen a woman who tallied exactly with the description of the Pyjama Girl. She was, he said a 'striking type', aged about twenty-eight, and had 'bobbed, fair, peroxided hair, plucked and pencilled eyebrows, light blue eyes and was of slim build'. The Melbourne *Star* quoted him as saying: 'Both the women were good-looking blondes, and of the theatrical type ... They were the type that would command attention anywhere.'

The colour of the hair attracted much attention. The Melbourne *Herald* said it was 'ash blond hair that has the appearance of having been treated with peroxide. Her hair was definitely ash blonde at the roots, but a little more golden in its longer strands.' A sample of the woman's hair was shown to 'a woman's hairdresser in Albury', who said that while the ends had been treated with peroxide, 'the hair closer to the roots was distinctly brunette.'

Speculation about the dead woman's appearance quickly extended to her background and character as well. In the absence of information, people seemed to construct the Pyjama Girl they wanted.

The Albury *Border Morning Mail*, on 3 September, asked: 'Whose is the body in the culvert? ask the investigators; surely a young attractive woman cannot disappear without someone knowing?' Maybe she has been brought from another town? This was perfectly possible, as:

> In these days of scanty work when the struggle to live grows intense, men and women must go far to find

> employment. Husbands and wives are separated, families broken up, and the parted ones are unheard from for weeks.

The *Herald* reported speculation of the woman 'having been married, or involved in an underworld feud'. Was she involved in another crime? 'Certain police officers do not believe it is impossible that the murder was committed in the underworld of Melbourne or Sydney.' In October, the criminal connection appeared again: was she a woman believed to have been 'engaged in smuggling goods into the Commonwealth'?

The Coburg mechanic was not alone in thinking her a 'theatrical type'. The Albury *Banner* reported on 7 September on 'the latest police theory' that 'the dead girl was a former amateur actress who recently left Sydney on a professional tour'. This was hard to check: 'theatricals and showfolk … are difficult to locate, as they are always on the move.' Was she the wife in a 'theatrical couple'? Or a woman called Gay Gains, 'last heard of as a member of a troupe of dancers who were touring principally in country districts'?

Another short-lived theory had the Pyjama Girl being an woman 'of independent means' who had stayed for two months in Shanghai and had 'mixed in good society'.

The *Argus* reported: 'The girl had refined features, well-shaped hands, carefully manicured and rose-tinted finger-nails; she was found in a suit of silk pyjamas of good quality; and it is surmised that she came from a family in, at least, reasonably good position.' That she had a gold filling in a back tooth 'seems to confirm this'. The *Border Morning Mail* was less charitable in its reading of the gold tooth:

> One prominent dentist in Albury, of considerably [*sic*] experience, expressed the view yesterday that broadly gold fillings are demanded by two classes of people. One is the person of means, who requires the best quality, while the other is the type which likes 'show', and will pay almost any price for a glittering filling, even though not of affluent means. The plucked eyebrows and lacquered fingernails, combined with other known details, suggests that the murdered woman belongs to the latter class.

The *Sydney Morning Herald* sided with the *Argus*: 'The victim bore every evidence of belonging to a respectable family, if not one prominent in society.' The *Age* agreed: 'The victim was not of the working class type,' and noted that it was improbable that 'a woman of the type in question' could disappear without being missed. 'The victim was distinctly not of the usual country-type condition. Her hands and nails show [this].'

Even the women's pyjamas were revised upwards. This famous garment was, quite literally, embroidered to fit the story, to an extent nothing short of fraudulent.

When the remnants of the pyjamas were produced at the 1944 inquest, there was a note of disappointment. 'The first murmur of interest ran through the court when Const. Kelly ... produced the tattered symbol of mystery – pyjamas,' reported the Sydney *Daily Telegraph*. 'At least, he said they were pyjamas. They were dirty burnt fragments of silky cloth.' *Truth* described 'the most famous pyjamas in the history of crime' thus: 'A few pieces of tattered, yellow rags, dirty and almost disintegrated, scorched and blackened with [illegible] of what might once have been a white facing.'

From the first, the pyjamas were subject to varying reports. The *Herald*, on 1 September 1934, said the victim was 'clad in white pyjamas bordered in yellow'. The *Telegraph* said they were 'expensive canary-coloured Canton crepe pyjamas ... the coat was edged with white crepe, but the white trousers were edged with yellow.' The *Border Morning Mail* also mentioned that, 'An oriental design in white silk had been worked in on the front of the jacket.' All these accounts tally with the official description.

But this does not seem to have been enough. Most of the cloth had been burnt, and new colours and designs filled the vacuum. On 8 September, the *Star* said the pyjamas were 'green and yellow'. Later in September, the *Telegraph* reported that 'the canary or maize coloured pyjamas had a large Chinese dragon worked on the front in silk.' This was the first appearance of a dragon which was indeed a mythical beast. At the 1938 inquest, the pyjamas were described both as yellow and 'green and cream'.

By 1944, the confusion was even greater. The *Daily Telegraph*, looking back on the case when the news of Agostini's arrest broke, said:

> … the pyjamas worn by the girl were made of kale crepe material, green and cream in colour, with a huge Chinese dragon stretching from the bottom of the jacket to the top.

But in fact this description is not of the pyjamas found on the dead body, but rather of a green silk jacket which the police claimed was connected with the case. This jacket first appeared in PIX magazine in 1938, in a photograph captioned 'Dragon Design on the burnt pyjamas which the murdered girl was wearing', which were said to be 'of a lemon colour'. Perhaps the implication is merely that the design is the same as on the original pyjamas.

The false pyjamas also make an appearance in Rupert Kathner's 1939 film. Here there is no ambiguity. The same dark-coloured jacket shown in the *PIX* article appears, and the narrator says it is 'the actual pyjamas worn by the murdered girl'.

Dr Benbow discovered this deception in 1940, and it was later admitted by the New South Wales police. Detective Sergeant Wilks, who had been a senior officer in the investigation from 1934 to 1939, confirmed at the 1944 inquest that the film had been approved by himself, another detective and Commissioner MacKay. Asked about the dragon coat, he prevaricated and said it was 'almost a replica of what the original garment was'. This astonishing deception was mentioned, matter-of-factly, in newspaper reports of the inquest, but no one made a fuss about it. Many subsequent accounts reproduce the pictures of the 'replica coat' without question.

*

In 1974, the Melbourne *Herald* published an account of the Pyjama Girl story. It began, as such accounts usually do, with the finding of the body:

> On a sunny Saturday morning, September 1, 1934, a young farmer named Tom Griffiths was leading a bull along the Howlong Road … The bull shied at a culvert and, investigating, Griffiths discovered the partly burned remains of a young woman.

Five years earlier, a magazine called *Criminologist* had described the same event:

> As he approached a brick parapet culvert about five miles from Albury, the animal lifted its head, snorted and was clearly disturbed. Griffiths went nearer, and in the culvert saw the partially naked body of a woman.

In 1965, veteran crime journalist Vince Kelly had written in his book *The Charge is Murder*:

> The animal smelt death, and snorting and baulking it refused to pass the culvert.

A pulp paperback about Australian crime published three years earlier had a similar story:

> … they came to a brick parapet culvert. Here the bull, which up to now had been lumbering docilely behind, stopped, snorted and backed away. Griffiths tried to urge him on. Then he glanced over the side of the culvert and saw what was frightening the animal.

There were eleven daily newspapers published in Melbourne, Sydney and Albury in 1934. Every one of them reported the finding of the body. Not one mentions the bull behaving oddly in any way.

The baulking bull's first appearance in the daily papers occurred in 1944. Reporting on Agostini's dramatic arrest, all the newspapers recapitulated the facts of the case. Most mentioned how the body had been noticed by a farmer; some noted that he had been leading a bull. But the Sydney *Daily Telegraph* added that the 'bull snorted as it approached the culvert, and would not move'.

This flourish did not come from the *Telegraph's* own reportage in 1934. Rather, it was picked up from the inventive minds of the staff at *Truth*, a scandal-mongering, sex-soaked weekly paper, the bawling bastard child of Australian journalism. The Sydney edition of *Truth* came out on Sunday, and the day after the discovery of the body it rushed into print with its account of how the body had been found. Tom Griffith is quoted as saying:

> I had reached a point about four and a half miles from Albury and a half-mile from our home when my horse exhibited signs of fear. It appeared to sense some danger.

This was almost certainly made up: Griffith had been on foot.

Undaunted, *Truth* had another try the following Sunday:

> [Griffith] was in view of his father's magnificent homestead on the Delaware Station when the big bull commenced to bellow and paw the ground. The animal was quivering with fear.
>
> [He then saw the partly-burned body, and said:] *'The same feeling of terror which had seized the prize bull overcame me.*
>
> *'With the big animal beside me I fairly galloped the half-mile which separated me from home, and I telephoned the police.'*

Which was also nonsense: Griffith tied the bull up and borrowed a bicycle to get home. But once the baulking bull crossed into the mainstream press, on 6 March 1944, it became part of the story and indeed 'would not move'.

The *Herald* article of 1974 contains the last confirmed sighting of the baulking bull. It was written by Robert Coleman, who later wrote the most authoritative book yet published on the case. Coleman's book does not mention the bull shying at the culvert or behaving strangely in any other way. Presumably he had done some additional research and discovered that no such thing happened. Coleman also makes no mention of the 'dragon pyjamas': again, perhaps he had come to doubt their authenticity.

The bull 'scenting death' was an occurrence so unlikely that any properly sceptical journalist should have questioned it. Once questioned, it could have easily been disproved. So why, then, did it survive in the story for thirty years? Part of the answer lies, literally, in the realm of fairytales.

*

The media's treatment of crime has been the subject of a vast amount of academic study and much popular debate. A common thread is unhappiness at how the media portray crime, although the reasons for this displeasure vary greatly.

Most critics fall into one of two sharply polarised groups. Defined crudely, the first believes the media are irresponsible and sensationalist in their treatment of crime. They glamorise illegal behaviour, thereby threatening law and order, morality and social stability, especially among the young.

The second group sees the media as an arm of the establishment. Crime news is a means of marginalising minorities, exaggerating their 'deviance' and generating an unrealistic fear of crime which assists the election of conservative governments.

Such characterisations tend to ignore something basic. Crime is news because it is innately interesting. Illegal behaviour generally, and murder especially, fascinates people, more than can be explained away by the machinations of the media. Leopold Bloom, in Joyce's *Ulysses*, ruminates on the genuine popularity of tabloid crime news:

> Murder … They love reading about it. Man's head found in a garden. Her clothing consisted of. How she met her death. Recent outrage. The weapon used. Murderer is still at large. Clues. A shoelace. The body to be exhumed. Murder will out.

But the fascination with violent death is older, even, than mass media. 'Tabloid crime' has existed in various forms for many centuries, and in all its incarnations its depiction has followed remarkably similar patterns. In particular, crime news, along with crime fiction, has consistently emphasised violent crime, especially that involving sex. It has also focused on discrete, specific incidents of crime rather than on broader trends and problems.

One scholar of nineteenth-century ballads remarked that their subject matter was mostly 'the stuff of tabloid journalism – sensational tales of lust, revenge and domestic crime'. This is putting things back to front: it was tabloid journalism which appropriated the subject matter of ballads.

The first newspapers that regularly published large amounts of crime news in prose form appeared in the early nineteenth century. They borrowed their style and subject matter from broadsheet ballads. These were songs, usually set to well-known tunes, which were sold by street vendors and often dealt with topical events. They were, in fact, 'a kind of musical journalism'.

The reporting of crime through song was a long-running industry. It began modestly in England in the middle of the sixteenth century, but by 1861 broadsheet ballads were a major industry, described as 'an important, perhaps the chief part of the reading of a large class of our population'.

Among the most popular ballads were those that concerned crime, particularly infanticide, adultery and murder, usually of a woman and usually discovered through supernatural means. As one ballad seller put it: 'There's nothing beats a stunning good murder.' A good example of a 'popular crime' was the murder in 1828 of Maria Martin, who was killed by her lover in a barn.

With heart so light, she thought no harm, to meet him she
did go
He murdered her all in the barn, and laid her body low
After the horrible deed was done, she lay weltering in
her gore
Her bleeding mangled body he buried beneath the
Red-Barn floor.

The crime was detected, so the songs had it, because Maria's ghost appeared to her mother in a dream. The 'Red Barn Murder', as it became known, spawned a minor publishing industry in its own right.

No one cared very much about the accuracy of these ballads (nor, it seems, about the quality of the lyrics). That was not the point; what mattered was a good story.

Broadsheet ballads were themselves a continuation of the folk tradition of minstrelsy, and through that of even more ancient storytelling forms, such as fairytales. The modern mass media are not as distinct from folklore as we often assume. In the modern world the media fulfils many of the functions that folklore did in pre-media communities, and there are compelling parallels between crime news and fairytales.

Fairytales, like crime news reports, are bare, boiled down to short, condensed plots embroidered with memorable details. Both forms provide little explanation of external circumstances. Stories begin abruptly, develop quickly and typically offer little or no sense of causal connection. Instead, we are simply told 'and then … and then …'

C.S. Lewis wrote that fairytales provide a child with 'the knowledge that he is born into a world of death, violence, wounds, adventure, heroism and cowardice, good and evil'. Crime news serves a similar function in modern society, though chiefly for adults. Crime news is often a kind of morality play, allowing members of the public to share their indignation and horror and providing an opportunity to reaffirm basic moral standards.

In *The Country of Lost Children*, Peter Pierce explores the link between the fairytales involving lost children and what he sees as a pervading Australian anxiety about 'the lost child', an anxiety which underpins reportage of, for example, the disappearance of Jaidyn Leskie in Moe, Victoria in 1997.

Children like to hear fairy stories repeated over and over. Although the individual details differ, much crime news, too, is essentially repetitious. Leopold Bloom's musings, inspired by one particular murder, could apply to almost any murder.

Colourful details are a key element to fairytales. Nicholas Tucker, an authority on children's literature, argues that details such as Rapunzel's hair and Jack's magic beanstalk, 'have intrinsic interest, whatever they also happen to symbolise, simply because they are bizarre and therefore fascinating'.

Crime reporters, too, know the importance of the colourful detail. Had Azaria Chamberlain been killed by a domestic dog in a suburban backyard, the case would have been news, but only locally and not for long. And had the victim of the Albury murder been a middle-aged man dressed in overalls, the case would be forgotten. The silk pyjamas and the beautiful young woman preserved in formalin: these are the mythic elements that make the story of the Pyjama Girl memorable.

The fairytale most closely evoked by the story of the Pyjama Girl is 'Snow White'. The preservation of the Pyjama Girl's body in a tank is an echo of the glass coffin in which Snow White is preserved after she has been poisoned by the wicked Queen.

> The dear child was dead, and dead she remained … They were going to bury her, but she still looked fresh and alive, and she still had her beautiful red cheeks. 'We can't lower her into the black,' they said, and they had a coffin made out of glass, so that she could be seen from all sides, and they put her into it … Snow White lay in her coffin for years and years. She didn't rot, but continued to look as if she were asleep.

This particular detail is older even than the Snow White story. The Grimm Brothers recorded another story, 'The Glass Coffin', with a similar theme, and there is a story of a beautiful woman enchanted and preserved in a *'casse di cristallo'* in *The Pentamerone*, a collection of stories first published in Italy in the early seventeenth century.

Another correspondence: when Snow White is poisoned by the evil Queen, the dwarfs try to revive her.

> They lifted her up, looked to see if they could find anything poisonous, unlaced her, combed her hair, washed her in water and wine, but nothing helped.

If only they had properly checked inside her mouth. Years later, when the coffin is moved, the piece of poison apple stuck in Snow White's throat is dislodged, and she revives.

In the usual story of the Pyjama Girl, the police and their experts inspect the body and do everything they can think of to identify her. If only they had properly checked inside her mouth! Ten years later, a porcelain filling is dislodged and she is finally identified.

In Benbow's reconstruction of the crime, the Pyjama Girl, like Snow White, seeks refuge in a remote cottage and is safe there for a time, but is killed because she yields to temptation: overtly sexual in one case, symbolically so – the poisonous red apple – in the other.

Dr Benbow believed that the Pyjama Girl was killed by 'snowy-haired Mrs Quin', an apparently respectable local matriarch rather like the evil Queen. 'Quin' even sounds like Queen! … but perhaps we are getting carried away.

The beautiful, apparently dead, maiden is a strong theme in fairytales. In the oldest known version of the Sleeping Beauty story, an enchanted maiden, Talia, is discovered by a passing king who falls in love with her. Although he has a wife, the king takes advantage of Talia's state to consummate his passion, and the woman bears him several children while she sleeps.

The sexual attractiveness of the Pyjama Girl is explicit in many of the fictional versions of the story. In Nigel Krauth's 1993 story, 'Worry No More', the police chief, who had been a client of 'Philomena Franki', a prostitute accidentally killed by another policeman, visits the room in which the Pyjama Girl is kept:

> Under the light she was perfectly still in the bath. He would stand on her right, with the collapsed side of her head away from him. He would run his eyes down her. Down the good cheek. Over the breasts, still perfectly upright, though translucent now. Down the dead still flank, blooming under the light. Down to the slim hips, slim as a schoolgirl's, slim and firm. Occasionally, when he couldn't help himself, he put his hand into the formalin and stroked her. Stroked the parts of her he remembered perfectly stroking.

A 1978 film based loosely on the story, *The Pyjama Girl Case*, directed by Flavio Mogherini, is equally unabashed. The 'novelisation' of the film describes how:

> The body in the tank of formaldehyde, for all the world to see, had become more than a local sensation. Hardcore porn magazines all over the world had got hold of the pictures … a syndicate, with faked press passes, had been shooting full frontals of the body, shaking the tank to spread the legs.

The Pyjama Girl's body was, manifestly, not sexually attractive. It was a horrific sight, something attested to by almost everyone who saw it, and evident even from the black and white post-mortem photographs of the body. The fiction writers have made the body beautiful because it fits ancient narrative patterns for it to be so. Doubtless they were inspired to do this partly because, in 1944, the police did attempt to beautify the body. Before it was presented for identification to several people who had known Linda Agostini, the body was taken from the formalin, washed and dried, and the face was heavily made up with cream, face powder and lipstick and the hair was prepared by a hairdresser.

But both art and life had, in fact, been anticipated – by the *Truth*. On 19 September 1934, *Truth* reported that the embalmers, Charles Kinsela and his son, had 'preserved the murdered girl with a secret formula'. More than that:

> She is now lying in a polished oaken casket and looks as if she is merely asleep. Mr Kinsela and his son shampooed

> and dressed her pretty hair, rouged her lips, darkened the eyelashes, creamed and powdered her face and pencilled her eyebrows.
>
> Were it not for the waxen pallor of death, the unknown pyjama girl might be in a doze, she looks so natural.
>
> There is now not the slightest doubt of her exceptional good looks. She is small and very prepossessing, with nicely-moulded full lips and slumberous thoughtful grey eyes: the sort of girl who would have had scores of admirers.

Nonsense, all of it. The coffin was of pine, lined with zinc and painted black. The body remained a horrific sight.

But whatever their faults as journalists, those who wrote for *Truth* had tapped into what people *want* to hear about a crime. We want a murder victim to be an 'unknown young beauty'. We much prefer it if burnt oily rags found on the body are glamorous silky pyjamas with an embroidered dragon. And, remembering the animal that warns of evil or reveals murder in fairytales, we are untroubled when a journalist invents a bull which scents death and refuses to pass a hidden dead body. These things fit the story. They belong.

The Pyjama Girl case first attracted attention because of its mythic elements. These elements were emphasised and exaggerated and even made up, to such an extent that the story, as it were, floated free from reality. We have the Pyjama Girl we want: a strange merging of tabloid crime and fairytale. She has become an Australian myth.

Pure Evil

Andrew Rule & John Silvester

THE OLD BLUESTONE COURTHOUSE in Bendigo is one of the most imposing in Victoria. On the first floor is the main courtroom, with a large oil painting of an English lord hanging on the rear wall and a huge chandelier over the bar table.

But on this day the case did not fit the majesty of the surroundings. Standing in the dock was a plump, nondescript man facing the relatively minor charge of false imprisonment.

The accused wasn't even going to fight, having earlier agreed to plead guilty to the solitary charge. This would save court time and public money, allow the female victim to avoid the trauma of giving evidence and enable the justice system to move on to the next, and seemingly more important, case.

But the accused was not motivated by remorse. He had a powerful incentive to plead guilty to this one charge. In return the prosecution had agreed to drop more serious charges, including kidnap, assault with a weapon and indecent assault.

The man in the dock was Peter Norris Dupas. And for all his mild looks, he had a history of committing increasingly violent sexual crimes over four decades. At least one policeman and an experienced psychiatrist had warned years earlier that he was a potential killer, but that didn't prevent Dupas from being allowed to plead to the least significant of the charges laid against him.

The year before his trial, the Victorian Government had passed a controversial law that enabled courts to sentence criminals such as Dupas to indefinite jail terms. The law was to protect the community from serial sex offenders – and if there was a stereotype of the man the Act was designed to catch, it was Dupas. But for the law to be activated the offender had to be found guilty of a so-called 'serious offence'. Unlawful imprisonment fell just short – it was considered too minor for the draconian legislation.

It would not have seemed a minor offence to the 26-year-old woman whom Dupas had attacked and slashed in the public toilets at Lake Eppalock in January 1994. Dupas was wearing a balaclava when he followed the woman into the toilet block where he threatened her and cut her with a knife. He clearly intended to rape her before he was frightened off. In the boot of his car were handcuffs, knives … and, chillingly, a shovel. A weapon might conceivably be used only to frighten someone, but a shovel has only one use for a violent abductor – to bury a body.

Defence and prosecution lawyers do deals all the time. In this case Dupas's lawyer made it clear his client would plead to 'appropriate charges'. Perhaps the evidence would not support the more serious charges, and jury trials are always a risk, but there can be no doubt that the defence lawyer did well to cut a deal for his client. He was aware that a guilty plea to unlawful imprisonment would protect Dupas from the possibility of going to jail forever.

In the Bendigo Court on 18 August 1994, Judge Leo Hart was also interested in whether he could deal with Dupas under the indefinite sentence rules. He asked, 'Is the offence for which he has pleaded guilty an offence which, together with his prior convictions, brings into play –'

Defence lawyer: 'No.'

Judge Hart: '– the provisions introduced by the *Sentencing (Amendment) Act* 1993?'

Defence lawyer: 'No, it is not, Your Honour.'

With his record Dupas was going to go to jail anyway. The trouble was, it wouldn't be for long enough. He was sentenced to three years and nine months with a minimum of two.

Dupas was released from jail on 29 September 1996, and went on to kill at least one and possibly three women. He was convicted in August 2000 of the murder of psychotherapist Nicole Patterson, who was stabbed to death in her Westgarth home on 19 April 1999.

He is also strongly suspected of killing Margaret Maher, who was killed in October 1997, and Mersina Halvagis, who was stabbed to death in the Fawkner Cemetery while tending her grandmother's grave in November 1997.

*

Peter Norris Dupas was just fifteen and still in school uniform when he first attacked a woman with a knife. Now, more than thirty years later, police believe he may be one of Australia's worst serial killers.

Dupas is a criminal oddity of a kind that the criminal justice system cannot handle. A man considered sufficiently mentally twisted to need treatment, yet too 'sane' to be institutionalised for life. The police, prison officers and many of the psychiatrists who knew Dupas wrote reports suggesting he would re-offend, yet he was released from jail to do just that.

An insignificant little man who was once a fat lonely schoolboy, he has carried a knife since he was a teenager and attacked women whenever the opportunity has arisen. And like many serial offenders, his crimes have become progressively more violent, despite medical and psychiatric treatment since the 1960s.

Dupas was born in Sydney and his family moved to Melbourne when he was a baby. His brother and sister were years older than him, and he was effectively treated as an only child by his mother and father, who were old enough to be his grandparents. He was later to say he was spoiled when he was growing up. He went to Waverley High School, repeated Year Seven and was seen as a slow learner with no friends and an unhealthy array of complexes. 'He did not participate in sports and describes himself as having been obese and the subject of ridicule by his school mates,' concluded a psychiatrist who examined him in 1990.

It was in October 1968 that Peter Dupas first showed his dark side. A few weeks earlier, a female neighbour had returned home after having a baby when she heard a knock on her back door. It was Dupas, wearing his Waverley High School uniform. 'Young Peter Dupas got on very well with my husband and he used to call in to our house and talk with us,' she would later tell police.

The boy asked if he could borrow a small knife to peel some vegetables. 'I remarked to him about him peeling the potatoes for his mother and what a good boy he was.'

Then Dupas suddenly attacked her, slashing her fingers, neck and face. As he tried to stab her, he said, 'It's too late, Pam, I can't stop now. They will lock me up.' Finally he stopped and began to cry. When asked by police why he had attacked the woman, he said, 'I must have been trying to kill her or something. I didn't know why I was trying to do this. As far as I am concerned there is no reason for me to do anything to Pam but I could not help myself.' He was put on probation for eighteen months and given psychiatric treatment.

Like many loners who turn into sex offenders, the nerdish and spoiled Dupas craved power. He had applied for and been rejected from the police force, for being one centimetre too short. According to a former FBI crime profiler, John Douglas, 'frequently serial offenders have failed in their efforts to join police departments … one of their main fantasy occupations is police officer.'

In the next few years Dupas began a pattern of committing low-level sex-related crimes. In March 1972 he was found hiding in the backyard of an Oakleigh home as he watched a woman undress. Two years later he was caught in the female toilet block at the McCrae Caravan Park watching women shower.

He was seen to follow women and young girls and his behaviour became increasingly aggressive. In 1973 he began to attack women in their homes. He would knock on the door, pretend to have car trouble and then ask to borrow a screwdriver. In one case he threatened to hurt a woman's baby if she attempted to struggle against him.

It was during their investigation into this incident that police started to believe Dupas was in a league of his own. It was not the crime he committed, violent as it was, nor his looks, as he appeared quite harmless. It was the way he answered or, more accurately, didn't answer questions, that worried detectives.

Senior Detective Ian Armstrong interviewed him at the Nunawading police station on 30 November 1973. Dupas was twenty-one and looked younger. He had a pudgy, baby face and the manner of a person who lacked resolve. To Armstrong he looked the sort of suspect who would easily crack under questioning. But as everyone who was to deal with Dupas over the next twenty-seven years would find, looks can deceive.

Many experienced criminals know how to lie their way through a police interview, but a frightened young man usually confesses quickly. Dupas was different – dangerously so. 'We tried everything and he would get to the point where he was about to talk. Then something would snap and he would go blank, then deny everything,' recalled Armstrong, a senior sergeant at Warrnambool when Dupas was found guilty of murder.

'He stood out. To me the guy was just pure evil. He committed a rape in Mitcham and would have committed more given the opportunity. He looked so innocuous but he was a cold, calculating liar. His attacks were all carefully planned and he showed no remorse. We could see where he was going. I remember thinking, "This guy could go all the way [to murder]."'

Dupas was being interviewed over the Mitcham rape which had happened six days earlier. 'It wasn't me, I didn't do it … I don't know anything about the incident … She must have been mixed up with someone else,' were his answers. Nobody believed him. He was convicted in 1974 over rape and burglary charges and sentenced to nine years with a minimum of five.

Ian Armstrong felt worried enough about the young offender to write a report which said in part: 'He is an unmitigated liar … he is a very dangerous young person who will continue to offend where females are concerned and will possibly cause the death of one of his victims if he is not straightened out.'

In his first few months in custody Dupas was examined by one of Australia's most experienced psychiatrists, Dr Allen Bartholomew. He noted that Dupas refused to admit his problems. 'I am reasonably certain that this youth has a serious psychosexual problem, that he is using the technique of denial as a coping device and that he is to be seen as potentially dangerous. The denial technique makes for huge difficulty in treatment.'

Late in 1977, a group of parents who lived near the Dupas family in Mount Waverley contacted the Parole Board and urged that he not be released as they believed him to be still dangerous.

But Dupas had started to learn how to play the system. According to Bartholomew, he began to talk about his crimes, not because he wanted to be treated but because he wanted to get out of jail to re-offend: 'I feel that when he realised that his hopes for parole might be jeopardised by his denials, he began to admit his guilt.'

Despite a warning by Bartholomew, in September 1978, that Dupas 'was a danger to female society', he was released from prison on 4 September 1979. Within two months he attacked four women in just ten days.

On 9 November 1979 he forced his way into a toilet block in Frankston and raped a woman. Two days later he chased a woman and threatened her with a knife. On 18 November he dragged an elderly women into a vacant block and stabbed her, and the following day he attacked another woman in the same area. For each attack he wore a balaclava and carried a knife. He told police, 'I've had this problem for about six years. I'm glad I got caught.'

Bartholomew could not resist pointing out that his view had been ignored. 'The present offences are exactly what might have been predicted,' he wrote when Dupas was again charged with rape and assault. He concluded that Dupas was unlikely to change. The trained psychiatrist and the experienced detective, Ian Armstrong, both saw something in this harmless-looking man that compelled them to commit to paper their fears that he was a potential killer. Bartholomew warned that Dupas's increasingly violent rapes and knife attacks 'could have fatal consequences'.

Even parole officers who had believed Dupas could change began to give up hope. 'There is little that can be said in Dupas's favour. He remains an extremely disturbed, immature and dangerous man. His release on parole was a mistake,' stated a report added to his file in September 1980.

Dupas was found guilty of rape, malicious wounding, assault with intent to rob and indecent assault for the 1979 attacks. He was sentenced to six and a half years jail with a five-year minimum.

It was to become a pattern. Dupas would do what he was told in jail, attend the courses, do the therapy and appear to be changing, only to attack women whenever he was out of jail.

He was released again on 27 February 1985, although no one seriously believed he would not attack again. It didn't take long. On 3 March he raped a 21-year-old woman who was sunbathing at Rye ocean beach.

After the beach attack he gave police his trademark speech of remorse: 'I'm sorry for what happened. Everyone was telling me I'm okay now. I never thought it was going to happen again. All I wanted to do is live a normal life.'

He was sentenced to twelve years with a minimum of ten. The beach rape was near a spot where a woman sunbather, Helen McMahon, had been bashed and murdered in remarkably similar circumstances only weeks earlier. Her body had been found naked, covered only by a towel, and her murder was never solved.

A counsellor who tried to help Dupas wrote: 'Through long-term association with various professionals he has learned to manipulate any individual who has endeavoured to challenge his offending behaviour by way of saying the right things and behaving in a convincing manner in a supervised environment.'

Despite treatment his crimes became more violent. Despite repeated claims he was dealing with his problems, he just became more cunning.

While in jail Dupas met and married a female nurse, sixteen years his senior. They married in Castlemaine Jail in 1987 while he was still a prisoner. He told parole officers his marriage to a 'beautiful person' would help him to stop sexually offending.

It didn't. He was released in March 1992, and in January 1994 attacked a woman at knife point in a toilet block at Lake Eppalock. The woman's boyfriend, an off-duty Australian Federal Police officer, grabbed Dupas after a car chase. He was held until two Victoria Police arrived. He even whined pathetically, 'They're hurting me!' while he was pinned as the police approached. He was found guilty only of false imprisonment and given a two-year minimum.

Dupas was released again in September 1996 and eventually moved into a house in Coanne Street, Pascoe Vale – near a shopping strip in Cumberland Road. Margaret Maher, a local prostitute, regularly went shopping in Cumberland Road – that is, until she was abducted and murdered in October 1997.

About a month later Mersina Halvagis was stabbed to death in the Fawkner Cemetery while visiting her grandmother's grave. Dupas's grandfather is buried at Fawkner in the same area.

*

Everybody liked Nicole Patterson. She was a psychotherapist who devoted much of her time to trying to help young people with drug problems. Those who knew her described a vibrant and compassionate young women. Her sister, Kylie, said, 'She was the most beautiful person I've known and she had a lot of special gifts that not many people have.'

In early 1999, Ms Patterson, then twenty-eight, decided to broaden her client base and converted the front bedroom of her house in Harper Street, Westgarth into a consulting room. She began to advertise in local newspapers. On 3 March a man calling himself 'Malcolm' telephoned. Over the next five weeks he was to ring her fifteen times before he made an appointment for 19 April.

Malcolm said he wanted to be treated for depression. He didn't say that he was a violent sex offender. Ms Patterson wrote the name

'Malcolm' and his mobile telephone number in her diary and circled the time of 9 a.m. on 19 April.

Police believe Dupas knocked on the door at 9 a.m. and was ushered into the consulting room. Ms Patterson made plunger coffee and entered the room with cups, sugar and milk. Then, without warning, he attacked, stabbing her repeatedly.

She managed to scratch his face and yell before she was overwhelmed. What followed was almost beyond belief in its savagery. But despite his frenzy, Dupas's cold-blooded instinct for self-preservation asserted itself. After the murder he searched the house for any evidence that he had been there. He missed her diary, which was under clothing on the couch in the living room.

It would lead police to him.

When police raided his home three days later, they found the newspaper advertisement for Ms Patterson's psychotherapy sessions, with her name handwritten by Dupas on the border. They also found a blood-splattered jacket. DNA tests established the blood was 6.53 billion times more likely to have come from Ms Patterson 'than from an individual female chosen at random from the Victorian Caucasian population'. Finally, they found a black balaclava and a front page of the *Herald Sun* report on the murder. The picture of Nicole Patterson had been slashed with a knife.

The head of the investigation, Detective Senior Sergeant Jeff Maher, is used to dealing with killers, but he found Dupas unsettling. 'He was pure evil. He was not physically intimidating but he really sent shivers up your spine.'

Maher said Dupas refused to talk of the crime or co-operate with the investigation in any way. 'Nothing he did was on impulse. Everything was planned in the most calculating manner.' FBI expert John Douglas says that each serial killer has a 'signature' that links his murder victims. Nicole Patterson and Margaret Maher were killed in almost identical ways. There is also evidence to suggest a connection with the way Mersina Halvagis was killed in the Fawkner Cemetery in 1997.

Nicole Patterson wore a silver choker-style necklace. When police found it next to her body it had been broken and repaired with sticky tape. Friends who saw Nicole the night before the murder said that the necklace was then intact. Detectives believe the killer may have ripped it from her and worn it himself while he was in the house.

Police said many of his attacks were concentrated on the breast area of his victims. The doctor who examined Dupas when he was arrested said that he was 'an anxious, timid-looking man wearing bifocals. I noted that he had prominent deposits over the pectoral muscles which had the appearance of female breasts.'

*

Bill Patterson and George Halvagis were old mates. They watched their children grow up together when they lived in Warracknabeal, in country Victoria, in the 1970s.

But like any families that move to big cities, they lost touch over the years. Now they are linked by a shared grief. Both men have had to deal with the death of a daughter. In both cases these deaths were murders and now, in a bizarre coincidence, it appears that both women were killed by the same man.

In August 2000, Bill Patterson and George Halvagis sat in the public gallery of Court Four in the Supreme Court and watched as Dupas, forty-seven, was convicted of killing Nicole Patterson. George and his wife Christina sat in the back of the court and watched most of the seven-day trial. Police were concerned the grieving couple were there to take justice into their own hands. On the last day of the trial police checked them for weapons before they were allowed into the court.

'I do not know why they would do that. We were here to support Bill and his family, not to do anything to the man who was charged,' Mr Halvagis said later. 'We were old friends and now it may be that the same animal killed our daughters.'

If the accused man knew who was behind him he didn't show any concern. He sat in the dock looking straight ahead. Dressed in a blue suit and a 1970s-style tie, he looked composed, his hands resting on his lap. Only the occasional fidget with his thumbs betrayed any sign of nerves. He looked harmless enough, the sort who might be given the role of the librarian in an amateur play. But his looks belied his criminal history.

When the jury began to file in to hear the judge's final summary, Dupas was on his feet, even before the court was asked to rise. Dupas didn't need to be told – he knew the rules because he had been in the criminal dock many times before.

The Patterson family sat through the whole trial. They listened to evidence about how Nicole died, about her last moments. They learned facts that grieving relatives should never have to hear.

George Halvagis is a driven man, but not a vindictive one. He says he is not looking for revenge, only justice. He, too, sat through the entire trial and, like the Pattersons, wept after the jury found Dupas guilty. The Pattersons cried because they finally knew what had happened to their daughter, the Halvagises because they still don't know for certain what happened to theirs.

George Halvagis has one dream left. He wants the man who killed his daughter to be put in the dock in the Supreme Court and to stand trial. 'I don't want anyone to harm him [Dupas] in prison. I want him to live so we can find out what happened to Mersina.'

*

The police also have unfinished business and unanswered questions. They want to talk to Dupas about the murders of Mersina Halvagis and Margaret Maher. Homicide detectives obtained the court's permission to speak to Dupas about the Halvagis murder while he was in custody but he refused to co-operate.

Dupas's arrest record already indicated that he was unlikely to talk. The days of heavy-handed police interviews are long gone and an investigation based on the need to gain a confession is usually flawed. Police need evidence that cannot be recanted later.

The former head of the homicide squad, Carl Mengler, who retired as a Deputy Commissioner, believes juries should know when a suspect refuses to answer questions. 'In a murder case the formal interview is video-taped. Why not play it to the jury? If the suspect declines to answer questions, then let the jury see it. If the police are unfair in the interview, then the jury would know from watching the tape. If juries are to make decisions based on the facts, then let them have all the facts, in fairness to both the defence and the prosecution. A suspect does not have to answer questions, but a jury should be aware of what they have and haven't said.'

*

What makes a man evil? Peter Dupas was not beaten as a child. He did not come from a broken home. His only complaint was that he was spoilt by his elderly parents. Some men are driven to greatness, others can never overcome their compulsions.

Another sex offender, Ian Melrose Patterson, cut a nipple off one of his victims and slashed her more than 250 times. In his cell he collected pictures of Princess Di and Jana Wendt and in each picture he would cut off the nipples. He drew elaborate pictures of naked women tied up while in jail and yet was released after serving his bare minimum sentence.

When freed in 1992 he was found to have inoperable cancer. He had tumours in his liver, kidneys, lungs, bones and chest wall. When released from hospital he went straight out and bought eight bondage books and a boning knife. He told associates he intended to commit more sex crimes before he died. 'What has been done can be done again. I have thought about it. They will have to take me out with a bullet this time,' he said.

He sexually assaulted a woman with a knife two weeks after he was diagnosed as terminally ill. When he returned to hospital he was so sick that he needed constant oxygen. Even then he wouldn't stop, removing his mask to sexually harass the nursing staff. Eventually only male nurses would treat him. Only when he lapsed into a coma was he no longer a risk to women.

It would be convenient to blame someone for Dupas's life and, by extension, Nicole Patterson's death. But no judge gave him an unrealistically light sentence and no jury ignored compelling evidence. Every time he was charged with a serious sexual offence he was convicted. The problem was that, while many in authority believed he would one day kill, they appeared powerless to stop him.

Nicole Patterson's sister, Kylie Nicholas, said that, while the family was relieved when Dupas was found guilty, they still felt betrayed by a criminal justice system that had freed Dupas when it was almost certain he would attack again.

'Why did they let him out? I just don't understand the system. I only hope that people listen so this never happens again.'

*

After being found guilty of the murder of Nicole Patterson, Peter Norris Dupas was sentenced to life in jail. Justice Frank Vincent told him, 'You must, as a consequence of the commission of this terrible crime which has brought you before this court, be removed permanently from the society upon whose female members you have preyed for over thirty years. The sentence of this court is that you be imprisoned for the rest of your natural life and without the opportunity for release on parole.'

Justice Vincent was a criminal barrister who specialised in murder cases, an experienced Supreme Court judge and chairman of the Parole Board. He has probably seen more killers than anyone else in Australia. During his closing remarks he captured the mood of the wider public in one sentence: 'At a fundamental level, as human beings, you present for us the awful, threatening and unanswerable question: How did you come to be as you are?'

Serial Killers Are Losers

Vikki Petraitis & Terrence Gardiner

Serial killers are losers. This rare breed of animal gets off on the pain and suffering of others. We try and rationalise their behaviour, looking for clues of a bad childhood or past trauma, but let's face it, if a bad beginning was a prerequisite for a murderous adulthood, then every child who survived the Nazi concentration camps would be a serial killer.

Whatever drives them to kill, ultimately, it is their choice whether they resist or yield to the temptation. They plan, they stalk, they kill – but they are wily enough not to kill in front of witnesses. They don't leave an obvious trail of evidence behind them. They don't reveal their murderous notions to their mates. In short, they choose a secretive life filled with violent killing fantasies. Then they start to act on them and good people die.

Mary Jane staggers down the street, arm in arm with her boyfriend for the night. She sings one of the latest songs at the top of her voice, much to the disgust of her neighbours, disturbed from their sleep. The song, 'A Violet from Mother's Grave', has a new-age beat but is still not appreciated at midnight. The man with her is nothing to look at but Mary Jane isn't too discerning in her choice of partner. If they pay, they make the grade.

Serial killers will often choose prostitutes because they are easy prey. Prostitutes represent all 'loose women'. They don't have to be stalked or hunted, they'll get in your car or go down an alleyway with you. You beckon, they follow. Of course, that isn't enough for your more energetic serial killer. He wants to stalk. He wants the thrill of the hunt. He wants to choose the weak gazelle, then pounce like a lion. The thrill is in the power. But how hard is it to stalk someone when you know that you have the upper hand? It's like a schoolyard bully picking on the weak kid with glasses. He knows that the weak kid can't fight back.

Bloody Jo! Mary Jane's de facto, Jo, had walked out on her a fortnight ago. But she can't afford to care. Men come and go and a girl's got to be able to look after herself without factoring in their fear of commitment. He had come round to visit a couple of days ago, looking defeated. He was unemployed and he said he'd nothing to give her. That'd be right. At the end of the day, a girl's gotta do ...

Serial killers are in fact a lot like hunters. They have a victim in mind. They select a weapon. They go to the places where they know the victims are. They stalk. They hunt. They kill. And like a hunter, they take a trophy: hair, jewellery, clothing or – as in one US case – feet. Eeeuuwgh. You've got to wonder about a bloke with feet in his freezer.

Mary Jane slurs when she sings, and the man carries a beer in his hand. His face shows signs of drink, blotches and lines, and his step is uneven. They make their way to Mary Jane's room where he can get his money's worth of her.

Much has been said about nature versus nurture where your serial killer is concerned. Are they born or made? Most experts say a bit of both. When the FBI investigators started looking into the phenomenon they discovered an extraordinary set of similarities in the backgrounds of serial killers. Unexpectedly, many had suffered malnutrition or at least poor nourishment in childhood. Most were bed-wetters. A lot had been dropped on the head – or received some kind of head injury. The list of commonalities surprised them. Even so, there was still the X-factor. Not every hungry bed-wetting youngster who was dropped on his head became a serial killer.

Mary Jane has known men. Lots of them. In her wildest dreams, she never thought she'd become what she is. At her wedding almost a decade ago, she promised till death do us part with her first love. With shocking irony, death parted them soon after when he was killed in a tragic accident. Without him, Mary Jane was bereft. Bit by bit, her system shut down and she was hospitalised for the best part of a year suffering from nervous breakdown. Who would have thought? She was such a sweet child, always smiling, cherished by her family.

Your typical serial-killer-in-the-making is not raised in an affective, nurturing environment. Rather, fathers usually nick off, and mothers are unlikely to qualify for Mother of the Year. When Charles Manson was a toddler, his single mother swapped him for a jug of beer down the pub. These youngsters grow up mutilating animals, wetting their beds and setting fire to small things around their neighbourhood. John Travers, Anita Cobby's vicious killer, was notoriously cruel to animals. His mother, Sharon, later shrugged off her son's actions by saying, 'You know what eighteen year olds are like when they get together, biting the heads off kittens, swallowing goldfish … a lot of kids go through that stage.' Not.

Mary Jane and the man disappear into her corner ground-floor apartment. She stares at the ceiling while the man flops up and down on her like a dying fish. His gravel chin scrapes against her throat. His mouth hangs slackly open and a line of spittle escapes and runs onto her face. A final clumsy thrust and it's all over.

A lot of serial killers don't have sex with their victims. Instead, they use a penetrative weapon such as a knife. Some confess that they can't even ejaculate until the woman is dead. Others are completely impotent. The knife is their erection. And not only can't they have sex with a woman, many of them can't even talk to one. While some serial killers are suave enough to establish a rapport with their victims, many prefer the snatch-and-grab method.

After the death of her husband and her lengthy hospital stay, Mary Jane went to stay with her cousin. Big mistake. At first, she wouldn't consider the life her cousin suggested. But after the pain she'd suffered, did it really matter? Did anything matter?

Your average serial killer objectifies his victims. Mostly these are strangers. The serial killer doesn't want to know their name or their history. He wants them to represent whatever it is that he hates.

When the man has cleaned himself with a filthy handkerchief, he tosses some cash on her bedside table and walks out of her life. And since Mary Jane has replaced 9 to 5 with dusk till dawn, she quickly dresses and hits the streets again.

Prostitutes epitomise evil – they are whores and harlots who boil the blood of your run-of-the-mill serial killer. They are the temptresses who lead men to sin. They are responsible for the downfall of society. Men are mere helpless victims led by their wanton genitals towards the pit of wicked lust. Poor blokes.

Not far from her apartment, Mary Jane spies a man in the shadows. At first, she is cautious. A girl like her can't be too careful. Before he left, Jo read her articles from the newspaper about the murders. But as she gets closer, the man looks okay. He is around forty, short with a black moustache. A man, like this, in a brown overcoat, could hardly be the killer. Surely any murderer worth his salt wouldn't wear brown?

Serial killers create the ultimate mystery to be played out on the news and in the papers. Many rush out to buy the morning newspaper to read all about it. How clever these killers are. Public's in a panic. Dumb coppers haven't a clue. Lock your doors or you'll be next. Serial Killer Strikes Again.

She raises her eyebrows and smiles out of the corner of her mouth. He knows what she means and nods, moving towards her. Transaction begun. Mary Jane hooks one of her arms through one of his. In his other hand, unseen by her, he holds a small shiny black bag.

An organised serial killer prepares a murder kit. He takes his favourite knife, maybe a rope or handcuffs. Anything he needs to make his fantasy perfect. But it must be the right girl. Ted Bundy, your classic casebook serial killer, was jilted by his fiancée who had long brown hair, parted down the middle. Bundy put all his efforts into becoming the kind of bloke whom he thought she wouldn't jilt, won her back again and then *he* dumped *her*. He then started killing women with long brown hair parted down the middle. Doesn't take Einstein to figure out who peeved him enough to start killing. Bundy sought revenge and the body count rose. Estimates range from around thirty victims to over one hundred. Only Bundy knew, and he met his end in Florida's electric chair, affectionately known as 'Old Sparky', in 1989 – so he ain't talking.

Mary Jane smiles and leads her client into her apartment. She shuts the door against the cold. They are alone. She doesn't waste much time; these men aren't paying for her personality. She sits on the bed and slides up her skirt. Then she notices his black bag.

Ideally, serial killers want to get their victims to an isolated place so that they can take their time. The fantasy is so strong; the pattern must be followed. Each slice and dice has a particular reason, a hatred built up and punishment measured out. Jeffrey Dahmer enticed young homosexual African-American, Asian and Hispanic males back to his apartment. There he would drug them, strip them, kill them and have sex with their corpses. When his lust was sated, he would dismember the bodies. When he was caught, Dahmer had various body parts in vats and fridges spread around his apartment and had made trophies of his victim's skulls. Dahmer, a former chocolate factory worker, was the epitome of evil, so it was fitting that he was murdered in prison by a man, Christopher Scarver, who claimed to be Jesus – because he was a carpenter by trade and his mother's name was Mary.

'What have you got there?' she says as seductively as she can muster. Each man has his own little fantasy. She's seen it all. He moves closer and brings the bag in front of her face. He is standing by the bed. She can feel his heat as she moves her hands to his thighs. She lowers her head and raises her eyes to meet his. He gently pushes her back. She takes the hint and lies supine. She pulls her skirt around her middle and she opens her legs as he opens his bag.

It's just like the movies, only real. The serial killer is playing the role that he's had written in his mind for years. Her fear excites him.

Her pleas give him power. Her death makes him quiver with pleasure. He is a small man in charge of his own sick little game. With one killing, he causes immeasurable suffering. His victim's family will never get over their loss. When serial killers are active, people lose their sense of safety. The pebble is dropped in the pond, but the ripples reach so much further. Hollywood movies never show this side of it. He came, he saw, he slashed. Scary music, fade to black.

This one is strangely silent. Some make embarrassed small talk. Some just grunt in an alcoholic stupor. But this one is different. Something about his eyes ... something missing ... it is then she sees

So why does Hollywood get it so wrong? Maybe it's us, the audience. Maybe we need to be scared out of our wits by someone all-powerful who can walk through locked doors and evade capture till the death toll hits the appropriate number. And it helps if they wear a scary mask while they're killing. We can eat popcorn and drink flat Coke in a darkened movie theatre and know it's not real. Every big carving knife that slices through some poor unfortunate carotid artery is a fake, and every spurt of blood is raspberry sauce.

the knife

But we pay to have our spine tingled. Just like we pay good money to go on a roller-coaster to get reacquainted with our breakfast. It's a safe scare. Hollywood has succeeded in convincing us that a serial killer lurks behind every potted palm waiting to slice our collective jugular. Cut to reality. You have more chance of being struck by lightning. In fact, Hollywood's real accomplishment has been to glorify the whole serial-killing business, so that when a serial killer is caught he is able to declare proudly, 'I am a serial killer!' and bask in the glory, hoping that the guileless public is impressed. Jeffrey Dahmer's grave simply reads: 'Jeffrey Dahmer, Serial Killer, 1960–1994'.

she doesn't have time to scream before he

And the media fascination with nom de plumes adds to our fear. 'The Silver Gun Rapist' sounds a lot scarier than Fred the Social Misfit with Erectile Dysfunction. Jack the Ripper killed five prostitutes over a period of a few months in 1888 and yet everyone has heard of him. The reason for the fascination is our not knowing who he was. If the police had caught Percy Smith, a clerk from Surrey, soon after the final victim's entrails were scattered around her bed, nobody would remember the case. But the fact that the killer remained at large made him literally larger than life. Or her – Jill the Ripper has a certain ring to it …

Hollywood picked up on the mystery of Jack the Ripper and ever since then has been contentedly turning out serial killer movies. What we don't know scares the popcorn out of us. The phantom killer is all-powerful, all-sinister and all-scary-carving-knives. Until we know his name. The known killer just can't compete.

plunges it into her gut.

Detective Sergeant Mick Hughes knocks on the flimsy wire door. The officer hears footsteps approach as a figure walks down the hallway. Appearing through the wire is a tall fat young man with pimples. He has short brown hair, which is flicked down his forehead into his eyes. Dressed in track-pants and a T-shirt, Paul Denyer invites the officers in.

Twelve hours later, in a sparse interview room at the Frankston police station, Denyer begins his confession looking straight into the video camera. 'I saw her get off the bus,' he says. Then he tells the officers how he followed eighteen-year-old Elizabeth Stevens in the rain on a cold Friday night in June. He said that he'd picked a rainy night because he knew that if anyone was around, they would be too busy trying to get out of the rain and their heads would be bowed. It would make him impervious to witnesses. He told how he'd taken Elizabeth to Lloyd Park in Langwarrin and how she'd begged for her life. He'd assured her that he wouldn't rape her. Didn't make any promises about murder and mutilation, though. Because they would have been promises he wouldn't have kept.

As soon as Denyer looks at the camera and begins his confession, the shadow man who hunted, stalked and murdered, who cleared the streets of Frankston after dark, becomes a fat, pimply, ugly, cruel young man.

He goes to work slowly. Happily. For a few seconds, she looks at him, puzzled. She doesn't understand. Then she does. He has just stabbed her. She searches his face, desperate to read his reasons. She sees only his absolute lust for power. One hand caresses her gently. The other takes the knife which is wobbling slightly as though her stomach were made of jelly. His hand grips the knife. His eyes, sparkling with wicked delight, never leave hers.

It's all about power. Jack the Ripper could walk the cobblestones of Whitechapel with his fancy nickname and his devil-may-care attitude and no one could hurt him – he chose who would die. He was like a god in his own mind – and in the London tabloids – because he held the power over life and death. This woman will live; this woman will die, eeny-meeny-miny-mo.

Mary Jane reads his intent. 'No ...' she whispers, but he is beyond hearing as he tears the knife upwards releasing her final breath with a hiss while the air escapes from her lungs.

Australia doesn't revere its serial killers in the way that America seems to. Certainly, Aussie women as a rule don't rush off marriage proposals in perfumed envelopes, address c/o Port Phillip Prison. We live in a society where Mark Brandon 'Chopper' Read can write a balaclava-full of bestsellers recounting his bloody murders and horror stories with his own brand of Aussie larrikinism, and the public lap it up like a cat. Chopper seems less abhorrent because he's a funny bloke who can spin a yarn over a beer at the local. Frankston serial killer Paul Denyer, on the other hand, didn't write ten bestselling books about shooting friends and influencing people, and so we just think of him as a cold-hearted, evil killer. If Denyer had a publicist, he would probably be advised to get a torso-full of tattoos, cut his ears off and write his memoirs.

She is dead, he has claimed another soul.

Chopper's a little like Hannibal Lecter if you think about it. You can't help but be fond of Hannibal – particularly when he isn't skinning security guards. In the end, you don't really want him to be caught because, quite frankly, you like him – you like his bravado, you like his super-humanness, you like the way he knows just which wine to have with which organ. You want to watch the relationship develop between Hannibal and Clarice. You have fallen into a trap set by morbid curiosity and perpetuated by Hollywood.

He is the artist and she is his canvas. He has lived this act over and over in his mind. First, her breasts must go. His razor-sharp knife cuts in a circular motion and in minutes, her raw, red ribcage is visible where her breasts had been.

It is not unusual for a serial killer to 'de-womanise' his victims. If you kill women because you hate them, then it's only one further step to want to strip them of those facets that make them women. Their lives, for a start. Next, their breasts and sex organs. And ultimately, their beauty.

She is open like a carcass in a butcher's window. An acidic odour emanates from her. He inhales and the smell of her blood is heady. Next extraction, her uterus. His hands penetrate her stomach and her warmth heats him. Her insides slurp as he locates her reproductive organs and cuts them loose. Now he must take her face. The mouth, so coarse in its suggestions, this mouth and others just like it; the ruin of so many. He carves deeply from her bottom lip to her chin, then he strips away the features that made her beautiful. He leaves her eyes so she can see him.

He – and it is almost always a he – develops a hatred for a person or a type of person (mother, jilting girlfriend) and will kill, over and over, the metaphoric object of his hatred. His madness comes in waves. Afterwards, some small amount of reason returns and he feels remorse. But mostly it is remorse for himself because he tried to release his pent-up rage and lust, but relief has only been temporary.

He is happier now because he's reduced her to pulp. Like a fussy mortician, he lays her out for whoever finds her. He spreads her internal organs around her corpse and in a final act of indignity spreads her legs wide to show the whore she was. He looks over his work and is pleased.

Once the serial killer comes down from the euphoria, he realises that life is just the same. He is still a socially inept loser. Then the fantasy builds up, takes over, and he begins to hunt again. The time between each killing shortens, and he continues to kill until he gets caught – or dies.

Thomas Bowyer hunches his thin shoulders against the bitter November cold and wraps his scarf and tattered coat tightly around himself. His cheap leather shoes click over the wet path as he makes his way to Mary Jane's place. He wonders whether she will be sober. It's a bit hard to tell with Mary Jane. When she's sober, she's fine but when she's drunk, she's wild.

Serial killer Ed Kemper hated his mother and was sent to live with his grandparents as a youngster. Aged fourteen, he killed them both and was sent to a mental institution for five years. He was then released into the custody of his mother. Hmmm, perhaps not such a good idea. Not surprisingly, Kemper had undergone no miracle cure while incarcerated. Still hating his mum, he went looking for substitutes and found himself regularly enticing young women into his car and then decapitating them. He buried the head of one victim under his mother's bedroom window.

Bowyer's job is to collect the rent. His boss, John McCarthy, who owns a row of small apartments in the street, has calculated that Mary Jane is six weeks behind on hers. Bowyer, known around the traps as 'Indian Harry', arrives at Mary Jane's door and knocks officiously. When no one answers, he tries the handle. Locked. Suspecting that Mary Jane may be hiding inside, he walks around the corner to her grimy side window.

When interviewed, Kemper explained how he grappled with his madness. He recalled sitting on his bed with the severed head of one of his victims in his lap. At first he thinks that he must be mad, but then reasons that if he *knows* he's mad, he mustn't be, because surely if he were mad, he would be unaware of it. Confusing stuff. In the end, Kemper kills the real object of his hatred, his mother.

On Easter Sunday 1973, he cuts off her head and dumps her body in her closet. Afterwards, he cuts out her larynx and throws it in the rubbish. Not the kind of bloke you take home to mother – unless you don't like your mother very much.

One of the four panes of glass is broken and has been stuffed with rags. A dirty coat doubles as a curtain. Bowyer removes the rags and reaches through the window. As he pushes aside the makeshift curtain, he sees two small lumps of what looks like meat lying on a table. Wondering why Mary Jane would have meat on her table, he looks further into the dim room and sees Mary Jane. Or what is left of her.

One of the key features of serial killing that Hollywood doesn't portray is the 'magical thinking' inherent in the serial killer's thought processes. Such magical thinking is something that we all do – just not so dangerously. You're running late for an appointment and the traffic is banked up. You get within fifty metres of a traffic light and think you can squeeze through, but it turns amber. You screech on the brakes and mutter, 'Bloody traffic light!' Ringing any bells? It's a small dose of magical thinking – it's not the traffic light's fault but you have just transferred your anger onto an innocent traffic light, an inanimate object. That's just what serial killers do, except that they transfer their anger and frustration onto innocent people.

Gasping for breath, Indian Harry runs back down the alleyway to his boss's shop. McCarthy knows immediately that something is wrong.

'Oh my God! I knocked at the door and I looked through the window and saw a lot of blood.'

Both men run back to Mary Jane's squalid room. McCarthy peers through the windows and sees for himself what has been done to her. For a moment he can't speak for lack of words to describe what he sees.

'You'd better call the police,' he says finally.

Do they know what they are doing is wrong? Hmmm … this is another case in which magical thinking comes into play. You're driving along in traffic again. You see a sixty kilometres per hour sign.

You look at your speedo and you're doing sixty-five. You know it's wrong, but do you *feel* it's wrong? A serial killer *knows* it's wrong to kill people but it doesn't *feel* wrong. So he does it. And instead of showing remorse, he will remember the event fondly.

Returning to the apartment with the police, the men break down the door. They enter the room, which has the vague warmth of a fire not long burnt out. In front of the fireplace, Mary Jane's boots rest side-by-side. Her clothes are neatly folded on a chair. But that is all that is normal. The men have never seen anything like this.

Why does Hollywood get it so wrong? Maybe because we would be bored with the real thing – bumbling ordinary human beings with a penchant for killing who have carved, poisoned and strangled their way into history. In real life, serial killers don't kill in ways that mirror the seven deadly sins. In real life, there are no Hannibal Lectors, or cunningly planned killing strategies or letters taunting police with cryptic clues that only university professors or resourceful lone-wolf cops can decipher. In real life, serial killers claim victims, ruin lives, leave clues behind, get caught and go to jail.

Mary Jane's outline is human but what has been done to her is not. Her face is gone and her skull, grotesque, is visible. Her body is lying on her dingy bed. Most of her insides are strewn around the room, leaving her abdominal cavity empty.

Any study of the pathology of serial killers will conclude that it is highly unlikely for a manipulative psychopath suddenly to decide to kill thematically. Hmmm, Seven Deadly Sins sounds like a hoot of a theme, think I'll be on the lookout for a fat bloke. Or gee wiz, I think I'll copy all the most infamous serial killers and become known as Copy Cat. What a blast! Or hey, I've got a good recipe for human liver with fava beans and a nice Chianti.

Dr Thomas Bond, a police surgeon, is called to the scene. He discovers some of her internal organs beneath her head; her liver at her feet. This mutilation must have taken quite some time. Bond hoped that the victim had died quickly.

We watch serial killer movies to be scared and then to go home tingling pleasurably, leave the lights on for a couple of days and then forget all about it. These celluloid creatures aren't real and they aren't like us.

Mary Jane's killer has struck at least four times before but always in the open and always in a hurry. Mary Jane is the first victim where he has had the luxury of time. He may have been in her room for hours carving himself into the criminal hall of fame.

It's the poor man's way of making it big, the nutter's fifteen minutes of fame. From reading the news to making the news. Head case becomes headline.

Mary Jane Kelly died on 9 November 1888. She was Jack the Ripper's final victim.

There is no cure for a serial killer – apart from 2000 volts or an injection of potassium chloride. Aside from that, civilised nations lock them in prisons, give 'em three square meals a day and keep their collective fingers crossed that they don't escape or get released twenty-five years later by a bleeding-heart parole board. Cases in which serial killers have been released show that they will kill again – just as Ed Kemper did.

We'll leave the last line to Brad Pitt's Detective Mills, trying to convince the Seven serial killer, John Doe, that he is nothing but a nutter. He says, 'You're not a messiah. You're a movie-of-the-week. You're a T-shirt … at best.'

One Kind of Bad

Lindy Cameron

It's mostly at night that people get murdered.

Rose Eden remembers everything. Her first case, not her first murder, but her first case as lead investigator is the one that stays with her the most. That, and the nightmare of being on call the night two colleagues were gunned down simply because they were cops.

Three years after leaving the police force, she still talks of her experiences mostly in the present tense: 'When I go to homicides I get the butterflies. The nerves are jumping because I never know what I'm going to see, and I always worry about how I'm going to react.

'It's hard enough knowing, without a doubt, that I'll see things which are often brutal beyond words, but there's also the given that everyone else there will be looking to me and my crew to fix everything. And it's not just the family and witnesses who are waiting, it's the other police as well, who can finally say, "Here are the homicide detectives, they'll deal with it, they'll sort it."'

When Detective Senior Constable Rosemary Eden joined the Homicide Squad she was thirty-three years old and had been a member of the Victoria Police for twelve years. She joined a crew of seven, one of seven crews, to investigate any and all suspicious deaths in the State.

At the start of her first shift, Rose was instructed to go over the files of a recent murder to familiarise herself with every aspect of the investigation. While this was standard practice to ensure all crew members were up to speed, Rose could have been forgiven for thinking, on that first day, that her new colleagues had chosen that particular case to see if the 'new girl' could stomach the job.

Detective Senior Constable Rose Eden was, after all, only the third woman – ever – to officially join the Homicide Squad of Victoria Police.

While Rose hoped that the case was not indicative of what a homicide detective had to face on a regular basis, she also told herself that fronting up every day to face any kind of death would be, in itself, more than most people could stomach. And even now, years later, she is thankful that her first case was the only one that involved children.

Rose was also to find that, with a couple of exceptions, facing death or the deceased was not the hard part of the job.

A trained detective learns to be objective, to see the whole as a sum of its parts; to treat the scene of the crime as the focal point of a larger investigation that follows on from the gathering up of all the tiny pieces that make up that crime scene. It's a circle that brings the police back to the killer, too late to save the victim but hopefully before any murderer comes close to feeling as though they got away with it.

A homicide investigation follows a precise standard operating procedure because the procedure is known to end, usually, in a positive result. A crime is solved, a killer is caught, justice is served, the victim can 'rest in peace', those left behind can …

What? Get on with their lives?

Most murders are solved because most murders are domestics. That means, tragically, that most murder victims are killed by someone they know; and often by someone they loved or trusted.

So the hardest part of a homicide detective's job, according to Rose, is dealing with those who are left behind in the midst of the worst imaginable time of their lives. Informing them, comforting them, sometimes having to interrogate them, can be more taxing for the homicide cop than bearing witness to the murder scene – no matter how horrible.

'Working with the victim's family is gut-wrenching – absolutely gut-wrenching because they are looking to you to solve their problems and they want you to take it away, make it not happen.

And often they want to know everything, all the details, even though you know they don't. That no one should know. Ever.

'You're the detective but you also become a counsellor; you become a friend, in a way, because they need you and you have to be there for them because the families, the loved ones, the friends will *never* understand, even if they find out why.

'They also see that the murder creates all these other problems, and because you deal with the murder then they think you can deal with everything else too. It's a big job; it's a big ask.'

So Detective Senior Constable Eden began the first shift of her long-sought-after stint on the Homicide Squad by going over the case notes, crime-scene video and photographs of a murder that had happened a couple of days before.

A woman, who lived with her de facto, had gone to play bingo with her mum and had left her two children in the care of the boyfriend.

'While she was out, he handcuffed and sexually assaulted the daughter, who was about six years old. He stabbed and murdered her, then stabbed her three-year-old brother to death. Then he took off. The woman, the mother, came home and found her children dead and him … just gone.

'A little while later there was an accident on the Western Ring Road, because a truck driver could not avoid hitting a man who just *walked out* in front of him. Of course the man, this coward, was just splattered everywhere.

'So I looked at the video and the photographs – they take photos *in situ* and then photographs during the post-mortem – and I saw the images of those children and photographs of the offender … and then I went to see the children's father and get a statement.

'That was so hard because he was absolutely devastated. I was on my own, which is not uncommon because taking a statement can sometimes take hours. And in his case only one officer was needed because he wasn't a witness to anything; it was only a background statement. He was only the absent father.

'But it was harrowing – for me, for him. He was already out of the full-time life of his children but losing them forever like that was unimaginable. And he had so many questions, the biggest one, of course, being, "Why?"

'It was distressing that I couldn't help him with that one, because in a case like that there is no reasonable answer to that question.

'So that was my first day in Homicide, made worse because it was children, and that really tore at me.'

Why did Rose Eden want to be 'in Homicide'? Why would she stay when her introduction to the job was a devastated father and the ruin left behind by a sadistic bastard who molested and brutally murdered his partner's children and then threw himself in front of a truck?

What kind of madness could allow any human to do what that man did? And why would anyone want to deal with the likes of him and the wreckage he caused?

According to Rose there are two main reasons: 'Murder is the worst crime there is – the one most worth solving; and because *someone* has to tidy up the mess.'

For Rose there was a third reason, too – when she joined the Victoria Police in 1984 there'd never been a woman on the Homicide Squad.

How did she get there? How does any police officer get to be in Homicide? And what was it, after three years, that prompted Rose to leave – not only the Squad but the police force itself? Was it too much death, too much violence? She does remember every little thing.

'You have to be strong, inside, when you approach a murder scene. I always used to … not get panicky, but get quite anxious about what I was going to find, because you can *never* guess what it might be.

'Strangely, though, once you get there you're so busy that you don't have time to acknowledge your own emotions. You're drawing diagrams of the room, writing notes about where the body is positioned in relation to everything else around it; noting that there's a wound here and a mark there, and that you can see blood splatters going in this or that direction.

'It takes a long time to go over a scene, because you have to do the whole environment, every room, for instance, if it's a house. And this can take ages, especially if there's been a disturbance other than where the victim is. You have to record what furniture has been knocked over, what's in what position.

'It has to be a thorough record of everything you see, so you know that you don't even have to look at the video to be sure you have the best record of what *you* saw.

'Once you've done all that, you're so busy that it really doesn't have time to hit you. And I guess by the time it would hit you, you're over it to a certain extent. Except that, *because* of that attention to detail, every one of those details becomes embedded forever in your memory.'

In 1984 Rosemary Eden was working at Leader Newspapers selling advertising – but she wasn't very good at it. At a party, her sister's boyfriend of the time, a policeman himself, suggested she join Victoria Police. Rose laughed, a lot, but he insisted that the force really needed people like her. In the cold and sober light of the next day, Rose thought, 'Why the hell not?' She didn't like what she was doing and she quite liked the rather corny idea of helping people.

Recruitment needs in the police force go up and down but Rose happened to fluke the right time. Some recruits she started with in December 1984 had applied two years before. Rose's application took three months – which wasn't even enough time to change her mind.

'It was like, "What have I done?" I had no real idea what I was getting myself into.

'What I *did* think, though, even back then, was that if I am going into the police force then homicide is the area to aim for. It is the ultimate crime. Also, the fact that there'd never been a female homicide cop presented a huge challenge.

'The police force then was *such* a male bastion, a semi-military organisation and a bit of a boys club. It still goes on a bit, but things have changed from when I joined.'

Rose spent the next five years in the uniform branch. Police officers then could not become Detectives until they were Senior Constables, and couldn't do the exams for the latter until they'd been in the force for five years. Rose did those exams at the earliest opportunity and became a Senior Constable, but it was another seven months before she got a CIB placement.

'Fairfield CIB was my first detective spot. While there I did DTS – Detective Training School – which is where I first met

Sandra Nicholson, who was not only one of my instructors, but one of the most fabulous women on the force. And believe me, there weren't that many women role models back then.'

When Detective Senior Constable Rose Eden went to Fairfield CIB and DTS, only 15 per cent of Victoria's police force – which numbered about 10,000 – were detectives. Of those 1500 or so detectives, only eighty were women; or, looking at the big picture, there were only eighty female detectives in a force of 10,000 officers.

The year was 1990.

Women had been part of the police force in Victoria since the 1920s, although back then they were not sworn in, had no arresting powers, were not permitted to wear uniforms and were only there 'to look after the welfare of women and children'.

From one end of a century to another, over a span of seventy years, women on the force had gone from hand-holders to Detective-Sergeant – well, one of them had. 'Three score years and ten' and the Victoria Police still had only eighty female detectives. That *one* high-ranking woman, who also happened to be the first woman lecturer gazetted to the Detective Training School, was Rose Eden's best inspiration.

'I looked at Sandy Nicholson, and thought, 'She's a woman, she's a Senior Sergeant. If she can do it, then I can do it too.'

(Sandra Nicholson, now Detective Superintendent, actually notched up a number of Victoria Police firsts. She was the first female detective in three different CIBs in 1978, 1979 and 1983; the only female detective seconded to the Ash Wednesday Bush Fire Task Force in 1983; the first female Detective Sergeant (1988) and Senior Sergeant (1990) at Russell Street CIB (then Police HQ); and, as Detective Superintendent, was not only the first woman of that rank in Victoria but was the most senior female officer in the State until the appointment of Ms Christine Nixon as Victoria's Police Commissioner in April 2001.)

'With women detectives so thin on the ground back in 1990, it meant that everyone knew of you; or knew exactly who or where you were. I was, for instance, not just Rose Eden but *the* female detective at Fairfield.

'And I loved it there. I did a bit of everything. I worked with eleven men, which was a bit of an eye-opener for them, working with a female detective. But we became just like family; they were my closest friends.

'Fairfield was a very busy division, so after five years of long hours and early or all-over-the-place shifts, I decided I needed a life. I went to the Fraud Squad, which being basically Monday to Friday, was a nice change. Two years later I decided I needed to get back out amongst it, so I applied to go to Homicide. I then just had to wait for a vacancy.'

In 1996 Detective Senior Constable Rose Eden became the third female police officer to join the Homicide Squad as an active member of a homicide crew (not just an officer seconded for the duration of an investigation that simply needed more hands).

Three months later, having already done the exam, Rose completed her Sergeant's Course, but didn't take the promotion as it would have meant going back into uniform and transferring out of Homicide. She'd given an undertaking to stay in the squad for at least two years, and besides she wanted to do the work.

The Homicide Squad. Seven crews, each comprising seven people, who spend all their time together and who even live in similar areas to make getting to a scene together more efficient. Each crew is a senior sergeant, two sergeants and four detective senior constables.

At any time two or three crews might be unavailable for on-call duty because of an ongoing investigation or court case. The others take turns to rotate through the on-call shifts … waiting for a death, from causes other than natural.

On weekdays, all crews work their current cases but one crew is also on call from 3 p.m. to 3 p.m. The members work a normal shift, go home, then return in the morning to work another shift – unless they get called out. And that could happen anytime during that twenty-four hour period, but for some reason it's more likely to be at night.

An on-call weekend shift runs from 3 p.m. Saturday to 3 p.m. Monday, so that only one crew's weekend is wrecked. Whatever shift it is, the on-call crew needs plenty of clothes ready because the Homicide Squad operates State-wide and the call might come in from Mildura or Mt Bulla, which could mean days away from home. Sometimes it can even take a couple of days to determine that the death was an accident.

The Homicide Squad gets called out to many more jobs than it investigates because a lot of 'suspicious deaths' turn out not to be homicide. If a crew gets a death that is a murder, then the next on-call crew comes on duty and takes over the waiting.

'One on-call weekend, we started by taking witness statements pertaining to a domestic murder that had happened some months before. We were then called out to a death in Windsor which turned out to be natural causes. We went home at the end of the day, still on call.

'Sunday lunchtime we attended a scene in Lalor – also not a murder, although in that case the local CIB could not have guessed "the victim" committed suicide by stabbing himself to death. Another job followed that one: it was something about an abduction, a body, then no body. Again, not a homicide; so I was home by 11 p.m.

'Three time-consuming jobs in twenty-four hours but none of them was murder. It meant we were still the on-call crew, until we picked up a case that was.'

The first official contact with a possible homicide is usually the uniformed officers from the local station who have responded to a specific call about a suspicious death or dead body; or who are, perhaps, investigating a complaint or disturbance.

The officers first call their own CIB detectives who determine whether the death was suspicious or not. If necessary, they place a call to D24 to request the Homicide Squad, and usually call in their own Detective Inspector.

The Senior Sergeant of the on-call homicide crew takes the job, calls his members and organises for them to be picked up. The crew is fully briefed at the scene by the local CIB detectives, but the Homicide Senior Sergeant takes control of the scene on arrival. He allocates tasks and nominates the crew member whose turn it is to take charge of the investigation.

'Not everyone goes into the scene. Every contact leaves its traces, so you don't want to contaminate the scene any more than you have to.

'Two detectives might go in, have a good look around, not touch anything, then come back out again and call for the services to video and photograph the crime scene. Basically we don't do anything else at the scene itself until it's all videoed.

'In the meantime we're making pages and pages of notes – usually in the dark with a torch under one arm and outside in the freezing cold.'

The forensic pathologist goes in next, makes a determination and organises for a post-mortem. A body is never moved until all of this has been done, and may sometimes remain in place for five or six hours. The government undertakers then remove the body.

The post-mortem is attended by one or two of the on-call detectives, who sit with diagrams of a body on which they mark each injury and make notes of everything the pathologist says.

Meanwhile the other detectives collect evidence, take statements and organise a door knock to look for witnesses. All of which needs to be done quickly while information is still fresh.

Sometimes all of that groundwork gets done for no reason. Well, at least for no reason as far as the Homicide Squad is concerned.

'We had a case that involved some druggies in a park in Footscray. The neighbours had apparently decided enough was enough, so they came out with five irons and just belted into these two blokes and a girl. The girl died, so the local cops called in the Homicide Squad.

'Out we go – in the middle of the night, of course – to do what we do. The pathologist came out, couldn't see any marks on this girl, but was happy to do a post-mortem straight away. I sat in on the PM at something like three in the morning. It turned out the girl had died of a drug overdose, not a beating of any kind. So, tragic as it was, it wasn't murder; and at half past four we all went home to bed.'

Rose remembers everything. Four murders after she joined the Homicide Squad, Detective Senior Constable Eden took on her first case as the detective in charge. While this meant she could delegate tasks to other crew members, it also meant she was the 'one' responsible for everything associated with that case, from evidence collection and witness interviews or other statements, to follow-ups with family and, ultimately, for putting the Brief together for the court.

Again it was night time. Again it was a nasty, brutal murder.

The victim was a Cambodian woman in her fifties. She lived with her thirty-year-old daughter and niece, who found her when they came home and then ran to the neighbours to get help – to call an ambulance which was not needed. The ambulance team called the police, who in turn called the Homicide Squad. Rose's crew arrived at the scene at about 9.30 p.m.

'She was on the floor in the lounge but had obviously been dragged there; there were blood marks across the floor. Her teeth were knocked out and the side of her head was caved in by a heavy-based glass ornament which had also cut her. And it was not one nice clean blow.

'I did a walk-through, making notes of everything I saw, indicated a few things I specifically wanted videoed and photographed, then I went to talk to the daughter. She'd already given a statement but I needed to know where she had gone in the house when she got home.

'Cambodian families don't wear their shoes inside, and as there were bloody footprints up the hall I had to know *exactly* where the daughter had walked. If the prints were not hers, then they more than likely belonged to the killer. And if they *were* the murderer's, the fact that they'd been made by socked feet, not shoes, indicated that the woman probably let her killer into the house.'

Rose was soon to discover the wider tragedy of the victim's life. Witness statements and details from her daughter and others revealed a good woman, a quiet woman with no known enemies, who had worked as a machinist in a furniture factory. Her husband had been killed in Cambodia by the Pol Pot regime; two of her children had starved to death before she reached a refugee camp in Thailand. She had migrated to South Australia and later moved to Melbourne. She worked hard to give her two remaining children a secure home, a good education; she lived a quiet life in a safe place, and then she was murdered.

'During her interview the daughter told us that the only trouble her mother may have had was with a man she'd called "Uncle". The daughter was not sure how he was related, but said her mother had lent this man some money, and when he had failed to repay it, she'd spoken with *his* mother. This had apparently embarrassed "Uncle" and perhaps made him angry.

'The victim's son knew where this "Uncle" lived. As it was rubbish night we checked the bins out on the street where he lived for blood-stained clothing, but found nothing. It was 6 a.m. when we knocked on his door.

'He was home, as were his wife and three daughters. He was cagey and nervous and at first denied all knowledge of the victim. He had an injury to his hand which looked, to my Sergeant and I, like a human bite mark but which he claimed was from a gardening mishap.

'One of his daughters said her father had been out the night before and when he'd come home he'd – quite unusually – gone straight to the bathroom, taken a shower and then washed his clothes in the machine.

'A search of his garage later turned up the victim's car keys. We arrested him for murder.'

Often it may not be until the next day that the Homicide crew sits down as a group to work out what they've got. They pool all the information gathered so far, including physical evidence and all the statements, and then work out the plan of action. If there are *no* suspects they arrange to check out or re-visit the places the victim frequented, including their home or workplace, and start talking to family, friends and workmates.

If they *do* have an obvious suspect, as in Rose's first case, it's a toss-up whether arresting them straight away makes the job easier or not. The problem with an immediate arrest is that the crew doesn't yet have all the possible information and evidence, but as soon as charges are laid the court puts a time constraint on the investigation and its presentation.

'During his interview "Uncle" must have realised he wasn't going to get away with his crime so he suddenly made the allegation that the victim's daughter had met with him and asked him to murder her own mother. For some strange reason, it seemed to him that it was better that the murder he'd committed was a contract killing.

'We knew that he was lying but we had to cover every angle. I had to go back and re-interview a young woman who had not long found her mother – like that – and who was now being accused of conspiring to bring that horror about.'

There was no evidence to suggest there was any truth in the murderer's allegation and he ultimately received a maximum sentence of sixteen years – not nearly long enough, in Rose's opinion. But she 'got her man' in the first case that was *her* responsibility – even though she never found out why he did it.

Rose also made some friends, in a way, because of the time she spent with the family during the investigation, and the contact she kept up even after the case was over. The daughter invited Rose and her Sergeant to her wedding reception. They were the only non-Cambodians there.

Detective Senior Constable Rose Eden cannot forget anything. Her last case for the Victoria Police Homicide Squad was still making news three years after the fact, when two men were finally committed to stand trial for murder. She wasn't in charge on that August night in 1998, but her crew *was* on call, and she still feels the sensation of cold, cold dread when she realised what her Senior Sergeant meant when he rang to say he was en route to collect her because there had been 'a police shooting'.

'My first thought was that police had shot someone – an offender – which is one kind of bad. But then my boss said, "Two policemen have been shot." I just felt sick and I got the shakes. Even with 10,000 police on the force, it's amazing how many you know.

'The level of police radio traffic we heard on the way to the scene was unbelievable. By the time we got there, we knew that one officer was dead and one was in a critical condition in hospital; and that there were no suspects in custody.

'A mobile command post had already been set up, and as the shootings had taken place outside on the road, the area that was cordoned off was huge.

'It was a dark night and it was really, really cold. Unlike other murders I've been to, this one I approached in a state of surreal shock. We all did, to a certain extent. I'd never been to a police shooting and even though, as it turned out, I didn't know either of these men it didn't make it any easier. The whole police brotherhood thing has its positives and negatives: on one hand, they're always there for you; and on the other, there's nothing worse than losing one of your own.

'We didn't actually enter the crime scene itself, where Sergeant Gary Silk was lying, for a few hours. The whole area was being videoed and photographed, statements were being taken, evidence was being collected and searches were being conducted for the offenders.

'My Senior Sergeant was controlling the investigation and I was acting as his right-hand, doing all his running around and working his phone and mine. He kept asking me if I was okay. There was no toilet anywhere, of course, which doesn't matter so much if you're a bloke, but it's not so easy for us girls. Anyway the boss finally sent me down the road to the Chinese restaurant, to find out how the other detectives were getting on with their statement-taking.

'It was the restaurant staff who had called the police in the first place, to say there was a man outside waving a gun. That man turned out to be a badly wounded Senior Constable Rod Miller, who was asking for help.

'Anyway, I entered the restaurant and said, "Need your ladies," and just kept on walking. So there I was, alone in the loo, when one of my phones rang and it was our crew member who'd gone straight to the hospital, ringing to tell us that Rod Miller had just died.

'It was horrible. I had to walk back to the command post, up a hill I think, in the freezing cold weather and I was shaking like a leaf but probably more from shock, and I had to tell everyone there that he was dead too.

'Then my Senior Sergeant and I went into the crime scene and Gary Silk was … I got the shakes and I had to go, I had to get out of there. It was too confronting.'

Rose didn't know at the time that *one* reason for her uncharacteristically emotional reaction to those murders, more marked than her response to any other she'd attended, was the fact that she was pregnant.

'Back at the office I was given the job of getting the Task Force area organised. In those first days, especially, the whole squad was on deck working until really late. There was an amazing sense of comradeship that I'd never seen before; everyone just wanted to do as much as they could to help us. And I don't know how many phone calls we got from police stations all over the State offering their assistance, asking what they could do. Eventually we did use a lot of CIB divisions, but in the beginning – as usual – it was just us.

'The response from the public, too, was almost overwhelming. The phones were running hot, and we had a massive amount of information to process, which was partly why everyone stayed working such long hours.

'I didn't find out until three weeks into the Lorimer Task Force that I was pregnant. I then understood, in retrospect, why I was all over the place emotionally. I'd be simmering away one moment and then suddenly spurt out. I thought it was all "the case", and that the incredible tiredness was from the horrendous hours we were working.

'One night, about a month into the job, some of the guys brought in like sixty pieces of property for me. Doing the property is a long and involved process designed to ensure there's no stuff-ups, so that when it comes to court you can guarantee the continuity of evidence.

'I could see it was going to take me about two hours, and they just dumped it all so that I actually couldn't leave my desk because I was surrounded by all this stuff. I just hit the roof and demanded they sit down and go through it all with me. I told them I wanted to know where each piece came from, who it came from, what time, etc.

'I think someone made a flippant comment at that stage, which was just *not the right thing to do*, so I lost it and burst into tears. These guys did *not* know what to do, I mean they just weren't used to a police officer bursting into tears over property.

'By this stage I had told my boss I was pregnant, because I thought he should know why I was so delirious, and because it becomes an occupational health and safety matter and an issue for the people I was working with. Not that you think you'd ever let anyone down but you're a bit more cautious, you're a bit more hesitant because you realise, Oh my god, it's not just me here. Anyway, my boss took me home and I did the property the next day.

'I ended up doing a lot of the administrative work for the Lorimer Task Force. Had I just been on the crew – if we weren't on a task force – it would have been very difficult, because I couldn't have been called out in the middle of the night or do twelve or twenty-four-hour shifts. I would have felt that I wasn't pulling my weight, that I wasn't of any use or value. But there on the Task Force I was valuable right up until the time I gave up work, when I was seven-and-half months pregnant – and newly separated.'

Rose Eden remembers everything. She still maintains that her time on the Homicide Squad was the best and the worst of experiences. She built long and lasting, loyal friendships with fellow officers; people she had to trust with her life and who had to know they could rely on her.

'I saw awful things; I dealt with awful things. I can still picture every homicide that I attended. Those images will never leave me; and they're quite disturbing. I wouldn't wish anyone to see what's in my head because it really is horrible.

'But I also got huge understanding and solace from my colleagues, from my friends on the job – which was vital. I could say to another detective, "I attended a murder today where this woman was found by her daughter and she'd had her throat cut." That's it. I wouldn't have to elaborate and they'd immediately "get it" because they'd been there. I didn't have to explain myself, or my mood, any further.

'Not that I mind explaining myself, but it's very hard for someone not in the police force to understand. You have to go into a lot more detail, and often you just don't want to do that.

'Sometimes you just want to say, to your mates at the pub, "I had an dreadful day. It wasn't a murder but it was tough. An old bloke, who had every disease known to mankind, decided he couldn't take it any more so he went into his garage and put a gun to his head and shot himself. His wife and an old friend – they were all in their eighties – found him. It was awful but I dealt with it."

'Now, other people would need more information than that to even begin to understand, but fellow officers would just get it.

'One thing that never ceased to amaze me was the remarkable spirit that exists in ordinary people; that even in their darkest hour they can do incredible things, they can *be* kind and generous. Extreme situations seem to bring out the best in most people; and the worst in only a few.

'There was one woman who'd scream abuse at me every time I saw her because we hadn't arrested "the boyfriend" for her pregnant daughter's murder yet. We did in the end, but it took a while to get the proof and in the meantime we were on the receiving end of that distraught mother's grief and anger.

'Then we had another case where a minor drug dealer had been killed. We had to inform his elderly parents and realised the mother would not cope with the reason for her son's death, so we only told the father. We'd go around there to update them on the case and she'd just want me to hug her, while she cried. That's all she needed from us, from me. The guys I worked with also showed incredible compassion and patience because they knew that sometimes that is all you can do for the family.

'The extraordinary thing is that sometimes the family gives as much back to you, like my Cambodian friends. And, on one of our visits to the dealer's parents – this was in February and it was really hot – he insisted that we sit down and have a beer with him. He needed us to do that with him, but he was also genuinely concerned for us being hot and tired because we'd been working such long hours on his son's case. He'd just lost his only child but he was worried about us.

'So you keep in contact with them, the families, and touch base every now and then, even if there's not much progress. The case of the drug dealer was unsolved for ages and there was nothing really happening, but we still dropped in on his parents if we were in the area just to let them know that we were still there and we cared, and we were trying our hardest.

'No one likes an unsolved murder. No one likes any crime unsolved because you feel that you failed. But particularly with murder, because someone's life was taken, you feel compelled to solve it, to help the family and to bring someone to justice.'

Detective Senior Constable Rosemary Eden, who never took her Sergeant's promotion, took maternity leave from the Homicide Squad but ended up leaving the Victoria Police, not because she was pregnant or because the job got too much, but because in 1999 there were no measures in place that would allow a newly single, new mother to return to her job *and* raise a child.

Eighty years after women had joined the police force to 'look after the welfare of women and children', the police bureaucracy still hadn't found a way to connect the dots between working single parents (probably of either sex) and police work.

Rose Eden and her fifteen years of experience walked away from the job she loved because of a lack of foresight or imagination or interest on the part of the 'powers that be' to make police life match the real lives of modern police officers.

'I really loved being a detective. I doubt, though, even if I hadn't got pregnant, that I would have stayed too much longer in the Homicide Squad. You can't live with such a warped view of the world for too long. At least each of the three cases that I was in charge of was solved, so I had no unfinished business.

'The trouble is, murder is *always* unfinished business, because its aftermath is a ripple effect. It damages or touches so many people in so many directions, and not just the victim's friends and family. There are the witnesses, who may not even know anyone involved but who saw something they didn't need to see, so the murder has an impact on their lives and on their family. There's also the police, of course, who have to deal with the mess, and their families who have to wear the fallout. And no matter how much you might like to, you can't forget the effect on the offender, because of *their* family.

'And then there's people like that poor truck driver who could not avoid hitting that bastard who'd just molested and killed his own girlfriend's kids. It no doubt helped the driver to know that the guy deserved to be spread all over the road, but that still wouldn't detract from the horror of having someone commit suicide on the front of your truck. And his family would have to help him deal with his trauma.

'In the case of Sergeant Gary Silk and Senior Constable Rod Miller, murder has a permanent and chilling affect on every single police officer because you really do think, in that instance, there but for the grace of god, go I – every day.'

The Policeman's Wife

Shirley Hardy-Rix

I CAN REMEMBER THE TIME when he was working in the squads as if it were only yesterday …

The silence is broken by the voice of the overnight radio announcer. It is only 4.00 a.m. and for most people the start of the day is still a few hours away.

Not in our house – our day is beginning and it is not an ordinary day. An investigation is coming to a conclusion. The squad is going to raid a criminal's home. These raids are always around dawn – even crooks have to sleep sometime.

It has been a late night, because Brian and the other detectives have been up planning. They can't leave anything to chance. Every 'i' must be dotted and every 't' must be crossed. It was well after midnight when he finally crawled into bed.

When the radio bursts into life he turns it off as quickly as he can. He tries not to wake me – but I'm not sure that I was even asleep.

Now, after very little sleep he moves around the house trying to be quiet, but I can track his every move. He comes out of the bathroom and goes to the spare bedroom where he laid out his clothes the night before. Back in our room he sits on the side of the bed. I lie in the semi-darkness and listen. Our room is lit with an eerie glow from the hall light. I feel his weight on the side of the bed. I smell him – the clean smell of a freshly showered body and subtle scent of aftershave. I sense his concentration. I sense his anxiety.

I listen as he gets out his revolver. I will always be able to recognise that sound. He opens the chamber and checks that the gun is loaded. He then checks the speed loader that has sat on the bedside table overnight. He makes sure it too is carrying a full complement. The gun goes into his ankle holster and the speed loader into his suit coat pocket.

He has done this dozens of times but it doesn't get any easier. I am sure he is nervous, but he doesn't admit it. I am anxious, but I try not to show it. He doesn't need to know that at this very moment I would rather he was in a sedate, safe occupation.

He turns and kisses me on the forehead. 'I will ring when I can. Go back to sleep now. I love you.'

With that he is gone. He switches off the light and the room is now swathed in darkness. I listen as the front door opens and closes. I strain to hear the gate open and then slam shut. I don't hear the car door, but I hear the engine. It is the last thing I hear – the car moving slowly down our suburban street. It is a street that is still sleeping. In the homes the people may stir, but they wouldn't think twice about the car moving off.

How can I go back to sleep? I lie in the darkness trying to will myself to doze – even if just for a moment. Any time asleep will help the time pass quicker. I wait. I wait for the sound of a car pulling up outside the house. I wait for the sound of footsteps coming towards the front door. I wait for the knock on the door. It is every policeman's partner's nightmare.

*

I was lucky. It never came for me. My husband survived those years breaking down doors before dawn, arresting hardened criminals who might have shot him dead.

But I know many that weren't so lucky – devastated by the knock on the door.

I remember Steven Tynan's mother telling me that she knew it was coming before the police car even pulled up at the bottom of her driveway. A mother's intuition. Wendy Tynan knew her son was dead before the knock on the door.

That morning came just after Brian had left the armed robbery squad. He wasn't involved in the raid that they say led to the cold-blooded murder of Stephen Tynan and Damian Eyre. That morning my heart missed a beat. I fought back the tears as I got ready for work – yet I didn't know them. They were not friends. But they were part of the police family.

I am sure that in police homes around the country there were wives breathing a selfish sigh of relief, just like me, that they knew where their husbands were when they heard the news. Your heart goes out to the family, the friends and the workmates who have to deal with the death. But no matter how hard you try you can't avoid thanking your lucky stars that it is not your husband lying dead on the roadway.

Over the years I reported on the violent deaths of many police and it never got any easier. When I became part of the police family it became harder. I remember Stephen Henry – shot while he tried to intercept a car. Maurie Moore – shot dead when he pulled a motorist over. Lindsay Forsythe – set up by his wife and killed by another policeman. Stephen Tynan and Damien Eyre – lured into an ambush when they were answering a call about a car parked illegally in a suburban street.

I was on the streets of Melbourne the night Mad Max gunned down four officers. The men who apprehended him were my friends. They killed him, but not before he seriously wounded them both. I was too distressed to go to the scene of their shootings to cover the story for 3AW. I couldn't remove myself from the horror of knowing that mates were fighting for their lives, all because they were doing their job. Until you have been touched by this dread it is hard to explain.

Watching the news and seeing a friend and neighbour being lifted out of the air ambulance was in some ways surreal. There was even a laugh when the injured man obviously swore as the ambulance officers jarred the stretcher.

Everyone rallies when friends are injured. Visiting these friends in hospital or at home while they are convalescing, you push the 'I'm glad it's not me' thought to the very depths of your subconscious. You couldn't admit to feeling it, but you feel it.

Over the years I have sat through too many funerals with full police honours.

The first was Constable Angela Taylor – killed when a car bomb exploded outside the Russell Street Police Complex in 1986.

I was in the Russell Street Complex when the bomb exploded. It was Easter Thursday and I had been at work since the breakfast shift. I was thinking of trying to knock off an hour early – at 1.00 p.m. because it had been such a quiet day. Just as the one o'clock news began, an explosion rocked the building.

Only a tree on the street saved me from being showered in shards of glass. The sound of the explosion was completely inexplicable – my first thought was that a petrol tanker had crashed into the building.

My first reaction was to file for the news. I saw smoke and felt the subsequent blasts. I didn't see Angela Taylor or the others who were injured. I was filing news updates and speaking on air until the Special Operations Group evacuated me from the building. When I came out into Russell Street it was eerily silent. There was me, the SOG officer escorting me to safety, and a police dog and its handler checking other cars in the street.

My God, how could something like this happen in Melbourne?

All that seemed so far away when I sat in the choir stalls at the Police Academy chapel for Angela's funeral. I wept as I listened to the Police Surgeon, Dr Peter Bush, speak. 'Vale Angela Taylor,' he said, before the haunting sounds of the lone piper filled the packed chapel. I wept as I ran towards my car, but there was no time for emotion. I had a story to file, and I needed to get it written and contact the newsroom. It was only minutes before midday – our major news bulletin of the day. I nearly missed that deadline. It took me minutes to control myself and I almost broke as I began my news story.

I sat through the funerals of Gary Silk and Rodney Miller. I watched Rod's young wife, Carmel, nurse their son – only weeks old. It is probably the saddest thing I have ever seen. I didn't know Rod or Gary but I shed tears at their funerals. It is impossible not to be moved at such times when you are a member of the police family.

*

While many of my friends carry the physical scars of their encounters with criminals, Brian does not. He survived all those raids. He never had to fire his gun in anger. He bears no physical scars from his years at the front line. But did his psyche survive unscathed? I don't think so.

I was no longer working police rounds when it happened. I had opted for the life of a women's magazine, working lady's hours – no longer at the beck and call of news editors at all hours of the day and night. Brian was still at the Armed Robbery Squad, and one call-out, in particular, would leave a lasting impression.

The job was in 1987 in Queen Street in the heart of the city. It became known as the Queen Street massacre. You couldn't imagine a duller workplace if you tried – somewhere that sold stamps for collectors! Yet that afternoon it became the most dangerous workplace imaginable. A man they didn't know, with a grievance they could never understand, burst into the office and began to kill indiscriminately. It all revolved around a ruined tennis career and a perceived slight by a friend. Not reasons to kill – except to Frank Vitkovic. And kill he did. Eight people in all.

When the first call for police came through as an armed robbery alarm, the armed robbery squad was turned out – my man was among them. They didn't know what they would encounter inside the building.

Frank Vitkovic was dead before the police arrived. His family has to live with that pain. They are victims, just like the survivors and the families of those killed. And the police and ambulance officers who went into that building are victims too, although too often this, and they, are forgotten.

As Brian and the other police ran through the building, clearing floor by floor and helping survivors make their way to the ground, they had no idea of what they would encounter in the credit union office.

Brian would often talk of the young woman he saw there, lying behind a desk – a beautiful girl, her eyes staring blankly into space. Her face was perfect in every way, yet her life had been taken from her with a single bullet to the neck.

We would be at a dinner and he would talk about her. We would be lying in bed and he would talk about that day, always mentioning the beauty of the young girl and the futility of the deaths. The memory seemed to hit him at the strangest times, and it seemed to permeate our life. I couldn't persuade him to talk to a professional about it – he could cope, he said.

Years passed and I thought he was over it. It seemed as though an age had passed since he had last mentioned her, yet chatting to his mother she came up once more. 'I don't think I will ever forget that day,' he told his mother. I had my back to them. I couldn't turn around and face him. How could I help him? I am his wife and yet I don't know how to reach to those depths of his soul.

Even today, after years of policing, he is not immune. A murder scene will move him. A suspect will infuriate him. The media's apparent lack of concern for those left behind will frustrate him. I see him hurt and all I can do is hold him. I cannot put myself in his shoes.

At such times I feel a frustration so strong that I want to shout about it. I want to let others know what men like Brian go through day in and day out. I want to confront the armchair critics, so far removed from the reality of policework, who complain, demand inquiries, and call for sackings and changes to procedures. Have they ever faced an angry man? Sure, they have seen one – when his anger is subdued and his true nature is hidden beneath the respectability of a new suit, as he tries to convince twelve of his peers of their innocence. But this is not the same as facing up to threat, uncertainty and violence.

A friend took a life on the job. An escapee ran over a fence, heading towards a suburban street where children were playing. Someone shouted that he had a gun. As he came over the fence, my friend fired. All he could think of was the children playing and a desperate man armed with a gun. He killed the escapee. He was exonerated in court but he has to live with the fact that he took a life. One night he admitted that whenever sleep evades him, his thoughts go back to that afternoon. He goes over and over the events that led to the escapee's death. Could he have done things differently?

Just like their husbands, the wives don't talk about the pressures and the tensions. You would imagine that we would share our fears and console each other – but we don't. We are as bad as our husbands when it comes to talking things through. We keep our fears to ourselves – as though voicing them will make them come true. As though fate will deal us the death card.

Every day I thank my lucky stars that Brian is now an officer and, in theory, out of harm's way. He will come home at night – eventually – and we will grow old together.

But maybe that will not be the case. The horror of 11 September 2001 made me realise that a policeman is always at risk. Like so many Australians, I watched the events in New York and Washington transfixed. I listened to the mayor of New York describe watching police and firefighters walk into the World Trade Center to help those trapped inside. He watched as the building collapsed – killing those emergency service workers inside.

Had such an event occurred in Victoria, it would have been my husband and the other detectives from the Homicide Squad going into that building to begin the investigation. It would have been our friends and colleagues listed as missing and presumed dead.

It just doesn't bear thinking about.

The Trial of Annette Myers

Martin Wiener

FRIDAY, 4 February 1848, was a brighter than usual winter day in London. In St. James's Park, many of the fashionable world were taking advantage of the good weather to take the air and promenade, to see and be seen. Contributing to the charms of the setting were the smartly-uniformed élite Guards regiments parading.

Around 4:30 in the afternoon, soon after the parading had concluded, the almost-pastoral scene was shattered by the sound of gunfire. A Guardsman fell dead, and a young woman threw down a pistol and calmly walked away. A police constable very soon stopped her and heard her say 'I did it,' adding, on the way to the station house, 'I intended to do it a long time.' Her name was Annette Myers, and the fallen man was Henry Ducker, a private soldier of the Coldstream Guards. A murder (and by a woman) in St James's Park, the most fashionable of London parks, adjoining the seat of the nation's government, was unheard of. The self-satisfied calm of high society was broken.

The shooting was the atypical outcome of a common situation – the jilted lover. But it involved a number of special circumstances which drew public sympathy, high and low, towards the perpetrator. Annette Myers, who claimed to be aged twenty-six but was probably twenty-eight at the time of the murder, was a housemaid seduced by a young man (aged twenty at the time of his murder) who was not only handsome but possessed a most impressive uniform and was barracked by the royal palace; a young man, however, with little regard for women. It is clear that after he had won her, he used her with utter callousness, continually extracting money from her small stock, which he seems to have spent gambling and carousing, while also seeing other women. He seems indeed to have embodied most of the vices often feared from soldiers.

She stuck with him for over two years (beginning when he was only eighteen), hoping he would fulfil his promise of marriage, while she was gradually stripped of her savings and infected with gonorrhoea. Finally, when she had no more money, he dropped her in favour of another woman with more ready cash.

Myers then wrote asking for the return of a few small items of hers and pleading for a final meeting the following Sunday, when they could part amicably. Ducker scornfully sent this letter back without comment, postage due. Two days after receiving the returned letter, she collected together her last bits of money and proceeded to a gun shop. The gun dealer was taken aback by a female customer, and asked whether her brother or other male relative could come back with her. She explained that her brother was away, and that she needed it to kill a Newfoundland dog that had become dangerous. The dealer sold her a pistol for 10s, with powder and ball. The next morning she showed the gun to a friend; being warned against using it, she replied, 'Yes, I shall suffer for it, but it shall be a warning for others.' Later that day she went to the park, waited in Birdcage Walk outside Ducker's barracks and accosted him as he emerged from the barracks. From her account, he ignored her, saying not a word; she then fired her gun mere inches from his head and killed him instantly.

Myers's life story (not generally known at the time of her trial) was out of the purest melodrama: born in Paris, she had been raised in a Belgian convent (which she had entered as a supposed orphan of good family) and taken from there at the age of fifteen or sixteen to the home of an English baronet, Sir Francis Myers, who claimed her as his 'niece'. There she was allowed to take his name and was treated as a gentlewoman. It would appear that she was in fact Sir Francis's illegitimate daughter by an unknown Frenchwoman. Within a year, however, probably fearing scandal, he banished her from his home and arranged for her to be taken in as a dressmaker's apprentice in his country vicinity. Her succeeding history is a downward one: she eventually left the dressmaker and took up a position in London as a lady's maid, which did not last long. Dismissed as generally unsatisfactory (probably spoiled for service by her year as a gentlewoman), she found another job as a housemaid, only later to be let go and find yet another, where she lamented to fellow servants her unhappy life. On her way down, she had one serious relationship with a man, which ended with his departure. Into this cul-de-sac the alluring young lad Henry Ducker entered, and she was smitten. Soon he promised marriage, and they began sleeping together. When he dropped her so crudely, she snapped and determined on revenge. 'Revenge is sweet when you can have it,' she wrote in a letter for her mistress to find after the act. 'My love is too great not to have my revenge. It will be a warning for other young men not to deceive a girl.'

The crime caused a public sensation. Even the daily slide of states across the Channel into turmoil and revolution failed to crowd out Myers's case in the public mind, and accounts of the shooting and the trial appeared in papers around the country. Her trial at the Old Bailey was unusual in another way: though virtually penniless, she had first-rate legal representation, paid for anonymously by Sir Francis.

In her native France, she would have stood a good chance of acquittal, or at least conviction for the least serious type of homicide, involving a very short sentence. Although French law formally granted special dispensation only to husbands killing their wives if they caught them committing adultery, this dispensation had not only been extended in practice by Myers's time to wives in similar situations, but was often extended by French juries even to other sorts of 'crimes of passion', in which category Myers's case could well have fallen. English judges, however, ever more determined to subdue public violence, were set on halting that sort of legal laxity at the Channel.

Her lawyers discussed among themselves employing an 'English' variant of this defence – a state of temporary insanity, evoked by 'the provocation and treatment she had experienced' from the deceased. Despite the restrictive M'Naughton rules set out just a few years before, there were recent successful examples of temporary insanity defences. In 1845, two men killing their wives in separate incidents, men with no history of madness and no physiological evidence suggesting it, were found not guilty on grounds of insanity. The latter verdict was arrived at by the jury in the face of the trial judge's open attack on such a defence. In the following year, a ship's captain who shot to death an insubordinate crewman was also acquitted by reason of insanity. Each of these defendants, however, had been drunk at the time of their act. In England, unlike France, temporary insanity was rarely found for sober and deliberate killers – with the great exception of women murdering their newborns, in whose cases it was an increasingly common verdict. Myers's lawyers tried but failed to persuade several eminent medical men sympathetic to her plight to agree to give evidence as to her sanity in court, and they therefore reluctantly decided not to raise this argument. They feared it would only antagonise the judge, harming prospects for a reprieve from hanging.

Instead, they settled on a pathetic portrait of the accused and an assault on the victim's character, coupled with a request for a strong mercy recommendation. In court, Myers, as the *Times* sympathetically reported, 'looked very pale, and was evidently suffering severe mental distress. She was seated in the dock during the trial, kept her handkerchief to her face nearly the whole time, and appeared to be crying.' Her counsel read a portion of some of the love letters she had written to Ducker. 'My happiness in this world', he quoted from one, 'depends upon you – my very existence is bound up with your wellbeing and prosperity.' 'God help her, poor creature,' said her counsel, 'she was little aware how that expression would be realised.' The deceased, he declared, 'after having polluted and destroyed the wretched girl at the bar, had basely deserted her, because, having made use of all her wages to supply his cravings for money, she refused to comply with an odious suggestion which he had made to her as a means of raising more money for him' (a suggestion that she should go on the streets). Even without corroboration – indeed, the fellow servant and close friend to whom she had shown the pistol testified that Annette never mentioned his having suggested this – it was an effective claim.

Although the jury didn't have to leave their box to find her guilty of murder, they added (as the defence counsel had pleaded for them to do) a strong recommendation to mercy on account of the 'extraordinary provocation' Myers had received. Disregarding this, the presiding judge, Baron Pollock, called the act a simple revenge killing, meriting no mitigation, and pronounced the sentence of death.

The story did not end there; as soon as the trial ended, a strong public reaction set in. The next morning, the eminently respectable

Morning Post published a leader taking issue with Pollock and urging a reprieve. The paper enthused over her character, in contrast to that of her victim, 'the vilest of the vile':

> She had sufficient noblesse left in the very wreck of her character to reject the proposal of indiscriminate prostitution, and find that the man whom she had imagined devoted to her, and for whose sake she had ruined herself, was not only shocked at the idea of her becoming the bodily property of another, but actually counselled it for the sake of his own vile gain, she slew him as a monster ... surely never was murder committed under more palliating circumstances ... the perpetrator of the deed was a character who carried, even into a lawless attachment, such a fidelity as alas! is not always found in marriage itself; who, in the very wreck of her honour, showed a certain nobleness, and preferred to brave the utmost penalties of the law rather than prostitute herself for lucre.

Central for the *Post* and many other supporters was Ducker's supposed suggestion of prostitution; this plunged his image to the depths and raised hers to that of a tragic heroine. At a public meeting of about 1,500 middle-class men held very soon after in the City of London, John Bright depicted her as 'a victim of systematic and atrocious villainy. Every feeling in her woman's heart was wronged and outraged by the man who had fallen by her hand.' The meeting drew up a petition to the Queen for mercy. Other meetings in different parts of London followed quickly, and this petition was succeeded by others from towns around the country, dwelling on Ducker's villainy and the insult to her 'woman's heart'. It would appear that womanliness, like manliness, almost demanded, in extreme situations, extreme action. If the notion of temporary insanity was blocked by the law, it still reigned among the public. Nor did it hurt her cause that her betrayer was a young soldier; dislike of the military had been growing since at least the end of the French Wars. Writing to the Home Secretary a year later about another female murderer, one gentleman observed that the case of Annette Myers 'show[ed] what influence soldiers exercise upon their deluded victims – i.e. robbery and prostitution to aid them in their pleasures'. Under this mass effort, chiefly by gentlemen and middling men, and despite the judges continuing privately to insist that any mitigation would be wrong and dangerous, Home Secretary Grey, though a serious Evangelical and a stern man, commuted her sentence to transportation. She sailed in 1850 for Tasmania, less than three years before the transportation of women ceased.

Myers was typical of female transportees in her age, occupation and unmarried state, but very atypical in her crime and her degree of education. Like other women convicts at the time, she was assigned out within months of arrival for private domestic service. Her subsequent life followed a familiar pattern for female convicts. In woman-starved Australia it was much easier than in England to find a husband, though not one to match her own upbringing. Eight months after starting her new employment she married a 28-year-old illiterate shepherd from County Cork and had at least one child. Soon after, her husband received a free certificate and she a conditional pardon in 1856. They appear to have moved to booming Victoria, where she died in 1879, her age recorded as sixty. Whether she found happiness or not we do not know.

Myers never saw England or France again. Back in England, her story lived on in memory, largely as one of victimisation by a bad man: as Sir James Fitzjames Stephen remarked, soon after completing his *General View of the Criminal Law* in 1863, 'There are injuries which would exasperate a man, or woman either, quite as much as blows. The case of Annette Myers, in which a woman shot a soldier because, after seducing her, he pressed her to prostitute herself for his advantage, was one.'

*

Annette Myers's case is unique: how many daughters of baronets, even illegitimate ones, found themselves translated from a convent to a country house and then to a life of domestic service? Yet her story tells us much about attitudes towards violent crime in the Victorian age, especially crime committed by women. Given conventional views of 'Victorianism', the attitude of all concerned towards the defendant's being a soldier's mistress for two years was surprisingly relaxed. Women could gain relatively easy access to firearms in the heart of the metropolis. Temporary insanity was an increasing acceptable defence in murder prosecutions. Newspapers gave sensational coverage to dramatic crimes, and a melodramatic narrative of seduction and betrayal could overpower the growing determination of the judiciary to hang all deliberate killers. If those administering the criminal law were hardening their attitude towards interpersonal violence, a woman's tears and a Guardsman rake nonetheless formed a powerful imaginative combination in early Victorian England.

At least for men they did. Thomas Carlyle's unsentimental wife Jane, visiting Tothill Fields in 1849, where Myers was incarcerated awaiting transport, received a courtesy from her and formed an immediate impression: Annette Myers was 'the sauciest looking commonplace little creature that ever played the part of an heroic criminal.'

Jean Lee

Kerry Greenwood & Ashley Halpern

AND THEY CALL WOMEN the weaker sex!

I was sitting at the law library's big polished table, surrounded by volumes of reports in red and green, reading the appeal to the Victorian Supreme Court in the case of *R v. Lee*. Spread out in defiance of library regulations was all the information I had, two books and the photocopies of the *Truth* newspaper's accounts of the murder and of the execution of Lee and her co-offenders Clayton and Andrews on 24 February 1951.

As I puzzled over the appeal, I became aware of two faces, one on either side of me. Two colleagues were reading over my shoulder. One was my idealistic and very learned friend, straight out of Law School. The other was my been-there, exceptionally able and cynical colleague whom I would have thought unshockable.

Both faces were reflecting my own expression. Horror. This is what we were reading.

'Jean Lee who had been living in the hope that she would not be hanged suddenly went berserk … for days she raved and screamed, throwing the simple utensils around the cell … the wardresses were afraid of her … she spat and clawed … The hangman and his assistants entered the cell. They were carrying handcuffs and leather straps. When they appeared again they were carrying the limp body. Jean Lee was masked with a white hood which fell down to her breast. Her hands were manacled in front and her ankles strapped together. Together the hangmen set her on the chair … Jean Lee's head was still being held erect … the hangman placed the noose over her head and pulled the knot tight. At the feel of the noose Lee appeared to faint. Her head lolled forward and she began to slip out of the chair. The hangman thrust her shoulders back … the trapdoor fell … Jean Lee was dead.'

On the same page, *Truth* informs us that she went to her death wearing 'well-pressed khaki pedal pushers, a white shirt and strapped sandals'.

It is a truism that 'deadline', in law, used to mean the date by which, if you hadn't completed the paperwork, your client would be dead. It has been said by some of my criminal-law colleagues that it must have been exciting in the old days; the stakes higher and the risks greater.

Every single one of them, when taxed indignantly as to whether they want capital punishment back, denied it. 'But it was exciting,' they said wistfully.

I can't see it. Rather than run the risk of having my client die if I made a mistake, I would take up art embroidery for a living. But I had to know, having read that gloating account – what brought Jean Lee to the gallows in 1951, the last woman to be hanged in Victoria, and why didn't anyone try to save her?

*

Jean Lee was born in 1919. Her family moved continually throughout her childhood, eventually settling in North Sydney where Jean went to a good school. She was almost expelled because she was impatient and stroppy, defiant and irritating. She retained these traits into adult life. She married at eighteen and had one child, in 1939. Then her husband ran away with another woman and left her destitute.

She left the baby girl with her own mother and drifted into waitressing and subsequently into prostitution. There were a lot of American troops around, with money to burn, and Jean saw no reason why they shouldn't spend it on her. She had creamy skin, auburn hair and beautiful dancer's legs. Indeed, she worked as a dancer in various capital cities under the name of Valez, a fact which is significant. She formed a relationship with a petty crim called Dias, on whom she spent most of her money, which broke up when she met two soldiers, first Robert Clayton in 1946 and then Norman Andrews in 1949. Both men had been discharged from the army with 'anxiety neurosis', a blanket term for anything from full-blown pathological psychosis to hiccups or a stammer.

Together, they played the 'Badger Game', in which Lee would entice the mark into her room and a compromising position, then

Clayton would burst in playing the outraged husband/brother, suggesting that a lot of money would assuage his offended sensibilities and make it unnecessary to inform the mark's wife or boss. This garnered them a nice little living. Occasionally the mark would fight, in which case one of the men would beat him up. Generally they just took the money and ran.

Clayton was a dangerous, brutal man, but Lee, who had pathologically bad luck with men, stayed with him, even after he sexually assaulted a friend of hers and was jailed for it. Andrews had a long criminal record, mainly assault and robbery. When they met William 'Pop' Kent in the University Hotel in Carlton, Lee was thirty, Clayton thirty-three and Andrews thirty-eight, all of them practised criminals.

Kent was a 73-year-old S.P. bookie, a filthy old man with lice and a large bankroll in his pocket. Lee disregarded the vermin in favour of the money and managed to accompany him to his room in Dorrit Street, Carlton. There she failed to get him into the correct compromising position, possibly because of his age.

Accounts vary of what happened next. George Kent was left dead, trussed like a turkey, having been stabbed, beaten to a pulp and (possibly) tortured by having splinters forced under his fingernails and into the head of his penis. The cause of death, however, was strangling by someone with a powerful right hand. The three had ransacked his room, taken what money they could find and fled to the Great Southern Hotel where they immediately bought three air tickets to Adelaide.

They left no forensic clues to link them to the crime. Glasses and bottles that might have had fingerprints were smashed. The police searched the verminous room repeatedly, finding only a cigarette paper with the word 'Valez' on it. Jean had been talking to Kent in the pub about her career as a dancer and had written down her stage name for him.

A young constable, recently transferred from Perth, recalled that a certain Jean Wright alias Breen alias Marie Williams alias Jean Lee had been convicted of offensive behaviour (that is, soliciting for prostitution) under that name.

The airline rang to say that the tickets had been purchased and the three were arrested at their hotel.

What followed became the basis of a series of appeals, eventually to the Privy Council. Jean Lee denied everything. Clayton admitted the crime and blamed Andrews and Lee. Andrews admitted the crime and blamed Clayton and Lee. Jean Lee, confronted with these confessions, observed wearily, 'And they call women the weaker sex!' and immediately confessed to having done the whole crime herself. 'I sort of done my block and I hit him with a bottle and a piece of wood.' Pressed to implicate the others she said, 'There was only me. I am not saying any more.'

The trial, before Judge Gavan Duffy, began on 20 March 1950. Jean Lee, abandoned by her associates, denied her confession and explained, 'I confessed so I could have some peace and quiet … I was hysterical.' Both co-offenders blamed each other and Lee.

As usually happens in cases where accomplices try to throw the blame on each other, the jury believed all of them and convicted them of murder and robbery, and the judge had no choice but to condemn them all to death.

When asked if they had anything to say, Lee flung herself in Clayton's arms and wailed 'I didn't do it!'

There was an immediate appeal. The Full Court of the Supreme Court considered the matter in May 1950. The basis of the appeal was that the confessions were improperly admitted, having been extracted by police acting in breach of the Judges' Rules. It was considered that statements by each accused should not have been admissible as evidence against the other. The judges discussed the principles to be applied. They conceded that the detectives had a right to find out what each person would say about the events of the night. They said that s. 141 of the *Evidence Act 1928* applied in the circumstances 'no confession shall be rejected as not voluntary unless an inducement was really calculated to produce an untrue admission of guilt.' They also considered that common law gives a judge a discretion to reject admissible (voluntary) admissions if obtained by improper means. 'If a statement is the result of duress, intimidation, sustained pressure or preceded by an inducement taking the form of fear, prejudice, hope or advantage, the will of the individual making the statement is regarded as having been overborne and hence the statement ought to be rendered involuntary [and hence inadmissible].'

Judge Barry recognised that there was a balance of social principles involved: on one side, the apprehension of criminals, and on the other, 'the necessity of ensuring that the wide powers entrusted to those whose duty it is to investigate the crime should not be abused'. He agreed with Judge Smith, who said that the conviction should be quashed because, 'It ought to be inferred that the pressure exerted [on Lee] by telling her what her lover Clayton had said and showing her the written statement caused her to receive a violent emotional shock and by this her will was overborne.' He said that it should be recognised that when in custody, a person might lie in order to get out. Further, he stated that Lee had become emotionally unbalanced on seeing Clayton's statement and had 'ceased to desire to guard her own interests and desired instead to clear Clayton by putting the whole blame on herself', and that therefore there had been a miscarriage of justice and the matter should go back to be re-tried.

The other judge, O'Bryan, considered that although the means of obtaining these confessions were a little improper, they were not improper enough to quash the conviction.

It is interesting that both the majority and the minority considered that there had been impropriety in the obtaining of these confessions, particularly Jean Lee's. The different decision of Judge O'Bryan to Judge Smith and Judge Barry is explained by the weight he gave to the Judge's Rules as opposed to the apprehension of violent criminals. All of the judges commented on the fact that, apart from a few bloodstains, there was little physical evidence to link the accused to the crime. Their own words had condemned them.

The Crown, outraged that their hard-won verdict had been quashed, appealed to the High Court on the same legal point. The High Court decided that the confessions were possibly involuntary, but stated that the trial judge had heard all the evidence and therefore his decision should stand. It upheld the judge's decision, I might add, while finding that Jean Lee had not been properly cautioned and that she 'probably did not know that she was not bound to say anything' – which seems to this writer to indicate that the High Court did not want to get involved. My very learned friend comments: 'It seems as though the High Court has given undue weight to the circumstances leading up to the confession by transferring responsibility back to the trial judge …' He goes on to wonder why, with the Standing Rules becoming so flexible, it did not complete the job and find that the police had investigated the matter properly. That it did not seems to show that even the High Court has a sense of the absurd.

The prisoners tried for an appeal to the Privy Council, the only available appeal left, but the Government refused them legal aid on the grounds that they had no chance of success. Money was collected and documents were nevertheless prepared and the appeal was heard on 17 February 1951. 'In the case of the woman [Lee] it is impossible to come to any other conclusion than that the bulk of what she said shouldn't have been submitted at all,' roared S.G. Howard QC, a famous English barrister, but it did not work. Lord Diplock said that it should all have been left to the trial judge and declined to hear the case. Leave to appeal was disallowed. And the Privy Council is the end of the line.

Even today, the law is not entirely settled on the subject of the unsupported evidence of a co-offender. It was and remains a legal sore point. Yet this did not help Jean Lee. Had she been retried it is possible that she would have been acquitted. It is clear that her confession was not admissible. In law, she should not have been convicted and she knew it.

Her cry 'I didn't do it!' is perfectly explicable to anyone in the criminal law field. Hers was not the right hand that strangled William Kent, therefore she didn't do it. I have heard this statement many times, from the passengers in a stolen car – 'I didn't steal it!' – or the lookout for a burglary – 'I never even went into the place.' You will have heard the same justification from any child. In law, however, those who are part of any criminal enterprise are guilty of all of it. Lee was certainly in on the transaction which left William Kent dead, and therefore her conviction is no vast miscarriage of real justice, though it was certainly wrong in law.

That was not what puzzled me. In all other cases of women condemned to death, even when they have actually been executed, there has been a vigorous public campaign to save them. Child murderers, poisoners, husband-slayers or women who have committed much nastier crimes all by themselves – there has always been an outcry at hanging a woman.

Why did Jean Lee die on the gallows, drugged and carried to her execution shrouded in a white mask? Why wasn't there an attempt to save her?

She waited in her cell 'taking things very hard', said *Truth*, 'nervous and fretful, still hoping. She seems to think that something will save here – some miracle, perhaps.' Nothing in her life can have given her any confidence. The impatient, intelligent girl who had left school because she couldn't stand rules had been married and deserted while only a teenager, only to fall in love with two utterly unreliable and worthless men, the petty criminal Dias and the cold unscrupulous Clayton. She had spent all her money on defending Dias, then transferred her affections to Clayton who had, in his confession, accused her of murder and brought her to the gallow's foot.

But she had courage. She fought to the end. Her only public support came from John Cain the elder and seven parliamentary colleagues who protested to the Premier; and from Mary Barry, who raised a delegation of Labour Women to plead for Jean Lee's life. Premier McDonald told them, 'The day I had to order the hanging of a woman was the saddest of my life.' Yet this does not accord with the contemporary account of the matter in Alan Dower's book *Deadline*. Dower was a reporter with the *Herald Sun* and an habitué of criminal circles. He reports a conversation with Henry Winneke, who was then Solicitor-General. 'One man alone decided whether the three should hang, or two should hang or none should hang,' he said. 'The next morning he went into his Cabinet meeting and told his Cabinet that all three must hang. He was very firm about it. That man was Jack McDonald.'

Why did Jean Lee *have* to die? She was on the outside of the actual offence of murder. No one suggested that she strangled William Kent, and there were definite legal doubts as to the admissibility of her confession which could have furnished an adequate excuse for reprieving her.

Was it that she made the world unsafe for men who used prostitutes, that she made every lascivious old man feel personally threatened? Was it the fear of social disorder, the fact that there had been eight murders in as many weeks, so that everyone felt the world had become criminal and dangerous and some demonstration had to be made? As Dower suggests, was it necessary for Jean Lee to die to 'encourage the others', to warn the underworld that they were still subject to the unsleeping vengeance of the law? Was it that being a prostitute meant that Lee was no longer a women or a person, just a thing, and that two men and a thing were about to be hanged?

Was it just that a conservative government, feeling threatened by what they perceived as a rise in violent crime, decided that any show of mercy would be seen as weakness?

Was it that the war was over but rationing was still in place and the brave new world had not eventuated – and did the unemployment engendered by returning soldiers and the rush to get women back into the kitchen mean that no one noticed particularly? Dower says, 'General violence fermented overnight … the war had set a warped psychological and physical pattern for the hoped-for years of peace. Perhaps the best test of McDonald's actions is that there was little public outcry at the time. I do not remember more than a whimper here and there.'

Did people feel so disgusted by the crime – a poor old man murdered by a whore and her two pimps – that they didn't even want to think about it?

Was it, perhaps, that Jean Lee was alone? There was no mother tearfully addressing the papers, begging them to save her daughter's life. There was no child to lisp 'Don't kill Mummy,' as in some famous American cases. I have seen some clients in my years of criminal practice who reacted as Jean Lee did. They never have a network, unlike men, who have sisters and wives and mothers – even the most appalling have some female person who still loves them. The toughest female criminals stand alone, as Lee did, without a friend, husband, child or mother. They rely on themselves, are often likely to take the whole blame from some sense of responsibility or even contempt – 'And they call women the weaker sex.' They look for a loophole, a way around the law, and they usually find it. Lee could not, partly because she had tried to exonerate the worthless Clayton, and she could only do that by blaming herself.

I have before me the page of the *Truth* describing the hanging of Jean Lee. The police expected some trouble. The prison gate was closed. Urquhart Street, Coburg was blocked off and the place swarmed with uniformed officers and police vehicles.

There is a photograph captioned 'Scene outside Pentridge Gaol while the hangings were in progress.'

The street is empty, apart from a press photographer. No one cared enough about Jean Lee even to come and watch her die.

Another's Shoes

Richard Bourke

I DID MY FIRST MURDER when I was twenty-three.

It was funny, really. We'd moved out to the country after getting a reputation in the city. The local rag got hold of it and made a big deal – 'Notorious criminal moves to town', that sort of thing.

There was a middle-aged bloke up there, a bit of a loner, who'd managed to save up some money. He wanted to open a houseboat business but didn't have the funds. He must have read something in the paper.

He came looking for us in a bar with a business proposition – take his savings, invest them in a drug deal. High profits for him, a cut for us, everybody wins. It was arranged for him to come out to the farm a few nights later.

He got out there and we had a conversation in the kitchen:

'Did you bring the money?'

'Yes, it's here in the bag. $10,000 cash, like I told you.'

'You didn't tell anyone that you were coming out here, did you?'

'No, of course not. No one knows that there's any connection between us ...'

They found the bloke's body about six years later, buried under the chook shed.

I'll never forget how relaxed the trial was – you wouldn't have believed that a man was on trial for murder.

Two things took the heat out of it. First, it was so long ago that the sting had almost gone, even for the dead man's family. That's not to say that he wasn't mourned; he was. But the mourning had happened long ago, and the fact that someone had died had become a fairly intellectual proposition by the time of the trial.

Of course, the second thing was that the accused was already doing life for another murder – they'd found that body under the stables.

I must admit, he was a lot more relaxed than I was, but he'd had experience – this was his second murder trial. Nevertheless, the fact that he was the one on trial and I was just an articled clerk tagging along with the barrister should have made a difference.

I don't know what I was expecting going into the trial but it couldn't have been anything like what happened. When one of the jury pool put up his hand to be excused from the trial because of work commitments, my client wanted to ask if he could be excused too. It was all I could do to keep him quiet. He still called out 'Bingo' twice when the judge's associate was pulling the juror's names out of the ballot box. Not loud enough for the judge to hear, but loud enough for pretty much everyone else.

It was the first day of my first trial and I was beside myself. But after a couple of days I relaxed – it was hard not to in the face of the constant quips and jokes from the client. He was in his fifties, a short man with a little potbelly, a long grey beard and twinkling blue eyes. It was hard to credit the police claim that he was one of Australia's most ruthless killers. But every now and again, you would see some real steel in his eyes and the temperature in the room would drop. His smile wouldn't change, just his eyes. It made you wonder.

In the end, the prosecution got their version of events to stick. Our account involved some real twists and turns, but the jury didn't swallow it. Its high point was my client coming home to find a dead body on his kitchen floor and his girlfriend sitting on the table swinging her legs back and forth and twirling a pistol around her finger. She was supposed to have slapped the $10,000 down on the table and said, 'Now that's how you make money!' Without missing a beat we replied, 'That's all well and good but don't think I'm gonna clean this shit up.'

The real heat in the trial came from our claim that the cops had deliberately lost a surveillance tape. It was definitely 'us' and 'them' for a time. In the end there was nothing we could do. The police admitted they had lost it but claimed there was nothing important on the tape; we claimed that it contained a confession from our girlfriend, who was by now the main police witness. It was our word against theirs and the judge ordered that the trial had to go on.

We were duly convicted and got another life term. My client didn't make a joke, but he didn't look all that fussed either.

It was in that trial that I picked up the habit of referring to clients in the first person, a very common habit in the criminal law. Court corridors are littered with lawyers talking to each other about cases, asking questions like, 'What are you up on?' or 'What have they got on you?' and getting answers like, 'I've broken into a house and pinched some jewellery,' or 'We're meant to have pinched half a dozen cars, but Mum is going to come along and say that we were at home the night they went missing.'

I don't know if it's just shorthand or some unconscious side effect of trying to identify with your client. Maybe it's because talking about your client in the third person always makes it sound as though you don't believe them – 'My client is accused of stealing some cars but has arranged for his mother to come to court and give evidence that he was at home on the night that the cars were stolen.'

However it got started, it certainly has the effect of putting you in your client's shoes, and sometimes they are not shoes that you want to walk a mile in.

I still find it funny when people who are in the habit of talking in the first person drift back into talking about a client in the third person. Something about the case has made their tongue recoil from the traditional phrases. It's usually when their client has done something stupid that has got them caught. I think it is probably easier for a lawyer to say 'I am a murderer' than 'I am an idiot.'

*

My second murder was a very different affair from my first. This was serious business. Dismembered body, indemnified police witnesses, angry relatives and we were saying that the prosecution's main witness was the real killer. Of course, we did admit to helping to decapitate and dismember the body. It was well and truly one with the lot.

I got involved at the committal stage. The committal is a preliminary hearing in the Magistrates' Court in which witnesses are examined to see exactly what they are going to say and to determine whether there is enough evidence to bother a jury with a trial. It's a good chance for both the prosecution and the defence to get their cases in order.

This committal lasted a couple of weeks and was conducted with massive security. The tension was palpable as a brother and sister came and told the court about how they had watched us hack a body up with an axe.

The prosecution was bound to call all the evidence relevant to the death and the main witnesses were dealt with early on. This left time, on the final day, for a series of witnesses who claimed to have seen the deceased days or weeks after the prosecution said she had been killed.

That day turned into a bizarre dance, as one witness after another reeled into court to describe going to sleep stoned and waking up with the deceased lying in bed with them or running into her walking down the street. All this when she was in fact lying in four bits and two locations over an oppressively hot Melbourne Easter.

These 'witnesses' were mainly drug addicts who had just got confused about which week was which, but some became so attached to the idea that they were the last to see the deceased alive that they wouldn't budge from their evidence, even if the person they saw couldn't possibly have been her.

As the witnesses came and went, I took notes, resting my elbow on a two-inch pile of photos of the victim: 'Head half-submerged' … 'torso in undergrowth' … 'head on the autopsy table' … 'torso on autopsy table before cleaning' … 'after cleaning' and so on and so on. Her head and hands had been found in a lake two weeks after she was killed, and her body had been discovered a few hundred metres away a couple of days later. Forensics said it was a fascinating study in decomposition, with half the body in the water and the other half in the open air. Fascinating.

I'd somehow become quite fond of the victim. The first shot in the police photo book always shows the deceased when they were alive, allowing you to get a feel for what he or she was like. She had a pretty smile and the witness statements let you form a picture of her life. She was a drug user and a thief and she'd managed to annoy a lot of people, but she was so like people we all know – at least she was until she was cut up and left to rot.

I'm not sure what you're meant to do after a day like that. That afternoon another lawyer and I got a lift back to the office in our boss's sports car. Both of us are big blokes and we were crammed in with folders and files and two suits on their way to the dry cleaners. We started to joke about those last few witnesses and the questions we could have asked them: 'So, when you saw her did she look any different, for instance, did she appear shorter?' … 'You say she had her arm around you, where was the rest of her?' Maybe that's what you're supposed to do after a day like that.

The trial made the committal look like a walk in the park. About two days in, the police claimed to have heard a rumour of an escape attempt from court. Security was tripled, our client's relatives were made to sit in the upstairs gallery and Special Operations came down. It was January and the courtroom was already about thirty-five degrees, but you could feel the temperature rising by the minute.

There was a ruckus getting our client out to the cells a day or so later. One of his nieces had got too close to him as he was being led out and had been shoved by a guard. This caused him to blow up and he ended up being dragged up a flight of stairs feet first with his hands still in cuffs.

After letting the dust settle, we went up to see him. He had his shirt off because a bucket of water had been thrown over him to clean him up or calm him down. A very fit guy and obviously proud of his physique, he was not the slightest bit troubled to have a conference wearing nothing but a pair of pants. As we sat there, I kept watching the QC's eyes being drawn to our client's nipple ring.

When we went downstairs the QC and I had a surreal conversation. He kept asking how somebody could do something like that – have their nipple pierced. I pointed out that, even on his own account, our client had hacked the head and arms off the corpse of a young woman he had known for years. It still didn't sink in: dismemberment is one thing but nipple piercing is clearly something else entirely.

In the end we beat the murder and went down for helping to conceal the crime. We got the biggest sentence that had ever been handed down in Victoria for that offence. I was furious at the time, but when you think about it, you can't go around chopping up dead bodies and expect to get away with it.

*

A few years later, when I was presumptuous enough to think that I had seen a bit, along came another case to put me in my place. My client was charged with killing her two-year-old child – a child found with over one hundred bruises and a torn liver. He'd died of brain swelling, caused by a blow or by being shaken or both.

As always, there were hundreds of photos. In a lot of them the child looked just like a china doll and in some as if he were only sleeping. In a couple, though, he looked like exactly what he was: a tortured soul.

Then there were the autopsy photos. Because he may have been killed by a head injury, they peeled open his scalp to look for evidence of bleeding.

You cross a line in your life when you start looking at photographs of a baby with its scalp and face peeled off. You cross another one when you start looking at them dispassionately, as evidence, with no sense of what they portray.

Everyone who works as a criminal lawyer has to come to some sort of accommodation, a personal balance between how much one lets in and how much one keeps at a distance. Sometimes it's not much fun, being upset by photos, being put in a bad mood for days and weeks at a time by your work. Still, there are worse things than being upset by a book of photos, like not being upset by a book of photos. There are some lines I'd rather not cross.

The newspapers went nuts, of course. They sent a sketch artist to the first day of the committal hearing equipped with only the darkest crayons and came up with a picture of my client that reminded me of something from *The Hobbyahs*, a children's book involving small, bent creatures that feast on children after stealing them from their beds in filthy black sacks.

The police released photos of the baby's bruises which the papers published the next day. That morning, as I came into court, I expected to see someone throwing a noose over the limb of a tree outside the court. There was something about the grey, pendant skies that would have suited a gallows.

Whatever view you may take of what you have read so far, believe this. There is only one thing more pitiable than a two-year-old boy who has been killed by his mother, and that is a mother who has killed her two-year-old boy.

My client had been born intellectually disabled and had her first child at thirteen, a child of incest following years of sexual abuse by her stepfather. Her mother had kicked her out of the house for being a 'slut' and trying to steal her man. Apparently the child bore an uncanny resemblance to its father even when only a few months old.

So, an intellectually disabled teenage girl, thrown out of home, with a child the spitting image of the man who had raped her and cost her a home and a family.

A year or so later, the child was admitted to hospital with a broken leg – she said it was an accident. The Department of Human Services became involved and the child was adopted out. The adoption was obvious, logical, the only thing that could have happened. And with that certainty it is easy to forget that it might not have felt like that to the little girl who was the mother of the child. Never underestimate how much hurt a human being can suffer in their life – and just because they are struck a hundred blows, never think that each one doesn't hurt just the same.

There followed a series of abusive relationships and a series of children. As each relationship fell apart and each man abandoned his children, she grasped for another relationship and another man not worth having. Certainly none of them was interested in raising the children of a previous relationship, and so the kids were farmed out to a series of foster homes or relatives.

Finally, another broken relationship, a phone call to another man not worth having and the stage was set.

In the week before the child was killed, the lifts went out in the Commission flats and they couldn't leave the apartment for a couple of days. Tensions rose and I will allow your imagination to fill in a description of those last days.

Finally, the man who had come to stay, a man with substantial burdens of his own, became frustrated and struck the boy to the head when he was trying to put him into his pyjamas. The boy fell back onto the floor, fitting.

Mum, panicked and ill-equipped to deal with the situation, shook and shook but her baby wouldn't wake up. At least he stopped fitting. They turned off the lights and left him to rest, hoping that he would come right. Eventually they called an ambulance. He died in hospital as a result of brain swelling caused by the shaking.

I can't talk about 'we' any more when I talk about this case. Not because 'we' killed a child but because the miseries that my client suffered she suffered alone and to use language that makes it seem otherwise would be false.

As the committal proceeded and the details of those final weeks were uncovered, you could feel the inexorable tide of fate in the courtroom, a swirling black undercurrent to the words of the witnesses. As the picture became clearer you almost wanted to howl in frustration as one thing led to another and, inevitably, to the death of a child.

Each day the defence team and the prosecutors would shuffle through the gloom and drizzling rain to have lunch together. It doesn't normally work that way, but a solidarity was forged in the wretchedness of the case; and besides, we weren't really fit to talk to anyone but each other.

Although no one else was on our wavelength, others were aware of what was going on in the courtroom and everybody had an opinion. Each day, a new set of self-righteous witnesses would arrive to claim that they had seen this coming – only to leave, humbled and confused, when asked why they hadn't done anything about it.

If you are worried that I have forgotten that a child was killed, you need have no fear that the women out at the prison forgot. Visiting the prison was heart-wrenching – she was so grateful to see someone who would speak gently to her. The pathetic gratitude of a person so accustomed to being beaten that the simplest kindness is to be treasured.

Nearly all of my clients have been victims of one sort or another, but this case seemed to go out of its way to make that point.

The man ended up pleading guilty to assaulting the child. As for her, the prosecution agreed to a plea of guilty to negligent manslaughter – falling so far short of the standard of reasonable behaviour as to be a criminal offence, even by a woman simply incapable of meeting that standard.

The judge wanted an explanation, though. What about the bruises and the torn liver? Why was she being let off with manslaughter? The prosecutor knew; he had sat through the committal and that's what he told the judge.

It seems we have a particular fascination for women who kill their children. The judge never asked about the boyfriend. She was sentenced to seven years in prison. It was one of the most pointless things I have ever seen. Even the cops thought it was a waste of time.

In the months before her release on parole she was given supervised leave for a couple of hours a fortnight. On her first leave from the prison, after years in custody, she came down to visit her lawyers.

There was no one else.

Hit and Run

Shelley Robertson

IT WAS A DARK AND STORMY NIGHT. And cold. The sort of cold that rural Victoria turns on after a seemingly innocuous day. I was huddled in the front seat of a stationary police car, ignition on, trying to warm up with the heater on full blast.

Outside the car, the tall gum trees were whipping themselves into a frenzy and the dirt road stretched ahead into darkness, as did the paddocks on either side of the road. The flashing police lights lent a surreal touch to the whole picture. Crime scene analysts and photographers (obviously hardier beings than myself), clad in yellow reflective gear, darted about, trying to measure, record and generally search the area between flurries of rain.

The centre of attention was the crumpled body of a middle-aged male, lying on the roadside verge. He was slightly built and wore only a light jacket over his clothes. He too was cold, but then, he was dead.

The call had come as I was getting ready to go to a friend's place for dinner. My friend cooks wonderful hearty meals that warm one's core, something I was to reflect upon several times during the ensuing evening.

Greg was a senior member of the Homicide Squad, with whom I had worked on many cases previously. 'How would you like a nice drive to the country?' he said, adding, 'Lovely evening for it.' Many potential social occasions are terminated for a forensic pathologist with this sort of opening line. Choice is not really an option, as the forensic pathologist is required by both police and coroner to attend the scene of a death to help determine if suspicious circumstances surround the death and, if so, how the pathological findings can best contribute to the overall investigation.

'We have a body on the side of a country road,' Greg continued, 'found by a farmer, and the local boys thought it was probably a "hit and run" as no one or no vehicles were around. AIS (Accident Investigation Squad) were called in, but when they arrived they weren't real happy.' As part of their investigation of road traffic accidents, members of the AIS are trained to interpret tyre impressions, skid marks and patterns of damage to vehicles. Using this information, they calculate speeds of vehicles, forces of impact and braking patterns which, when correlated to witness statements, weather conditions, environmental lighting and so on, serve to build a complete picture of the circumstances relating to a particular accident and highlighting its cause. Their concerns in this accident were principally based on the tyre marks of a particular vehicle, visible in the gravel of the road and the muddy verge. They showed the vehicle running off the road and onto the verge, impacting the body then appearing to reverse, back over the body and onto the road. This is not what would be expected in a 'hit and run', where a vehicle strikes a pedestrian, usually standing on the road or at least close to its edge. The body is flung out of the path of the vehicle, which either stops before accelerating off or continues on, the driver sometimes being oblivious to any impact.

The tyre marks here told quite a different story, suggesting a deliberate collision with the body and a reverse pass 'to make sure' – that is, murder. AIS had decided that the matter would be best handed over to the Homicide Squad, assisted by a forensic pathologist, hence my phone call from Greg and disrupted social evening.

*

When I arrived a few hours later, it was early evening. I was escorted to the scene, several kilometres from the centre of a small to medium-sized country town, by local uniformed police who were concerned that I would become lost if I tried to find it on my own. The light was fading quickly and gum trees cast long shadows over the gravel road while dark clouds threatened to hide the sunset. I was still able to see the tragic figure of a man, lying on the grass and dirt of the roadside, with two sets of tyre marks leading to and from him. The dead man was lying face up, an arm flung up over his head and one leg obviously badly broken, jagged bone ends protruding through torn trousers. As I moved closer to examine the body, reflecting sadly that my job is to deal with the wrong end of life, the scientific part of my brain took over, and little alarm bells started going off.

Something was missing! In my long career as a forensic pathologist I have seen many bodies, often with horrendous injuries. One of the best indicators of what has happened is blood: either the spatter pattern where blood splashes onto surfaces, or the pooling or trickling of spilt blood. Clothes can show patterns of blood staining; implements such as knives or axes can leave distinctive imprints in blood; direction of blows can be calculated from the shape of a blood droplet. Blood, the amazing fluid that keeps us alive, can also tell the story of death, and it was telling me a story here.

There was almost no blood surrounding this badly injured man, neither on the ground where he lay nor on his clothing. Why not? The answer was startlingly obvious. He was already dead when the vehicle ran over him.

*

Larry had not had a fortunate life. Injured when a car collided with his pram at an early age, he had been left with an intellectual disability, suffering from epilepsy, and somewhat physically disabled. The Supreme Court had awarded him damages and the sum of money was held in trust for him. One of the trustees was his sister, Mary. He had been institutionalised for most of his life and now lived with supervised care in the country town. Life wasn't too bad for Larry, though. He was well cared for and able to get around independently. He took pleasure in simple things, particularly the countryside surrounding his home. He enjoyed taking long walks and the sight of his slightly lopsided frame and shuffling gait was familiar to the town's residents. He also had visitors. Mary would often drive from Melbourne to see him, and occasionally he stayed with her.

In fact, Mary had been to see Larry just that day, the same day that his body was found by the roadside. As police pieced the information together, it appeared that she must have been one of the last people to see him alive. She said she had left him in good spirits early that afternoon and had driven back to Melbourne in her small brown car.

Meanwhile at the roadside scene, the accident investigators were still taking measurements and photographs and the local undertaker had arrived to transport Larry to the mortuary for the last and most complete medical investigation he would ever undergo. I had now fulfilled my role at the scene. I drove back to Melbourne, thoughts of my friend's dinner table being replaced by visions of a vulnerable man, whom society had an undertaking to protect, having his simple life taken and his body callously discarded. I wondered what his body would tell me, what clues it would give to the investigation.

*

I performed the autopsy on Larry's remains the next day. The clothing was carefully removed and again the paucity of blood staining of the clothes was striking, especially given the nature and severity of Larry's injuries. The pattern continued with the internal examination. Larry had sustained the type of injuries that would normally bleed profusely, both internally and externally. I was now certain that he was already dead when he received them. But how did he die? Here was a problem. Take away all the injuries inflicted by the vehicle running over him and I was left with a man who may not have been a glowing picture of health but who really didn't seem to have anything much wrong with him. At least nothing more than had been the case for the last forty years.

I collected various samples of body fluids during the autopsy (including blood and stomach contents) and these were sent to the toxicology laboratory for analysis. The results were interesting. As expected, traces of the anti-epilepsy medication that Larry had been prescribed for most of his life were present. But also present was a drug used in treatment of insomnia. Lots of people take drugs to help them sleep, but not Larry. All his medication was administered under supervision and the records showed that he had not been prescribed any sleeping drugs. This particular drug was also interesting as it had been withdrawn from general usage some years previously when it was found to be too dangerous to be routinely prescribed by doctors. The problem was that the difference between a 'normal' dose that aided sleep, and a 'toxic' dose that caused side effects including coma and death, was not very great. The amount in Larry's body was only quite small. Certainly not enough to kill him. But enough, perhaps, to make him drowsy, particularly when combined with his daily anti-epileptic medication.

So why did Larry take this stuff? Where did he get it and who gave it to him? Could Mary have given it to him?

A scenario was starting to emerge from the facts. Was it possible that Mary, after supposedly bidding Larry 'goodbye' and driving home to Melbourne, could have taken him for a short drive out of town. Could she perhaps have given him some special 'medicine' which made him a bit sleepy, then held a rug or some clothing over his face until he suffocated (the 'medicine' had made him too drowsy to struggle much, so this wouldn't necessarily have left any marks). Did she push his lifeless body out of her car and drive over him, reversing the car 'just to make sure', hoping it would appear that poor Larry had died in a 'hit and run' accident? Did she then drive home to Melbourne, planning to wash her car as soon as she arrived home, ridding it of any traces of Larry?

If she did these things, the next question was 'Why?' Why, when Larry seemed so inoffensive, going about his life within his limitations?

This is a point in the investigation when the experience of the investigators comes into play. The majority of murders are carried out by persons known to the victim, usually closely. Fortunately, the true 'random killer' is a rare entity. The prudent investigator looks first to those nearest the victim. These are usually the ones with the opportunity and, more importantly, the motive to kill the victim. In this case, the investigators were already considering the victim's sister, Mary. Her story hadn't quite rung true to the experienced Homicide Squad officers who had questioned her. These officers are accustomed to delivering terrible news to people and gauging reactions to this news. Mary's reaction to learning of her brother's death was described as 'feigned concern'. She had certainly had the opportunity to murder Larry, having been one of the last people to see him alive. But what was her motive? Why would she have wanted to do away with poor harmless Larry? One of the strongest motives for murder in our society is money. Remember Larry's compensation payout, awarded to him following his childhood accident? Is over a hundred thousand dollars a good enough reason for a scheming sister to dispose of her brother, a sister who, under the law, will inherit her brother's assets? The Homicide Squad thought it was probably a good reason. Good enough for police to obtain a warrant enabling them to impound her car (freshly washed following its country trip) for forensic testing.

*

The investigation continued. Forensic scientists examining Mary's impounded car found traces of hair, blood and other tissue beneath the vehicle (a difficult area to reach in a car wash). Further testing matched this material with samples taken from Larry's body at autopsy. Impressions taken from the tyre marks at the scene matched the tyres on Mary's car. This was incontrovertible evidence that Mary's car was the vehicle that twice ran over Larry's body.

But how did Larry die? This question loomed over the whole investigation. Review of Larry's medical records confirmed that he was epileptic, and epilepsy is sometimes associated with sudden unexpected death. He had no other heart, lung or other natural disease that would lead to sudden death. I was left with the diagnosis that every forensic pathologist dreads – 'cause of death unascertained'.

'Unascertained' leaves everyone frustrated, including the deceased's relatives, friends, doctors, lawyers, police and most of all the forensic pathologist, who agonises over the diagnosis, wondering if he or she has missed something, finally giving in and making the unsatisfactory pronouncement. Such a conclusion is not reached without much checking and back-tracking. The internal and external examination findings are reviewed in meticulous detail. The microscopic slides of tissue samples collected at autopsy are re-examined and the results of toxicological analyses researched. Further information, such as past medical history or results of investigations undertaken during life, may be sought. But at the end of the day the forensic pathologist may be left with no alternative.

And so it was with Larry. Over and over, I sifted through everything I knew about his death. In my own mind, I felt that the 'smothering scenario' was most likely, but I had no evidence to support this. Forensic pathology is a science, in which conclusions are based on proof, and I had none. I could not exclude epilepsy as a cause of death and indeed, if Larry had been found by the roadside with no injuries at all, having collapsed, it would have been the most likely cause of death. Similarly, had Larry been alive when he sustained his injuries, they most certainly would have killed him. But he wasn't, and it would have been too much of a coincidence to suggest that Larry had died suddenly from epilepsy just before his sister bundled him out of her car and ran over him (twice). It didn't explain the presence of the sleeping drug either.

*

It was now up to the judicial system to determine what had happened to Larry. Mary was charged with his murder but she maintained her original story of having left him alive and well before driving home to Melbourne.

The jury members eyed the small middle-aged female seated in the dock. Were they going to find her guilty of the murder of her disabled brother? As witnesses gave evidence over the next few days, the sad story of Larry's life and death unfolded. The court and the twelve members of the jury heard about the accident in which a car struck Larry's pram. They heard of his disabilities, of his supervised life in care, of his penchant for country walks. They also heard of the money held in trust for him, and of Mary's visits during which she would give him money for small everyday items.

The jury heard my evidence, my opinion that he was already dead when run over by the car. They heard that I was unable to ascertain a cause of death for this man. They heard the AIS members give evidence about tyre patterns and they heard forensic scientists prove that it was Mary's car that ran over Larry.

What the jury did not hear was Mary's voice. She did not enter the witness box to give evidence or be cross-examined. This was her right under the law, and the law also states that the jury cannot draw adverse conclusions based on a defendant's refusal to give evidence. This jury never heard Mary's explanation of the fact that her car had run over Larry. She had steadfastly refused to answer this question (as was her right) whenever it had been put to her during the investigation and she maintained this position. The jury were also denied the opportunity to hear about the evidence relating to the sleeping drug found in Larry. The court decided that this evidence was not admissible, on the basis that the drug could not be directly linked to Mary, and 'it may have come from anywhere.'

A major obstacle to a murder conviction was the lack of a definite cause of death. In law, there are two components to murder, the '*mens rea*' or 'intent to kill', and the '*actus reus*' or 'act of killing'.

The problem in this case was the latter component, it being difficult to find that an act of killing had taken place without exact knowledge of what had caused Larry's death.

The judge directed the jury that, without a cause of death, they could not find Mary guilty of Larry's murder. But the jury members weren't fooled. They had heard the evidence and made up their minds. They found Mary guilty of the lesser charge of 'attempted murder' and the judge gave her a heavy sentence.

*

Larry had had an unfortunate life and an even more unfortunate death, but the justice system didn't let him down and the person who was responsible for his death is in prison.

A result like this restores one's faith in a system that sometimes seems so wrong. For me, this case more than made amends for a missed dinner on a cold night. I will have many more dinners but Larry won't be taking any more country walks.

Names in this story have been changed to conceal the identities of those involved.

Room for Disquiet

Mark Whittaker

CHRISTINE SHAW, feeling unwell, put herself to bed early on the night of 27 August 1993. She woke in the small hours, made a cup of coffee and was reading in bed when she heard a noise. A deep, primal, guttural noise. A crazed man's voice, she thought, followed by a woman's. Looking at her clock, she saw it was 3.57 a.m. A dog was barking.

As she lay there, three members of the Gilham family were being killed on the other side of Prince Edward Park Road, Woronora, a quiet riverside suburb in the far south of Sydney. A beautiful place to bring up kids.

Ted Warner wouldn't be sure of the time. He was roused by some terrible commotion nearby and would have gone over to investigate with the baseball bat by his bed, only he'd already been woken twice that week by the alarm going off at his café in town. He drifted back into sleep until – he thought it was an hour later – there was a loud banging on his door.

'Who is it?'

'It's Jeff.'

Warner recognised it as the neighbours' 23-year-old son, Jeffrey Gilham. He opened the door to the winter's night. Jeffrey was there in boxer shorts, smelling of smoke and kero. Events went by in a whirl, but he'd recall Jeffrey saying he had to use the phone.

'What's the matter?'

'Albert has killed Mum and Dad and lit them.' Albert, as in Fat Albert, was a nickname for Jeffrey's brother Christopher, twenty-five.

Jeffrey, mumbling, grabbed the phone on the wall just inside the front door. 'I got to use the phone, dial triple-0. The house is on fire.'

Warner saw Jeffrey wasn't capable of dialling, so he took the phone from him and sat him on the lounge, yelling to his wife: 'Jan, Jan, get out here. I need you.' She was already coming.

Warner dialled triple-0. It was 4.34 a.m. Thirty-seven minutes had passed since Christine Shaw heard the crazed man's voice.

Warner reached the emergency operator. 'Listen … ah … my neighbour's just run in the door and he's yelling that he's just … his brother's just killed his parents …' He gave the address and phone number, tried to explain what little he knew, then asked the operator to hang on a minute. 'It's not a bad dream, is it? Jeff, Jeff! It's not a …' He returned to the phone 'Hang on. It might be a dream.'

'Can you put Chris on?' asked the operator, confusing the names.

'Mate, he's … he's shaking. He's unc… He's out of it.'

'How old is Chris?'

'Twenty-two, twenty-three. He's [at] university.'

'He's what?'

'He's an engineering student.'

'Do you know Chris well?'

'Yeah, yeah, we've known them all our lives down here.'

'He hasn't been out tonight?' the operator asked.

With the phone in his hand, Warner bent over and sniffed Jeff's breath. It smelt like a fire that's had kero poured on it.

'He hasn't been drinking,' said Warner, increasingly frustrated that no units had been dispatched. The operator asked to speak to Jeffrey. There was a minute and a half's gap before he came on. The operator introduced himself as Mick Jordan, checked that the young man was okay and asked again what had happened.

'He killed my parents.'

'You haven't been out tonight?'

'No, I've been at home.'

'You've been at home? Now what … tell me what's happened.' There was the sound of heavy breathing. 'Easy. Calm down. Calm down and just tell me, mate.'

'I walked in … through the door …' Gilham's panting punctuated every word.

'You've walked in from where?'

'Mum called me … called me …'

'Right.'

'And I came up … and … I see him there … with a knife.'

'Your brother was?'

'Yeah. And they were alight.'

'They were what?'

'They were on fire.'

'Right.'

'Aa ... aa ... and ... and then ... then I killed ... I killed Albert. I don't know why.'

Meanwhile, Jan Warner had gone upstairs to the linen closet and grabbed her husband's burgundy sloppy joe and a blanket. She wrapped the blanket around Gilham as he sat on the floor near the front door. She saw a little smeared blood on his lower left shin. Just a little.

Ted had gone out to check the Gilham house, then returned.

'It's for real,' he told her. 'It's really alight.' He saw Jeffrey on the floor shivering, curled up in a foetal position, looking very scared with the sloppy joe scrunched up under his head.

*

Detective Sergeant Jeff Ahern was called out of bed and arrived at the smouldering triple-murder scene at 5.45 a.m. Smoke and steam were rising from the formerly neat brick house as the fire brigade mopped up.

Ahern had previously been in homicide for five years and had been involved in cases like the Surry Hills massacre, the disappearance of Samantha Knight, the murder of Anita Cobby. He'd also been with 'scientific'. Had seen domestics where you followed trails of dead children until you got to the father with his head blown off.

He'd been in Sutherland – 'the Shire' – for a year and it was a sleepy backwater, just as Tolkien would have had it. This case was out of the blue. As soon as he arrived at the smouldering scene, it was obvious he was dealing with a domestic, but the details were unclear. Someone told him there was a family member in the ambulance.

Jeffrey Gilham was taken back to the station to be interviewed. To Ahern, he seemed coherent, if a little distant, and he responded to questions logically. Everyone reacts differently, so Ahern didn't see anything unusual in the mechanical way Gilham described how he was asleep in the boatshed where he lived; how he was called on the intercom by his frantic mother; how he pulled on his boxers and ran to the house in about ninety seconds. He said that once there, he saw his brother standing over his mother with a lit match in his hand. He told Ahern that, as he approached Christopher, his brother said, 'I have killed Mum and Dad.' As he drew nearer, Christopher put the match to their mother's body which ignited immediately, the fire spreading quickly to the bedroom where he could see their father on the floor.

The video shows Ahern deadpan: 'Can you tell me what happened then?'

'Then I picked up the knife and chased my brother and stabbed him.'

He chased him down the spiral staircase into the lower part of the house where Christopher lived. There, he said, he stabbed his brother in the chest 'a few' times. He said he was not in fear for his life, and when Ahern asked why he did it, he responded: 'I just did. I just saw everything there and I just picked up the knife and chased him.' He said he then went straight to the Warners' house without washing.

When Ahern took Jeffrey for a walk-through later in the day, he asked him why the door to his boatshed was locked. Jeffrey answered that he had locked it out of habit while responding to the screams of his mother.

Ahern didn't know then that earlier that morning Jeffrey Gilham had told both the triple-0 operator and Detective Constable Narelle Parsons in the ambulance that Christopher was holding the knife when he entered the room. He'd also told Parsons that Christopher was sitting when he arrived. By the time Ahern learnt all this, the legal system had got hold of Jeffrey and he was being advised not to speak.

So when the clothes that witnesses had seen Jeffrey wearing earlier in the evening were found mysteriously rolled up under a cushion in the lounge, he could not be asked how they got there. Had he walked all the way down to his boatshed semi-naked? He could not be asked why he might have stripped in his parents' lounge.

*

If Fay MacArtney-Bourne were to write a book about this case, she'd call it *Where the Mullet Jump*. The suburb is so quiet at night that you can hear the fish down in the Woronora River. She first met Stephen and Helen Gilham when she moved in a few doors down, in the mid-'60s, before the boys were born. She and her now ex-husband, Barry Crouch, went for a swim and the Gilhams were pottering away in their boatshed.

None of the houses had fences. Every Sunday there was a communal barbecue down on the grassy riverbank where ducks and geese wandered. Each of the two women went on to have two sons born in the same years and they went through it all together. 'It was a very nice feeling down there. Everyone cared about each other,' MacArtney-Bourne recalls.

She describes the father, Stephen Gilham, as 'a wonderful and placid man who went with the flow'. Helen appeared quiet and gentle in her work as a nurse, but she ruled the home.

'Helen was very controlling. She controlled where the kids went and who they went with. She used to put them to sleep even when they were school age. An afternoon sleep. My kids would go over and stir the shit out of them and she'd run them away. Kids at that age aren't going to lie down and have a rest but she controlled them enough that they did it.

'Helen was really careful with money. Other people said she was frugal ... She was very tough as a person. She tied Chris to the toilet, for example, for toilet training. I said, "You don't do that to kids." Hers was a really tough, country upbringing, up near Lismore.'

Fay moved out in 1985 following her divorce but stayed in touch with Helen and the family. It took her a while to do it, but she summoned the wherewithal to tell the investigating detective, Jeff Ahern, about the last time she was down there for dinner, in Christmas 1992, eight months before the tragedy. 'Chris had said – and they used to joke about money and things – "Oh, we'll kill you and get all the money." It was definitely a "we'll". Everybody laughed, but I took offence at it so much I said to my son, "Ever say that and you'll get nothing." Money was always an issue in that family.'

*

Jeffrey Gilham waited almost a month in the psychiatric unit of Sydney's Long Bay jail before he was granted bail. MacArtney-Bourne visited him there. It was the only way she could cope with the situation. She knew she'd have wanted Helen there if something like this were happening to her boy. She held his hand and they talked. She was surprised by how rational he was.

'We started talking and somehow we got on to his parents' super. I don't know how that came up. And we got on to him not getting a job in the public service because he'd have a record, and how [his solicitor, Chris] Murphy told him he'd get off with a suspended sentence, and I said, "He can't guarantee you that. He's not the judge."'

Jeffrey came to the funeral in handcuffs and a suit, and the family did their best to make him feel okay.

*

His uncle, Tony Gilham, supposes that they started to feel all was not right about six months later, when the people at the Woronora cemetery called another uncle, Richard Gilham, saying that if someone didn't come to collect the ashes, they'd scatter them themselves. 'That's what made me suspicious. If you lost your family like that, you would want to put them to rest properly.'

But when the case came to trial, the family was still behind Jeffrey. He pleaded guilty to the manslaughter of his brother. The Director of Public Prosecutions did not oppose the plea and accepted Jeffrey's version of events.

On the morning of the sentencing hearing, a secretary from Chris Murphy's office had rung Tony Gilham. Tony recalls: 'I was asked to write a statement for my mother to sign. It said that the brothers got on well together. But both brothers hated each other with a passion. We wrote it and it was submitted to the sentencing trial.'

'I made a mistake there doing that, didn't I?' Tony's mother, Jessie Gilham, later said of the statement.

So it wasn't the full truth? she was asked. 'It wasn't, no. It honestly wasn't. I only said it because I was asked to say it, you know?' In fact, Jeffrey couldn't pass Christopher in the corridor without Jeffrey thumping his older brother. 'They was always like that,' she said. 'Always.'

At court Jeffrey had about forty supporters. His best friend Wayne Nolan gave evidence of 'Fat Albert' being a 'bit of a loner. He really liked his own company and had no friends who came over.' Nolan said that two weeks before the murders, Jeffrey had told him Christopher had been acting strangely, violently, towards their father. On the evening of the murders, he told Nolan he had to rush home to make sure their dad was okay.

When he got home, his girlfriend, Hayley Moskos, was there. She gave evidence that she saw no signs of friction that night, nor had she seen any in the past but, on leaving, Jeffrey pulled her aside and said: 'What am I going to do about my brother? It's pretty serious, Hayley. I've never seen him so psycho. He's pushing my father around; I don't know what to do.'

Fay MacArtney-Bourne remembers sitting in court as all these things were being said, thinking: 'That's not the Christopher I know.' She remembered him as the kid who always played beautiful music. 'He played the piano. Steve would always say, "Go on, play something for us." He gave lots of people a lot of pleasure. Nothing to show he had feelings came out [at the trial].' She recalled how neighbours would call the house when Chris was playing the piano to ask that the Gilhams open their windows and doors. How he was also a keen university fencer with a girlfriend and a life.

'Jeffrey was Helen's favourite. Chris would do something but "my Jeffrey can do this, and oh, my Jeffrey". It was really hard on Chris but Chris was pretty placid about the whole thing. Chris and Steve had a very nice blokes' relationship as Chris got older – they'd sit there and have port together.' She remembered, too, the more athletic Jeffrey always hitting Chris, as if to show who was the boss, who was the star.

The judge, Justice Alan Abadee, took seriously the copious evidence attesting to Christopher being a quiet loner who played Dungeons and Dragons and who fretted about his job prospects after his graduation as a chemical engineer.

Jeffrey, the evidence indicated, was the popular sailing champion. Justice Abadee was impressed with the testimony: 'That evidence discloses much loyalty and love [in the case of both relatives and friends] and discloses much warmth and friendship towards the prisoner ... The prisoner should be truly grateful for the support that has been shown to him ... the evidence to which I have just made reference is, to say the least, of a most impressive kind.'

Abadee placed Jeffrey Gilham on a five-year good behaviour bond. He was free to go.

In following months, it was argued before coroner Derrick Hand that since the Supreme Court had accepted Jeffrey's version of events – that Christopher had killed his parents – there was no point in holding a full inquest. Unaware of any contrary view, the coroner recorded a finding that Stephen and Helen Gilham had died at the hand of a person now deceased.

That's how the murder of two people can slip through the legal system without any in-depth formal inquiry.

*

Tony Gilham remembers talking to Jeff Ahern at the time of the murders and being told: 'If he is capable of murdering his brother, he is capable of murdering the others.'

'After that, all we heard was that there was no other conflicting evidence,' says Tony. 'We didn't want to go into it. It was painful enough finding out the grisly details. All we heard then was Jeffrey's side of things and naturally assumed that was the story. I would ring him up to see how he was going. Talk about football, that sort of thing. I believed his story. I was just trying to help in some way. He didn't seem to want help.

'After the murders he [Jeffrey] went straight back to university and passed with flying colours. I couldn't work for six months. I was in shock.' Tony lost his business in Brisbane doing architectural illustrations. 'I couldn't draw a straight line. Not him. He graduated three months later.'

'On the day of the trial he was surrounded by his friends. He didn't bother to come over to us or acknowledge we were there for him. My mother had just perjured herself for him and he didn't even say thanks for being here. The doubts started then. Just the way he would not come near us. I did find it strange at the time. I put it down to him being upset by the events.'

Jeffrey had got the ball rolling to collect on his parents' wills in February 1994, six months after the murders. He claimed 50 per cent of his parents' estate, with the half that would have been Christopher's going to the grandparents on Stephen's side, Jessie and William.

Four months after the sentencing and two months after the coroner's finding, Jeffrey's solicitor wrote to Jessie saying that Jeffrey had said it was her wish to give Jeffrey her share of the will, and could she please sign it over. That was not her wish and she did not sign.

Jeffrey, meanwhile, had begun renovating the house. He took time off work to lend a hand, and spent $80,000 on the repairs to the fire damage before selling the absolute waterfront property for just $380,000.

According to Tony Gilham, 'The clincher was that he even wanted $10,000 from Christopher's account signed back to him. That really started getting me. Then he would ring my mother every night saying, "Have you signed it? Have you signed it?" I told her not to sign it. I started having disturbing thoughts about his story, and not long after that I went to Sutherland police station and saw Detective Ahern to find out exactly what happened that night.'

For the first time, Ahern told Gilham facts that no court or legal forum had ever been asked to examine: the anomaly in the timing between the screams and the emergency call; that Jeffrey's clothes had been found rolled up under the lounge; that the knife had no blood and no fingerprints on it, indicating it had been cleaned; that both Helen and Christopher had received seventeen stab wounds to the same area of the body; that there was no blood on Jeffrey belonging to Christopher, yet when Ahern had asked Jeffrey if he'd washed himself after killing Christopher, he had said no; that there were no accelerants in the lungs of Christopher, who had apparently walked around the house dousing it, yet Jeffrey had smelt of 'kerosene' to Ted Warner.

Tony Gilham found out that two weeks before the murders $10,000 had been taken out of Helen's bank account, coinciding with $10,000 going into Christopher's. This was about the same time that Jeffrey started telling people that Christopher was acting strangely. He thought of jealousy.

Tony Gilham felt an incredible anger welling inside as he learned all this. Why hadn't he been told? Why hadn't Justice Abadee been told? Why hadn't the coroner been told? But most of all, why had the Director of Public Prosecutions accepted the manslaughter plea?

'Next day I rang Jeff in Canberra. "Jeff, I want you to come up and see Richard and myself. We want to ask you some questions about what happened in 1993. There's strange evidence here I want you to explain." He said, "I'm not saying a word to you unless I've got Chris Murphy with me."'

The uncle thought it a really strange reaction. 'Why are you saying that? You are sounding a bit guilty.' According to Tony, his nephew then hung up.

Jeffrey engaged another solicitor, who gave him advice that he was entitled to all of the estate. And so he was. He collected the entire assets of Helen and Stephen Gilham, worth $867,134. This included the little pink fibro house of his grandmother Jessie, who has life tenancy. On top of that, according to one document filed to the court, he already held $363,000 in bank bills. So, as of 1997, Jeffrey Gilham was worth more than $1.2 million.

Tony Gilham started writing letters to the Director of Public Prosecutions asking why the manslaughter plea had not been contested. Months later he received a letter from the DPP, Nicholas Cowdery QC, saying there was insufficient evidence to convict and if more facts were obtained the case might be reopened.

Gilham brought the perjured statement to the notice of the Law Society, but the statement he wrote and his mother signed was missing from the court registry. He took the complaint to the DPP, but says he was threatened with perjury charges. After several more attempts at getting a proper inquiry into the death of his brother and sister-in-law, he called the Nine Network's current affairs program *60 Minutes*.

*

Researcher Andrew Corbett-Jones and producer Steve Barrett filed freedom of information requests on behalf of Gilham for all the evidence held by the court registry. Of particular interest was the evidence of three fire investigators, who all agreed the fire began in the bedroom around the father's body and spread from there to the rest of the house. Once the DPP had declined to contest the case, Justice Abadee had no need to consider this in relation to Jeffrey's version that the match was dropped on his mother.

60 Minutes hired an independent fire expert, Wal Stern, to examine this. They also hired a forensic pathologist, Dr Gus Oettle, to examine the medical evidence, plus eminent Queen's Counsel Michael Finnane to look at the overall case. It cost the network a packet and took about a year, but the opinions started rolling in.

Finnane pointed out that Jeffrey's story required that in the time it took him to put on a pair of boxer shorts and run up the stairs to the house (it took the *Australian* Magazine fifty-one seconds to walk briskly up the same stairs), his brother had stabbed his mother seventeen times, got the turps (the actual accelerant used) and poured it over his mother and father and other parts of the bedroom, obtained matches, dropped the knife and was standing up holding a lit match just as Jeffrey came in the door. 'And his story involved acceptance of the proposition that instead of immediately trying to knock over his brother or knock the match out of his hand or seize him, he lets his brother light up his mother and then looks around, picks up a knife and chases his brother with a knife. That seems very unusual.'

Gus Oettle's opinion was: 'The position of the stab wound is more consistent with there being one killer rather than two … I think it is possible that there could be two, but I think the reasonable probability is that there was one.' Oettle couldn't see any evidence pointing to two killers, 'because I think that the evidence which was shown on the dead brother demonstrated that he wasn't involved, because of the lack of blood on his arms and legs and his coat as I understand it. I think that he wasn't part of that.'

'The dead brother wasn't part of murdering the parents?' asked reporter Jeff McMullen.

'My opinion is that he wasn't.' Asked again if there were any factors that would rule out the single-killer theory, he said: 'I think it would be remarkable if two people used the same area of attack in order to kill the person.'

Oettle said the photos of Jeffrey Gilham's fingers suggested that, 'there'd been some attempt to clean or to be in a situation where water was present.' The blood samples taken from his hands and feet were too thinned to be suitable for comparison.

Jeffrey Gilham claimed he dropped the knife and left the house immediately after stabbing his brother, but the knife was found wedged under Christopher's arm. 'That suggests that it was placed there,' said Oettle.

'There was no blood on the knife. Is that possible?' asked the reporter.

'Only if it was cleaned.'

Oettle's opinion in this field was not to be ignored, and a month after the *60 Minutes* program aired in November 1997, the coroner, Derrick Hand, announced he was re-opening the investigation.

It took a year of further investigation by Oettle and Ahern before the coroner sent the case back to the DPP – the same person who four years ago had decided not to contest the manslaughter plea – to consider what action to take.

The Gilham family waited another year before the next stage of the drama began.

*

In that time, surprised that no other media had picked up the story after the *60 Minutes* investigation, I decided to have a go at it. Three years earlier, in the weeks after Jeffrey walked free, I'd poked around the still charred house. Interviewed Ahern. Put it in the too-hard basket. But I didn't know of Tony Gilham then.

Tony Gilham's house in the Blue Mountains west of Sydney was bare but for a big TV and two lounge suites. His drawing board was near a window looking out on a eucalypt gully. My first impression was that no woman lived here. And so it transpired. As we stood in the kitchen sipping instant coffee, he told me how he had had a virtual breakdown in the twelve months after the murders. He had lost the business and his wife, but they were both back now. Only thing was, his wife was afraid to live in the mountains. Afraid of Jeffrey.

'How could a judge take the word of a person who has just murdered his brother, stabbed him seventeen times in a fury. How could he do that? And his mother died with seventeen stab wounds. What are the chances of two normal human beings going nuts at the same time on the same night in the same way? Nothing will convince me.'

Tony had become one of those people – familiar to journalists and bureaucrats' receptionists – driven mad by the system. His only means of redress was the phone. A list of numbers was nearby. It included his point of contact at the DPP who, he said, simply hangs up on him; Jeff Ahern, who took his calls but never parted with any information to Tony's satisfaction; the Attorney General's office; former ICAC commissioner Ian Temby; *60 Minutes*; and now me.

He had been told two months previously that a decision would be made in two weeks. The longer it takes, the more he wonders who is hiding what. 'How embarrassing is it going to be for them to make a decision on this case and admit they stuffed it up in '93? Why weren't they this diligent then?' he asks. 'The thing about the DPP is that they're not accountable to anybody. They can make these decisions and that's it … I wouldn't want this to happen to any other family. It's a disgrace. There's a tree out in the backyard. I don't know how many times I've looked at it thinking I'm going to throw a rope around it.'

*

Jeffrey Gilham got his government job. He became an engineer working for the Roads and Traffic Authority in Sydney. He declined to talk about the case. I wrote a story which was pretty much what appears above, but the story was only just hotting up.

The DPP came back some months later and said there was not enough evidence to proceed with a prosecution.

Jeffrey took out an Apprehended Violence Order against Tony, who had taken to phoning his nephew and asking him awkward questions.

The coroner proceeded to a full inquest. And in July 2000, after hearing months of evidence, the coroner sent the case back to Cowdery asking that he again consider charging Jeffrey Gilham with the murder of his parents.

And again Cowdery refused, saying there was no prospect of a jury convicting Jeffrey on the available admissible evidence. Tony Gilham appealed to the Attorney-General, but was similarly rejected.

Tony took out an Apprehended Violence Order against Jeffrey.

Then, in May 2001, he launched the big one. No one in legal circles remembered anyone doing it before, but that didn't stop Tony launching his own private, criminal prosecution of his nephew. He engaged the former independent Commissioner Against Corruption, Mr Ian Temby QC, also a one-time Commonwealth DPP, as his counsel. Temby said the case should be heard in open court, where a magistrate's thoughts on whether the evidence warranted a trial would be transparent.

'The same cannot be said for any decision you might make to terminate the prosecution,' he wrote to Mr Cowdery. 'You will surely understand that there is room for disquiet as to what has happened to date ... The time has surely come for objective reconsideration of the matter ... Surely you should permit the law to thus take its course.'

But Cowdery took the case off Tony Gilham and then promptly shut it down, in June 2001. No jury was ever going to hear this evidence.

He wrote: 'I have taken this action in the public interest. My decisions have not been influenced in any way by the course of proceedings against Jeffrey Gilham which resulted in his conviction on one charge of manslaughter or the circumstances in which that occurred. The law is taking its course … My preference does not enter into the matter, except to the extent that a course of action has been chosen in accordance with principle.'

'Go Hang Yourself'

Tom Austen

ALREADY AT SEVEN O'CLOCK in the morning you could tell it would be a burning day. The sky was clear over the port city of Fremantle, as over most of Western Australia. Passengers boarding the workers' train for the nineteen-kilometre ride to Perth tried to get a seat on the shady side. The date was Wednesday, 4 February 1903.

As the railway guard pulled a silver watch from his waistcoat pocket and prepared to signal the driver to pull out, he heard calls of 'Hey' and 'Wait!'

Five men and three women hurried along the platform. A porter helped with their laden wicker baskets, and they told him eagerly they were going to the tiny township of Smith's Mill for a picnic in the Darling Range.

Among themselves they chatted in French and joked as they climbed into a railway carriage. With a snort of steam and a short screech of the whistle, the locomotive started off. The eight were in jolly spirits, not knowing they had set forth on the strangest journey any of them was ever to make.

If they had a leader, it was the comely Marie Fontan, better known as Sweet Marie. In her late thirties and madam of a Fremantle bordello, she was wealthy. In the name of her husband Peter, whom she had married in 1902, she owned land around Suffolk Street, and several houses, some of which were let to others who purveyed pleasure.

With her in the train was a swarthy French-Canadian, Marie Dean, who had left her four-year-old daughter in the care of a friend. The third woman was Lucienne Volti, much younger than the first two, petite and exceedingly pretty. Each of the women was in the long-skirted attire of that era and wore a showy wide hat which shaded a smiling face.

Most striking of the five men was 23-year-old Ferdnand Maillat, a fisherman at Fremantle. He had black hair, a fresh face with a thin moustache and was 183 centimetres tall (nearly six feet). He wore a yellow silk suit. The only man not in a suit was Eugene Lechoix, who had on blue dungaree trousers and an odd jacket; he was more than twice Maillat's age and cooked for Marie Fontan's establishment. Making up the party were the 'puny and weak' Raoul Lintauf, bespectacled Leo Mousset and Benoit Volti, brother of Lucienne Volti.

In the train and at the stops travellers noticed the voluble foreigners. The picnickers were in marked contrast to the quiet cloth-capped workmen, male clerks wearing flat straw hats, shop-girls in black skirts and white blouses, and dour-suited businessmen with noses in newspapers.

Some of the Fremantle people who recognised the eight looked on them as a wild lot. The more rigid Anglo-Saxons labelled them Latins with Latin morals. The members of the picnic party were certainly different from most Australians. Perhaps, as the events of that day tumbled into their unhappy place, that was a sin.

The French changed at Perth, then took a train eastwards towards the hill where they planned to stay seven and a half hours. They had to wait a few minutes at Midland Junction. There Mary Ellen Hesford, who worked in her brother's drapery, sold Maillat a hat for 5s 6d.

Again the party just managed to get into the train before it moved out, at half past eight. Lazily the locomotive chugged into the hills. The rails shone white in the sun and despite the altitude warm air wafted through the open windows of the wooden carriages. At twenty-three minutes past nine the whistling locomotive pulled into the small brown and cream station at Smith's Mill (now Glen Forrest).

This was a settlement of farmers and orchardists thirty-two kilometres from Perth. The eight were almost the only half-fare summer excursionists – in second-class they paid 1s 8 1/2d each – alighting from the train there. They laughed and a couple sang as they strolled out of the station yard. The men took off their jackets as they all moved along Hardey Road.

A number of settlers in the areas were also from continental Europe. Most, though, were thrifty British or Australian-born who had worked hard to build up their businesses. Some among that fairly moralistic community frowned at folk who had time and money to enjoy a mid-week jaunt.

Glad of a quiet day away from bustling Fremantle, where all resided, the eight breathed the country air with much pleasure. Relishing the view of farm paddocks and vines, and the sweet smell of orchards, they reached the solid cellars of Glen Hardey.

Half the party had been to other picnics at Smith's Mill and were pleased to meet again Hardey's cellarman, Henry Kiesewetter, who greeted them in French. They returned three empty five-gallon wine casks. Marie Fontan ordered ten gallons of wine to go to the station for the five o'clock train by which the party would return.

They also wanted wine for the picnic. A regulation demanded a minimum purchase of a gallon of wine from any off-licence outlet. Gallic minds had difficulty in comprehending the logic of this rule but the visitors took the required six bottles. The wine was Colonial Claret, 21 per cent proof.

Most of four bottles of this claret, which at least one of the men complained was too strong, was drunk with water during their bread-and-cheese lunch. This they had at about eleven o'clock in the cool of the Hardey barn.

Kiesewetter tried out Maillat's five-chamber .38 Smith & Wesson revolver. One of the women had a light shotgun and when they asked Kiesewetter where to bag birds, he said farther along the valley. Maillat shot two pigeons with the revolver while the other shooter also aimed at birds. Both weapons were carried openly.

The remaining three men and three women walked in the noon-day sun along the dusty road which passed the Helena River Nursery. One of the partners of that enterprise, which in fact was chiefly a vineyard, was Charles Lauffer. He was thirty-eight, heavy and stood even taller than Maillat. He lived there in a weatherboard house with his wife Frencienne, from France, and four healthy children.

Lauffer, who said he was Swiss, had come to Western Australia from Europe in 1887. He possessed a thorough knowledge of viti-culture and had £1000 to invest, a large sum in those days. Once established, he sent home for his fiancée and they married. Three of their babies died and four years ago an eight-year-old son had drowned in the river. Now, however, life was looking up and business expanding.

Lauffer was solid and cautious, and his life was insured for £500. Although his wife and children were Roman Catholic, he was a Protestant and popular in this predominantly Protestant locality. All in the picnic party were Catholic.

The six asked Lauffer if they could buy a bottle of the wine he made. He stood there, in his wide-brim hat, cotton shirt, moleskin trousers and slippers, and insisted they take six bottles. Little Lintauf, waiting in the open heat, primed by the luncheon wine, argued with burly Lauffer. A scuffle developed and Mrs Lauffer and an Italian employee, Francisco Rocchiccioli, came to help the winegrower. Mrs Lauffer was held back by a woman from the group. Rocchiccioli was knocked down.

The six were to swear Lauffer had provoked them. Maillat said the winegrower told him, 'You go and hang yourself,' called for his gun and threw a stone at them. Even the Italian said he saw Lauffer pick up a rock 'half the size of my head'. The Lauffers declared the visitors had picked the fight.

What is certain is that during the row Maillat's revolver discharged and Lauffer fell dying. Marie Dean fetched water for Marie Fontan to bathe the shot man's face as she supported him in her arms. The two women placed leafy pear-tree branches on his head to keep off the sun and flies. The temperature there in the shade was just about its maximum for the day, almost touching forty degrees Celsius.

The Italian dashed 400 metres to Hardey's. Kiesewetter telephoned the police. Mousset and Benoit Volti reappeared and the eight sat down for an hour before a lone constable arrived. Maillat said the revolver went off accidentally but all eight were arrested. Without the slightest trouble they consented to be handcuffed and were chained to a tree outside the station, awaiting a train for Guildford, halfway to Perth, and the lockup.

A crowd, angry that a local man had been slain, gathered near the prisoners. A leading resident said the onlookers were 'itching to have command of the picnickers for about ten minutes'. When the train drew back the locals hooted and the prisoners replied with mocking bows. At Guildford, too, feeling ran high against the prisoners.

The police quickly gave currency to what they knew, or in some instances merely believed, concerning the prisoners.

Maillat had deserted a French barque at Fremantle five years earlier. On a drunken spree with two shipmates he threw half a brick through a Perth shop window. His friends escaped; he spent three months in gaol.

A year later Maillat was at Kalgoorlie during the gold town's roaring days. There he had a high old time with other young French people, among whom were 'ladies' plying a certain trade of the night with gold-laden miners. There he also met the lovely divorcée Marie Renaud. Almost the same age as Maillat, she fell for him, lived as his wife and was his staunchest friend till the day he died. She waited for him when, after a knife fight in the gold town of Coolgardie, he was sentenced to twelve months of hard labour. He looked older than he was and in the Smith's Mill inquiries told the police he was twenty-seven (although in fact only twenty-three).

Mousset was said by the police to be an ex-convict from New Caledonia who stowed away in the French liner *Armand Behic*, which docked at Fremantle only five days before the ill-fated trip to Smith's Mill. Benoit Volti was described as a bookmaker at unregistered racecourses.

All three women were 'known', the police said. The officers told reporters the Voltis were not brother and sister, a story that was not verified. They further besmirched the Volti girl's name with the cryptic information that 'she was prominent some years ago with the taking of a girl' to the goldfields.

All in all the prisoners were cursed, by reputation and association, before the inquest was completed and before their lower-court appearance, let alone the trial. Whether any or the lot of them had led an insalubrious life, of course, ought not to have had any bearing on their court hearing, any more than ought the report that Maillat, from the northern French port of St Nazaire, came of good family.

Two days after the killing the case took an odd turn. The *Morning Herald* quoted prominent settler T.R. Smith as saying that Lauffer had been in dread of French people. The winegrower had told Smith he was driven out of a place in France 'for a certain reason' but 'they won't move me from here.' Next day the *West Australian* lamented that the apparent lack of motive complicated the detectives' work. However, it was now known there was 'some event in the deceased man's past life which made him fear meeting

French people'. Twenty-four hours later the Perth *Sunday Times* elaborated at the top of its front page:

> It is … alleged that the trial will disclose a chapter in the deceased vigneron's past of which his closest friends and relatives are entirely ignorant. Suffice it to say that Mr Lauffer is suspected to have been implicated in a tragedy in his native country, many years ago, that made Maillat swear to be revenged upon him if ever they should meet.
>
> Last Tuesday evening Maillat and several of his associates were carousing together in the house of ill-fame kept by Marie Fontan in Suffolk Street, Fremantle. Lauffer's name cropped up and Maillat is said to have become apprised, for the first time, that his enemy was in Western Australia.

Despite this somewhat loaded report, the narrative of Lauffer's fleeing a French town was not raised in the courts. Yet the appearance of this speculation in the newspapers was effective in sowing confusion and undermining the defence case.

France's acting consul in Perth announced categorically that Lauffer was not Swiss but from Poiseux in the eastern French *department* of Nievre. Contradicting this, two writers of letters to the press, including a partner who had known Lauffer for sixteen years, were convinced he was Swiss. In his will, Lauffer left everything to his widow and expressed the wish that his family in Australia would go to join his family in Switzerland.

Whatever the truth of the situation, if the feud story was deliberate misinformation, it was clever stuff. Australians had no wish for a foreigner's vendetta and public vehemence increased against the prisoners.

Each day of the inquest and for their appearance at Guildford police court, the accused were brought by train from Fremantle, where they were kept at the gaol. Sightseers at stations along the line hoped for a glimpse of the 'bloody foreigners' and the chance of hurling an oath or two. The prisoners were followed by a catcalling crowd when constables marched the eight, the males handcuffed, from Guildford station to the courthouse. When the lower-court hearing began, many rushed the courthouse and had to be restrained.

The State's major newspaper said of the prisoners, 'They were all typical foreigners, the man being stolid-looking.'

There was conflicting evidence and downright confusion concerning the fight with Lauffer. Dr J.E. Fergusson Stewart, who gave evidence, examined the body but seemed unable to say if a second bullet had taken the same course as the first bullet. Some experts thought it unlikely that one bullet would follow another exactly in entering the victim. The firing of one bullet could be accidental; two suggested otherwise.

Utter surprise was caused by the committal of all eight for trial for wilful murder.

When the trial went ahead in the middle of the following month and the legal big guns fired their respective questions, much of the evidence seemed increasingly inconclusive. General opinion changed. Demands for punishment which had been bandied about the streets and in pubs lessened appreciably.

The trial was before Mr Justice Burnside, middle-aged and an enthusiastic yachtsman although in bad health. Robert Bruce Burnside had been on the Bench for less than a year. He had made the leap forward from Crown Prosecutor on £750 a year to become a puisne judge at £1700 (roughly ten times what Maillat earned).

One observer wrote of the judge, 'A master of cold and contemptuous sarcasm, there is something in the sharp curve of the underlip, in the impatient sniff of the nostrils, the gleam of the eyes, which effectually demolishes elaborate but specious argument … excels in cutting remarks.'

The four-day trial ended on Friday, 13 March. A big crowd had been clamouring outside for hours. Inside the wood-panelled courtroom the afternoon air was stifling.

During the hour and thirty-five minutes it took the judge to sum up, he said it was well known that the French were more excitable than Anglo-Saxons. The jury of 'twelve good men and true' – women were not then eligible for this duty – left the courtroom on the stroke of noon to consider its verdict. The atmosphere was electric when the jurors trooped back at twenty past four.

Their names almost exclusively were of the sort associated with the British Isles: Henry Howell (foreman), John Harrigan, James Harris, Francis Hedges, Charles Helm, Michael Hickey, Thomas Hogan, Charles Holland, William Holmes, William Houston,

Benjamin Hughes and Thomas Hutchinson. (The common 'H' indicated the stage reached in the alphabetical jury-service list.)

Mousset and Benoit Volti were found not guilty and discharged. The jury then found the other six guilty of murder, not wilful murder. There was a strong recommendation of mercy for all but Maillat.

Mr Justice Burnside, making more of a mark than expected, even by the Empire sodality he represented, sentenced to death the three men and three women. Benoit Volti, who had just been freed, heard his sister sentenced to the gallows. She cried out towards Mrs Lauffer, 'God Almighty will punish you!'

Maillat was the first to be addressed by the judge, who donned the black cap – the small square cloth of terror that was such a tradition of the British Empire. 'I order that you be taken from here to go to your former place of custody and at a time and a place to be appointed by His Excellency the Governor-in-Council you be hanged by the neck until you are dead.' One by one each was similarly sentenced.

If the public had been astounded that eight were committed for trial and aghast that six were found guilty, it was dumbfounded that so many, including three women, were sentenced to execution.

On the following morning at Midland Junction, Dr Fergusson Stewart wrote to the Attorney-General (Walter James, who also was Premier), to clarify his evidence during the trial: '… the misapprehension under which the Judge summed up seems to me to have perhaps led the Jury to decide that two shots may have been fired, whereas I am certain that only one bullet entered Lauffer's body.'

Senator Edward Augustine St Aubyn Harney – a big, witty, Irish-born lawyer respected throughout the State – championed Maillat's cause. He had taken no part in the trial but agreed to represent the hapless young man in the appeal. On Sunday, 15 March, Harney penned a letter which was delivered by hand to the *West Australian*: 'All the circumstances seem to me irresistibly to point to an accidental shot in a drunken affray, where both sides were equally to blame … [the case] may even be viewed by some as another of those astonishing extravagances to which our objection to all alien immigration is leading us.'

On St Patrick's Day, 17 March, the *West Australian* disturbed its readers' breakfast with some short but startling news. On the previous day Frencienne Lauffer, who with her children was staying with a lady at Cottesloe Beach, had returned with the lady to the house at Smith's Mill. Mrs Lauffer wished to collect some possessions.

While the two women were there the post arrived. The widow of forty days received a chilling message. A secret society would avenge those sentenced to death. If Mrs Lauffer were caught in her garden at Smith's Mill members of the society would burn out her eyes and destroy her. The Lauffers' Italian employee was also threatened. A police watch was placed on Mrs Lauffer and her children but no more evil messages, let alone deeds, came to public notice.

At a time when a good part of public opinion had shifted against hanging the group, the threat made some people think again. Was the letter the work of a twisted busybody? Or was it a contrived frightener, the brainchild of somebody concerned to reinforce the duty of the police and the courts to be hard?

It does not stretch credulity too far to hypothesise that attempts may have been made to manipulate public sentiment – firstly with the story that Charles Lauffer received his comeuppance in some mysterious years-old row, secondly with the threat to his wife. But there was never any public proof of such manipulation.

The *W.A. Record*, the major Catholic journal in the State, said it was probable that the threat was designed to excite public alarm against the sentenced men and women, 'to lessen the chance of their escaping the capital penalty'.

The *Morning Herald* published an editorial on the public hostility provoked by the verdict. 'The mere fact that a verdict of murder, instead of one of wilful murder, was returned indicated the extreme probability of a commutation of the death penalty,' it said. The newspaper called on the Executive to give a reasonable and not a vindictive interpretation to the jury's verdict.

Letters to the press increased. H.T. Jenkin of suburban Leederville complained, 'Things have come to a pretty pass if a party cannot spend a pleasant day in the hills without being tried for their lives.' Italian sculptor Pietro Porcelli, one of the most highly regarded of non-British migrants, asked, 'Is it not astonishing to find a jury giving such a verdict as that of the Smith's Hill tragedy without a moment's hesitation? The verdict may be according to the law but it is opposed to all humanity and logic. Six persons sentenced to death, for what I do not know.'

While some sent letters, others signed a petition aimed at stopping the hangings. Hundreds from all walks of life and representing every nationality signed the petition, which went to the Government and on to the Governor, Admiral Sir Frederick George Denham Bedford, who took up office on 24 March.

On 25 March, twenty-two lawyers signed a new petition seeking to save Maillat, for whom the jury had not recommended mercy. Later names brought the number to twenty-seven – out of a total of thirty-five practitioners in Perth.

One of their points was that the judge had told the jury he believed it was plain that when the Frenchmen and women left Fremantle on 4 February, 'there was no intention on their part to do harm or interfere in any way with the deceased.' The lawyers also argued that, whether Maillat's shot had been accidental or intentional, he had been experiencing great excitement induced by the row.

Only on the morning of the appeal, a week later, did Premier James forward this petition to Sir Frederick. Soon to be labelled hard-headed and pushing, the pipe-smoking Premier lashed out publicly at the signatories: '… I am very much surprised that any members of the [legal] profession should have signed a separate petition … The course is, I believe, quite without precedent and open to serious objection.'

The Premier, a barrister well practised in quoting English legal precedent, had either forgotten or chosen to ignore a celebrated case fourteen years earlier in Liverpool. A bright 26-year-old American, Florence Maybrick, publicly damned because she had a swain on the side, had been accused of poisoning her husband, a phlegmatic fifty-year-old Lancashire businessman. There were doubts but the jury had found her guilty and the judge had sent her to the gallows.

Sir Charles Russell, who led her defence, had with other lawyers signed a petition similar to that for Maillat. Immediately other petitions were begun and in a couple of weeks nearly half a million signatures were collected. Mrs Maybrick's sentence was commuted; she spent fifteen years in prison. Five years after the trial the judge died in an asylum.

In Western Australia in 1903, during the delay in delivering the petition, Mr Justice Burnside was 600 kilometres away in Kalgoorlie. There, far from the mounting anger in Perth, he set out detailed notes on the Smith's Mill case. These he sent to Sir Frederick, who was able to read them before he got the lawyers' petition.

The wording of this petition was duplicated for a hurried third petition which carried a further 246 names from among the public.

On appeal, the Full Court affirmed the verdict and judgment passed on Maillat. At the same time it upset the verdict on the other five and, having been in Fremantle gaol for two months, they were released that same evening. When they left the gaol they were greeted by scores of cheering people, many French.

Bitter humorists noted that the Full Court's decisions had been made on April Fool's Day. Others asked how it was that five prisoners under sentence of death in a few hours should be deemed blameless and freed absolutely. For many people there was something disturbing about this. Granted, Maillat fired the fatal shot, but if the courts had been mistaken about the five others could not the courts have erred in deciding that he was a deliberate killer? Was it not a case of manslaughter, if not accident?

Fremantle's *Evening Courier* said, 'The legal innocence of the others reduces his [Maillat's] crime to that for which a reasonable amount of imprisonment should amply suffice to meet the claims of justice.'

Senator Harney never gave up the fight for Maillat's life. Three days after the appeal he pointed out to James, who was wearing his Attorney-General's hat, that '... although "wilful murder" and "murder" both carry the death sentence it is highly improbable that the Legislature ever intended when creating these two offences that the punishment for them should be identical.'

General outcry, letters to the press and petitions were of no avail. The judges, Premier, Colonial Secretary Walter Kingsmill (who acted as Premier when James left in mid-April for premiers' talks in Sydney) and even the newly arrived Sir Frederick were accused of racism and judging citizens by their morals, of bungling and callousness.

The French acting consul vainly asked for the hanging to be set back a week while fresh inquiries were made.

Four days before the date set for the hanging, 21 April, Harney addressed a packed meeting at the Perth Town Hall. He said that in confirming the execution the Executive Council acted without legal advice, because Premier-cum-Attorney-General James was away.

When seventy-two hours were left, Harney and other prominent citizens desperately talked to Kingsmill but with no result. With forty-eight hours to go, further names were added to the original petition. These brought the total number of petitioners to more than twelve hundred.

On 20 April, the Executive Council, headed by the Governor and Acting Premier, refused petitioners' requests for the sentence to be commuted to imprisonment.

On the evening before the execution, Alfred B. Mayer, manager of the Cigar and Tobacco Agency in Perth's main shopping thoroughfare, Hay Street, scrawled a hurried note to Sir Frederick. Mayer was sorry that 'largely signed' petitions from the goldfields 'are on their road to Perth but not yet here'. What became of those sheets, and how many names were on them, is unknown.

Maillat's lover, Marie Renaud, sought the Governor's permission to marry her man before he died. This also was refused but she was allowed to arrange for the burial of Maillat outside the gaol. She was the last outsider to visit him, on a balmy Monday afternoon.

In a final plea she wrote directly to Sir Frederick: 'Ferdnand Maillat himself is no criminal. He is of good and loyal heart but young and impulsive and from the result of a severe attack of malarial fever easily excited, especially under the influence of drink.'

During his last hours Maillat wrote to his parents in Brittany, his two sisters and his brother who, like their father, was a naval officer. The grieving Marie Renaud sent his more precious possessions, as he requested, to the family in France. She had spent £600 – four years of wages for the average man then – on counsel to defend the picnic party.

Five hundred people waited outside the gaol at eight o'clock the next morning, Tuesday, 21 April 1903, as Maillat went to the gallows. Twenty men, officials plus four reporters, watched him die 'with great fortitude'. The doomed man's final spiritual adviser was the Very Reverend Father Cox, who commented, 'Religion is a great help to a man in that situation.'

The hangman was paid five guineas plus two pounds for incidental expenses. He used 'the new noose with metal thimble and leather button', but botched the job.

A drop of only 122 centimetres (four feet) was allowed, insufficient for a man of Maillat's build. The neck was dislocated straight away but the pulse remained beating for nine more minutes. A doctor present said, 'There was certainly something wrong, for death should have been instantaneous.'

The corpse was not cut down for an hour. At four in the afternoon a hearse, followed by a vehicle carrying Marie Renaud and friends, left the gaol for the Catholic section of Fremantle cemetery. A hundred and fifty people were at the graveside for a burial, which the authorities had tried to keep quiet. When the interment was finished and the mourners gone, scores of red roses among the flowery tributes left a rare splash of brightness in that grey place.

Thousands felt that the outcome of the Smith's Mill affray was outrageous. This was not only because someone had taken nine minutes to die on the scaffold but because there seemed to be something wrong with the whole process, from arrests to execution.

Government leaders, as representatives of the establishment and upholders of law and order, had been bent on the harshest punishment. A community sometimes can accept such punishment, provided it knows why. In this instance many did not perceive the reason at all.

The *Morning Herald* said on the day after the hanging, 'Perhaps no execution in recent years has been attended by such peculiar circumstances as have been wound about the murder of Charles Lauffer … These cries have had the effect of investing the condemned man to some extent with a halo of martyrdom, and even now, when he is beyond all human aid, public opinion is divided as to whether the penalty inflicted on him was just.'

'G.H.K.' said in a letter to a different newspaper, 'Another name has been added to the black list of our modern Juggernaut … For many centuries we have mercilessly lopped off these social excrescences and find that, far from our drastic action being a deterrent, they follow each other in cycles of crime and violence.'

When Maillat had been dead for eleven days, 'Omadhaun' wrote in the *Record*:

> Trial by jury has been on *its* trial … the trial really begins only when the jury have given their verdict; the decision of the Full Court has made that clear … the jury convicted five innocent people wrongfully. It follows, consequently,

> that these people must have been wrongfully arrested and illegally detained in prison. But, more than that, they were subjected to the utmost terrors that the law can impose in being sentenced to death … It is only reasonable to suppose that the Government will give suitable compensation to these five individuals.

Compensation? Oh what a fond hope was that.

If the five who were so abruptly freed amid a good deal of acclaim thought they could go about their ordinary lives, they were mistaken. Less than six weeks later, on a Saturday night, all five were apprehended again.

With ten others they were 'arrested in the streets or captured in their homes' during what the police described as a cleaning out of some of Fremantle's undesirables. They were charged under a section of a new *Justices Act* which disallowed bail, although they sought it. So they spent Saturday and Sunday nights in the Fremantle lockup. Considering that they had so recently been in gaol awaiting the rope, considering the execution of their friend only eighteen days ago, the police action was seen by many as partisan, harrying and cruel.

The five appeared in the police court to show why they should not be bound over to keep the peace. Marie Fontan said she had turned over a new leaf, had sold her properties and was about to return to France. She was arranging to send Marie Dean, with Lucienne and Benoit Volti, to New Caledonia in a few days.

Oddly, Fontan was discharged and the other women were each ordered to find sureties of £20 to be on good behaviour for six months despite evidence that they were in fact leaving the country. Raoul Lintauf and Benoit Volti, described by the police as 'bludgers' who did not work, each had to find sureties of £10.

*

Twenty-three years later there was still unease. The Comptroller-General of Prisons was asked to forward documents to do with Maillat. Some were missing. The new superintendent of Fremantle gaol replied to his chief, 'I cannot at present trace any more papers connected with Maillat's case. It does not appear to be complete. The superintendent's report that the execution was carried out is not to be found.'

ON MURDER 2

They'll hang me as the clock strikes eight.
All for a summer picnic in the hills,
When we sang in the sun and wined.
For a shot in the light
and for being a stranger.

Keitho and Davo

Steve Dow

KEITH HIBBINS IS A TALL, RAKISH BOY. Light brown hair, parted and slicked to one side. Freckles, toothy smile. Each lunchtime, he cycles from school back to the house for the main family meal of the day, past the weatherboard homes, through the familiar streets of Maryborough in western Victoria.

Keitho, as he is known, is affectionate, demonstrative. Bright, too, and outgoing. For his ninth birthday he initiates a party and invites his school friends. Then he gets around to telling his mother, who is forced into frantic last-minute shopping to cater.

At high school, Keitho has the hots for a couple of guys. Officially, though, he has girlfriends before he has boyfriends.

Keitho matriculates in the early '70s, and the country kid comes to the city to study architecture at the University of Melbourne. Perhaps the campus life speeds up the long coming-out process that gay men of his era usually face. He starts dating the daughter of one of his architectural employers, but it just doesn't work out right. He has to tell her that he really does prefer men. She turns around and tells him that, actually, she prefers women.

None of this fazes Keitho. He's a big party boy. All six-foot-one of him. Doesn't mind a drink.

*

'Look at that,' says David Campbell, handing me a black-and-white photograph of a boy aged about ten. Freckly, with hair diligently combed and parted to the side, big cheesy grin. Keitho.

'Isn't that an incredible photograph? Oh, I've got photographs of Keitho where he is a real dork! But that photograph I used to see up his mum's place when we went up, and it always took my …' he pauses and stumbles over the word, '… h-heart away.'

We're sitting in the kitchen of their Edwardian house, the one Keitho redesigned, in Collingwood. Sleek 1990s tones, polished timber floors. And Keitho's coffee machine. David Campbell is learning to master an espresso on his own.

'Later on he was a real lookin' dork, I mean you wouldn't bother with it. But I knew that even if I met him then, I would have loved him.'

This assessment includes the picture of Keitho with long wavy hair and '70s brown and beige woollen vest.

What was it about him?

'About Keitho?' says David Campbell, wiping his cheeks, his eyes rounding on me as though it is an odd question. He looks tired and drawn, and his bald 48-year-old head accentuates the effect.

'I don't know. A connection. I remember when I met him the first time, I thought he was somebody else …'

*

One beer, that's all David Campbell wants, all he is determined to have. Tonight he is going to behave himself in all senses of the word. He puts enough money in his pocket for one beer and flings his wallet into the glovebox of his ute, and heads into the pub.

He'd knocked off work as a self-employed gardener at about 4.30 p.m. It is now 6 p.m. The early November sun is yet to fall over Commercial Road in Melbourne's inner south-east; too early for the true bustle to begin along the burgeoning gay mini-mecca.

In the early '80s, long before it morphs into a handbaggy nightclub, the Market Hotel is a pub with a friendly rather than faceless facade. David Campbell is thirty and knows the gay scene. But he has never been in love before. That is about to change.

And then he sees him. That's his friend Robert, isn't it? Keith Hibbins, at the bar, waves back. David approaches him and he realises the mistaken identity.

Keitho – for that is what David will come to call him; in turn he will be called Davo – is tall and slender, twenty-eight, bearded, with hair already receding. He admits he hadn't seen who was waving to him; he needs his glasses. But they talk. And talk and talk. David thinks: 'This guy's great.'

They have dinner with Keitho's friends. And then they go to a gay nightclub in beachside St Kilda, Mandate. The pair head back to Keitho's to stay the night.

For some years, they live in Acland Street, St Kilda. Davo finds it hard to keep up with Keitho's love of the nightlife. Friday, Saturday, Sunday. Monday, even. Davo used to be a big reader, but virtually gives up the habit for a few years after meeting Keitho. He'd happily stay at home and be a hermit, but what he wants more than anything is to be by Keitho's side.

Keitho always buys Davo a book as a gift. Davo is not a present person, but Keitho loves to mark an occasion.

Old Jewish Mrs Carmel is among their favourite neighbors. 'All these men living in the flats and you're all bachelors,' she says with amazement.

A few queer facts of life are explained to old Mrs Carmel. Still, she loves the boys. One day, she decides to bake Keitho and Davo a plate of sweet pastries to show her affection. She enters the back door of the apartment, unperturbed by the noise from the lounge room. There are the two men busy confirming their bachelor status. Mrs Carmel stands there, face frozen, plate of pastries in hand. 'I just made you some piroshkis.'

*

Davo grew up a farmer in country Wandin and Yea. He doesn't know exactly where he was born. He was raised by grandparents and then lived with a teacher's family. But that is a whole other story.

Keitho and Davo buy a house together in Collingwood in 1992. When they move in, they attempt to dig the garden out. Keitho has about three hits at the green and says, 'Oh God, I'm going to make a cup of tea. I'm exhausted,' leaving Davo to do the work.

As they get older, they stay in a little more. On weekends, by the window near the stove in the kitchen that he redesigns, Keitho often presses his little lover against the stove.

'I love ya, Davo.'

And Davo will say, 'Ditto.'

Just like in *Ghost*, which Davo thinks is a stupid movie.

*

'This is the one I take to bed every night,' says David. Keitho is forty-something, in the right of frame, in front of an upright architectural drawing board.

'He's doing a plan. He might have been working for Melbourne City Council then; I'm not too sure where I took the photograph.'

'Somebody gave me this (small, wooden) picture frame for my birthday. Keitho said, "Why did they do that, Davo? You don't collect photographs."'

'I thought, "I know what I'm going to do." So I snapped him at work, and I put it away. I hid it. And then when he died I found it. Like, I wasn't even looking for it.'

'I never had worn pyjamas in my life. But now I wear pyjamas. And I stick this photo down my pyjama top when I go to sleep at night.'

'I talk to it then, and I talk to it in the morning, and I kiss it.'

*

The Fitzroy Gardens are located in East Melbourne, buttressing the central business district and comprising the equivalent of several city blocks. Keitho, now forty-five and slower after an accidental fall that left him with metal pins in his arms and in his legs, and Davo, forty-seven, would often cut through the gardens to get to the city, to buy a book or whatever.

Sometimes on a Saturday morning, they would call in at the automatic teller machine at the Peter MacCallum Cancer Institute, west of the gardens.

On the night of Sunday, 25 April 1999 – Anzac Day – Keitho and Davo decided to head for the Peter Mac ATM. They've spent the day in country Marysville in north-eastern Victoria, visited the falls. The day is perfect, the falls beautiful. They call in at a winery, and Davo buys Keitho a choice red.

Home in Melbourne, Davo decides he needs olive oil, which they normally buy in Brunswick. So they head to the ATM in the car.

There's football at the MCG, and the parking spots are all taken. So instead of pulling up near the teller, Keitho and Davo are forced to park the Volkswagen Apollo further out.

On the way back to the car, Davo says, 'Oh, let's go and look at the possums.'

But Keitho and Davo never get to see the possums. Instead, they meet two straight blokes – John Whiteside, a 28-year-old air-conditioning mechanic, and Kristian Peter Dieber, a 24-year-old economics graduate – who are running frantically across the grass.

Whiteside and Dieber run up to Keitho and Davo, enraged because they have met a woman who says she was raped in the park. Whiteside, the bigger of the two, seems the controller. The blond-haired Dieber runs on, and Whiteside calls him back to the site where they've encountered Keith Hibbins and David Campbell. Whiteside screams and carries on. Dieber follows suit.

Whiteside and Dieber both reek of alcohol. They have been drinking with friends at the nearby MCG Hotel. The friends are on the other side of the park, comforting Evgenia Tsionis, the woman who claims to have been raped (falsely, it will turn out; she was drunk and stoned and had had an argument with her boyfriend, who had dumped her on the edge of the park).

Whiteside and Dieber have not the faintest idea what the rapists they are looking for actually look like. David Campbell mishears them; he's half-deaf in one ear. He thinks they are looking for a rapist, as in singular. Keitho asks why they are so aggressive. Davo cannot hear the full conversation. Keitho senses their hostility. He thinks they are gay bashers. 'We've got to get out of here!' Keitho shouts. 'Run!'

So Davo and Keitho run back to Lansdowne Street, back to the Peter Mac. Davo is pushed to the ground. Feels a boot to his head, another to his hip and leg.

'I'm going to f— kill you!'

Davo thinks – he can't swear – that it's Whiteside who says this.

'Leave him alone!' That's Keitho, definitely.

Whiteside and Dieber round on Keitho, who runs away at an angle, rather than back to the lights and safety, where Campbell runs. With all that metal inside him, Keitho runs like a tin man.

From the seventh floor of the Peter Mac, Beverley Skinner, who is taking a break from caring for her dying husband, gazes down into the park. She sees Whiteside pin Keitho against a parked car. Several cars pass by. No one stops.

These are some of the words she will later use to describe Whiteside 'just punching the crap out of him': 'He was using fists and elbows – he wouldn't stop for no one. It was an outrage. He was a bloody animal. Savage.'

*

Keitho does not regain consciousness.

They say he's going to be OK, lying there bruised and battered in St Vincent's Hospital. The police, the doctors.

Then everyone starts getting gloomy.

'Even if he survives, he'll be just as happy as a cricket,' says the pastoral care worker.

Davo goes off the deep end. 'He's not a bloody insect.'

Davo swears that at one point Keitho hears his name and turns towards him.

On 6 May, Davo gets a call.

Hurry. He's going.

Keitho dies in Davo's arms.

For some days, they put Davo under watch. Won't even allow him to shower without supervision.

*

The Office of Public Prosecutions is ecstatic. Justice Philip Cummins has been named as trial judge in the state versus Whiteside and Dieber, to hear charges of murder. It is almost like a cheer-squad atmosphere. Cummins is known as a tough sentencer. Hates violence.

Then plea bargaining enters the picture. Just days before the trial, the game changes. Whiteside and Dieber will answer charges of manslaughter. They plead guilty. This means they have elected not to give evidence. This means we will not know what was going on in their minds on the night of 25 April.

And then, unexpectedly, and with much community outrage, Cummins lets Whiteside and Dieber walk.

On 23 June 2000, having served six months pre-sentence detention, they are released. Cummins sentences each to three years' jail, but suspends the rest of their sentences. Head trauma, says Cummins, was the cause of Keith Hibbins' death.

Thus: 'The final step in this unfolding tragedy is that the death of the deceased was unexpected, unintended and unlikely.' Hibbins' death was not a purposeful bashing of a homosexual. Nor, he says – surprisingly – did he consider Whiteside and Dieber's conduct to be that of vigilantes avenging a rape, 'for vigilante conduct is premeditated'.

What exactly the killing was is not made clear by Cummins.

Some questions David Campbell must sift through and ponder along with his photographic memories.

Was there an element of gay-hate in the bashing of Keitho?

Why had the Office of Public Prosecutions suddenly swung

from being confident about having a murder case to pursuing a manslaughter trial?

If the victim had been anything other than a gay man, would the hard-line Cummins have treated Whiteside and Dieber's sentencing differently?

Cummins, through his associate Nick Cummins (his son), refuses to be interviewed.

David Campbell feels anger towards Cummins. He feels nothing for Whiteside and Dieber. 'When I went to their summations of the outcome at the committal, I actually stood and stared at them. And I felt nothing. Isn't that strange? I would love to be able to hate them. I really would. I really would give anything to be able to hate those two.'

Was the fact that Keitho and Davo were two gay men important in the first instance?

'I think they were looking for rapists,' says David. '(But) something clicked in, either an automatic drive – they had a bloodlust – or something else and bingo, they lost it.'

What do you mean, 'clicked in'?

'Well it clicked in that we were gay. Because it doesn't make sense to me that they were attacking rapists. To me it just doesn't ring true.'

*

In what seems record time, Cummins' sentence is appealed by the Director of Public Prosecutions. Justices Winneke, Brooking and Phillips on the appeals bench share few of Justice Cummins' perceptions of Whiteside and Dieber's crime.

John Winneke emphasises the severity of the assault on Keith Hibbins. 'The injuries to the neck resulted in extensive bruising over the left side of the neck extending to the angle of the jaw,' says Winneke. 'There were three adjoining bruises.' Consistent with punches, the court is told.

There is 'not a word from the respondents themselves about their own state of sobriety and state of mind and their own roles that night', says Brooking. 'His Honor described the death as unexpected, unintended and unlikely, a phrase on which the respondent's counsel relied without, however, analysing it … When it turns out not merely that the victim was entirely innocent, but that the supposed crime had not been committed, the case becomes very striking.'

Whiteside and Dieber received six-year jail sentences on 4 August 2000.

They are appealing.

Davo can't leave the house he rebuilt with Keitho. He hates the house. Gets confused by the plethora of switches for the downlights in the kitchen. Doesn't play music there any more. There are lots of things he used to do there that he won't do any more. But he can't leave it. When he is cooking, he notes the tick of the stove timer, and thinks, 'Another minute gone before I'm with Keitho.'

He raises the question of ending his life. But he stops short of suicide, he says, because he now is unsure there is something else beyond this life. Just a little unsure.

So life goes on. Davo sits in the doctors' waiting room, and notices two women. They are sharing a magazine. Their arms touch. That way they look at each other. A couple, obviously.

He thinks to himself: 'That's Keitho and me in a female form. The blending of souls.'

The women stand and disappear behind the door together.

Lady's Day

Andrew Rule & John Silvester

JOHN AND HELEN MAGILL packed the boot of the family car with two fold-up chairs, a portable wooden table, a thermos and some fresh Christmas lilies picked that day from their neat suburban garden. They were off to see their youngest daughter. It was her birthday.

John didn't look at a map. Every week they travelled the same way, in the 1982 white Ford Fairlane that had taken their girl to church on her wedding day fourteen years earlier.

It was a beautiful autumn day for a birthday picnic – cloudless, sunny and almost still. They parked and set up their picnic gear on the manicured grass in the shade of a tall claret ash.

They sat, listening to the wrens that had been missing in recent visits, and could hear the rustle of the leaves directly above them. They could have been in the middle of the country but for the noise of a lone motor mower in the middle distance.

It is a peaceful scene but the Magills are not at peace. They are at a Melbourne cemetery and the daughter they have come to visit is dead – murdered by two men who have never been found. Their daughter is, or was, Jane Thurgood-Dove. She was shot dead in the driveway of her Niddrie home in front of her three children on Oaks Day, 1997.

In racing, they call it Ladies' Day, when thousands of women turn out in their finest clothes to see the best thoroughbred fillies in the land battle for supremacy at Flemington. But for the Magills, it will always be Lady's Day. Their sweet Jane's day, the saddest one on their calendar.

They sit, as they always do, next to the bronze memorial plaque in the Garden of Eternal Memories and ask why.

Thursday, 6 November 1997 (Oaks Day): It would have to be the worst day in the life of this family. Around 3.45 in the afternoon I was watering the back garden and as I often do at that time, thinking of Jane picking the children up from school to bring home. Jane was a very caring mother; the mum who stayed home and took care of the kids and the house.

Being Thursday and payday they would wait for Mark to come home from work and then as a family would do the weekly shopping at the supermarket and get fish and chips on the way home. They all looked forward to that.

Helen and I ate an early dinner and around 5.45pm there was a knock at the front door. There were two men in dark suits who identified themselves as homicide detectives.

The police asked to come into the house as they had some bad news to tell us. Sitting in the sunroom waiting to hear what the police had to say seemed to take an eternity but, in reality, only seconds passed.

It was Sergeant Michael Baade who said: 'Your daughter Jane has been shot and is now dead.'

Helen and I looked at each other, stunned. Why Jane? The outpouring of emotion and grief seemed endless.

With the terrible shock we had just suffered our first thoughts were for Mark at work and most of all, for the children.

– from John Magill's diary

Society is becoming increasingly conditioned to acts of senseless violence, but the murder of Jane Thurgood-Dove seemed to touch the broader community in a way that many don't.

Here was a young mother who was stalked for days by two men in a stolen car as she went about her daily routine of taking her children to school, shopping and living a normal, productive life.

The Victorian Premier of the time, Jeff Kennett, was personally moved by the case and intervened to double the $50,000 reward requested by police for information.

Two men in a silver-blue VL Commodore sedan had been spotted in the area in the days before the shooting and detectives believed Jane was followed on her way to drop two of her children at the nearby Essendon North Primary School.

As she pulled into the driveway of her Niddrie home the stolen Commodore pulled up, blocking in her four-wheel-drive. A man, aged in his forties, and with a pot belly, chased her around the car before shooting her three times in the head with a heavy calibre handgun.

Her children were left cowering in the car as the killer sped off in the stolen Commodore, driven by a younger, thin-faced man.

The stolen car was burnt a few streets away. The men have not been identified, nor has a motive.

Police now think the killers were waiting for the perfect moment to kill her and may have been thwarted on several previous occasions by the presence of possible witnesses.

What they don't know is why two killers, possibly paid hitmen, were so determined to kill this suburban mum.

> *Saturday, 8 November: The phone today never stopped ringing, with calls from well-wishers for sympathy and support, and also throughout the day friends and relatives coming and going.*
>
> *Rod Iddles (the Homicide Squad Senior Sergeant in charge of the investigation) called early, around 7.30am, had a cup of tea and told us how hard the investigation was going, being short of information. I don't know what it was but this hard-nosed cop did appear to be emotionally upset with what he saw in this family.*

There was nothing special in the Magills' family barbecue on Easter Sunday, 1997, except that it was a chance to catch up with the kids and the grandchildren.

It was the sort of get-together held in backyards around Australia every weekend – often fun but mostly forgettable.

John Magill took the opportunity to practise with his new toy – a video camera. He and Helen planned to head to Europe for the overseas trip they had promised themselves as a retirement present and he thought it was better to make mistakes with the video in the backyard than during a once-in-a-lifetime holiday.

The video, filled with the typical close-ups and zoom shots of a practice tape, captures Jane's three children, Holly, Ashley and Scott hunting for hidden eggs. The Magills' three daughters are there – Sandra, the eldest, Susan and Jane, the youngest. So too is Jane's husband, Mark, and Susan's husband, Steve.

Jane is wearing a green top and black skirt, the same clothes she wore when she was photographed about two weeks earlier at her birthday. That picture now sits on the Magills' glass coffee table and is always published in the newspapers when there is a story on her murder. It's the one where she gazes at the camera and you look back, wondering why such a woman would be stalked and murdered outside her suburban home. But on that Easter Sunday the nightmare was in the future. For John Magill, it was a good time to practise with the camera.

It was no big deal and the tape would have eventually been used again to capture a more important event – something worth remembering. As it was, John Magill forgot about the tape and it remained in a drawer untouched.

Now it is one of the family's most precious possessions.

Saturday, 6 December: Came across the video of the last family Easter gathering together in 1997, I was trying out the new camera before going away in May, the tape has given us a lot of memories of Jane and we can't believe she has been taken from us.

Helen sits forward on the couch and John leans closer in his comfortable lounge chair, though they are both no more than a metre from the screen. Their faces crease in smiles as they watch the family as it once was.

For the moment they can block out their loss and wrap themselves in the protective warmth of nostalgia as they watch the Easter video again.

People pull faces at the camera, the kids ham it up. A watcher eavesdrops on snatches of conversation between sisters who are, or were, good friends. Jane is sitting in a white plastic chair at the outside table. Holly is on her knee and Jane has her arms draped around her in a relaxed pose, unaware the camera is on her.

She makes all the kids paper hats. Gets up and makes an attempt to do a River Dance routine with Susan. 'We really miss her laugh,' says Helen with warmth, not bitterness.

Jane waves at the camera: 'Hi Dad,' she says. Few say anything witty when they have a video camera pointed at them.

Later the music is louder and the party moves inside. The three sisters dance in the same room where they would have danced when they were kids. Jane stands, swaying to the music. Holly walks up and stretches her arms in the air. She wants to join in. Almost without looking Jane sweeps the two-year-old into her arms and continues to dance with her child clutched to her chest. It is the unconsciousness act of a natural mother.

The shock has long worn off for the Magills. It has been replaced by bitterness, almost unbearable grief and a sense of helplessness that will not go away. If there is a more crushing burden than losing a child and not knowing the reason why, they can't imagine it.

From the outside, there is little to betray the torment that this nice retired couple in their neat Niddrie home go through every day. The garden is immaculate, with a row of flowers adding a splash of colour. They are well-dressed and try to push on as best they can. They don't show obvious signs of their grief. They have been brought up to keep such things private.

But it is not private. It is front page news. Their friends and neighbours know they are the family whose daughter was murdered by a two-man hit squad for reasons that no one knows, but many speculate about.

Inside their neat house the Magills cry every day. They won't go on any long trips in case the police have a breakthrough in the case. John has started to read crime books to try and understand more about the underworld.

Every day they look at the clock around 3.50pm and think that this was the moment when their youngest girl was being chased around her own car by a man with a gun. Every day they ask why.

Few people can comprehend how their grief is doubled by not knowing why she was chosen as a murder victim. George and Christina Halvagis understand. Their lives were destroyed when a man with a knife killed their daughter, Mersina, at the Fawkner Cemetery five days before Jane's murder.

They know there is no tomorrow and the pain just doesn't go away. Peter and Sarah MacDiarmid know. Their daughter Sarah was murdered at the Kananook railway station in July, 1990, and her body was never found.

They had to move to Queensland to leave the memories, but distance does not diminish the injustice or bring any answers.

Ron Iddles has been a policeman for twenty-six years. He is married with children. He has worked in the National Crime Authority, the drug squad and has had two stints in the homicide squad.

He takes policing seriously and once quit the force when he felt an investigation was sold out through corruption, only to rejoin and then be fast-tracked to run a homicide team as a senior sergeant.

He is determined to find out the truth about Jane Thurgood-Dove. After more than two years on the case he was not prepared to say he knew who pulled the trigger, but he believed he was getting closer.

He has travelled down every orthodox path as an investigator and has begun to look at the unorthodox. He has used a lie detector on two men connected with the dead woman.

One is Mark, her husband. He passed every test.

The other was a man who was (and remains) obsessed with Jane. He agreed to the polygraph test, but failed it miserably.

The polygraph is not evidence. It is not foolproof, but it may be a start. Theoretically, at least, it establishes when people are 'being deceitful'. In short, it might find liars – but can it find gunmen?

A former Western Australian police commissioner, Bob Falconer, who introduced the use of a lie detector in the search for a serial killer in Perth, believes the use of a polygraph is a sensible way to reduce the number of suspects.

Using that theory the polygraph test has so far reduced the number of known suspects in the Thurgood-Dove case to one.

But two men stalked Jane Thurgood-Dove and police believe there are others who know what happened.

Detectives have been told the handgun used in the murder was a 'loaner' provided by a gangster from Ascot Vale, unaware it was to be used to kill an innocent mother.

Several times heavy criminals have come close to passing on information but each time they have walked away. One has said he would be prepared to make a death-bed confession about the handgun. But, until then, nothing.

There is no right way to deal with tragedy, no blueprint to grief. Some people find talking a cathartic experience. Some who are close to a murder victim want to share their feelings in a prime-time, multi-channel wake.

But the Magills are not like that. Their natural reaction is to grieve behind their wire screen security door, away from prying eyes. But they have learnt to play the media game. They talk, not because they enjoy it, but in the hope that publicity will prick a conscience and provide a new lead for police. It also helps provide a momentary release from their constant feelings of helplessness. They have been interviewed by Ray Martin for *A Current Affair* and have appeared in press conferences organised by police.

They are prepared to co-operate with this story in the hope it may help provide a breakthrough. They know it is unlikely but a slim hope is better than none.

They have kept a scrap-book on what has been written and a mental note on how some reporters have behaved. Two days after the murder a pair of reporters turned up at their door. They wanted an interview and a photograph. The female reporter then urged them to hurry – 'We've got a deadline, you know.'

That was the end of the conversation.

Another knocked on the door to ask if the family was related to an AFL footballer. 'I don't know how they live with themselves,' John says.

> *Thursday, 13 November: It is now a week since Jane's funeral ... it leaves you with a feeling of emptiness knowing there are no answers as yet.*
>
> *Ron Iddles was telling us yesterday that the police were going to do a media release ... the press will probably try to talk to us. The pressure on all of is very hard to handle.*
>
> *The children must be suffering dreadfully inside being without their mother.*
>
> *This morning's paper was on the kitchen table with a picture of Jane and a police report asking for any information about the two suspects in the photo-fit pictures. Ashley (Jane's daughter) was at the table and very gently put her hand on Jane's picture as if to say hello (that moment will never leave my mind) and with two fingers, pointed at the suspects and said 'bad men'. Holly saw the paper as well because Ashley said 'There's mummy.'*

Sunday, 23 November: I wanted to help Jane's cause, I wanted to get on the phone and ring people, anybody who might listen, I wanted to go to the TV stations to ask for help to assist the police to catch the two responsible for taking Jane from us. It is only a short time since her parting but it seems like an eternity. I do miss her so.

Saturday, 27 December: Nothing much today except Ron (Iddles) rang to say that the media wanted to speak to Mark or ourselves. They are desperate to try for a story, which they already have anyway. All they want to do is sell papers.

The Magills are a loving couple who were looking forward to life without the pressure of running their own butcher's business. After twenty-six years at the Victoria Market and twenty at the Moonee Ponds Market this was supposed to be their time.

John is wiry and still has the muscle definition in his arms of a man who has been active all his life. He sometimes struggles with breathing and requires constant medication for asthma – a legacy from smoking the roll-your-owns he gave up ten years ago.

The house is always clean. She drinks tea and he prefers coffee but they agree on almost everything else. They know each other's thoughts so well they can finish each other's sentences with the shared speech rhythms peculiar to close married couples.

They have a daily routine that rarely changes. They eat breakfast together at the kitchen table but split the paper. He reads the news while she tackles the crossword. He takes his asthma medication and then has the inevitable sneezing bout.

They can still laugh about the little things. It is a distraction from the almost constant ache of their loss.

They don't spend every day in a black cloud of grief. They emerge from it to talk about normal events – Essendon's great form in the football, stories about their grandchildren, reminiscences about family holidays – but the conversations always return to Jane.

They should be spending these years travelling and enjoying their family. They are doing none of these things.

The family will never be the same. When they gather it is a reminder not of what they have but what they have lost.

> *Sunday, 28 December: I'm just thinking what a close family we were and all the work to keep it that way is taken away by one evil deed.*

They won't travel in case they miss a development and they continually verge on tears. John Magill is a tough man and his wife is stoic, but their resolve is weakening. 'I just want to be alive when they catch these bastards,' he says.

It is always with them. The newspaper says a man was caught with illegal guns; they wonder if it could be a breakthrough. They go to the local shops and see a man who looks vaguely like the description of one of the suspects. They wonder, then ring the police for an update. They don't want false hopes. They are tired of well-meaning platitudes. They want a breakthrough.

'Those who want to help us can't and those who can, won't,' he says.

> *Friday, 21 November: I am alone at the moment, sitting at the table outside the back door, just listening to the birds, hearing the traffic on the freeway and quietly gathering my thoughts, looking at a family photo of Jane, Mark and the children, thinking what could have been. It is very hard to accept that Jane is with us no longer and I expect her to walk through the door. I want to believe I feel her presence all the time, the feeling comes and goes. I think she is there with me.*

Ron Iddles never met Jane Thurgood-Dove but he knows more about her than her best friend. He comes to the case with compassion but also with a detective's eye for detail. He looks more for weaknesses than strengths of character because he knows from experience that identifying flaws in victims and suspects can solve murders.

Every person means different things to different people. Jane was a wife, a mother, a daughter and a friend. She has been referred to as an 'ordinary' mum. There is no such thing.

Iddles had to break down all the little walls between roles to find out everything he could about the woman so that he could find out why she inflamed someone to the point of wanting her dead. He has looked in every closet and found every skeleton. He found her every secret. Or has he?

Rarely has a murder created such unsubstantiated gossip about the victim. There have been stories that she was a star witness in an armed robbery case, was a drug courier or was having a torrid affair with a gangster and was murdered by another underworld figure.

None of the stories are true. It is as if we want to blame the victim for her own murder. That if she is somehow responsible then we are somehow safer. If Jane was 'just' a suburban mum who was stalked and killed then it could happen to anyone. And that means none of us would be safe.

Saturday, 22 November: I tried to have an early night, but while lying there all I could see in my mind was the terrible situation in which Jane was cast, not knowing what was going on.

The more I think about it and what happened to our Jane, the madder and more disillusioned I am becoming about the law not looking after its citizens. I am so angry at the moment I just wish I could get out there and find these arseholes myself, but I would not know where to start.

It is now 10.10pm. I can't believe the information trail has stopped. It is constantly on my mind what that girl suffered and neither Mark nor myself could do anything to help her. I am trying to stay on top of things, but finding it hard.

Nobody needs to die the way she did and I looked forward to the time when the police catch these evil bastards for what they did to Jane. I look at Mark at the moment and all I see is despair.

Friday, 6 November, 1998: Another hard day ahead. Even though it is twelve months ago the heartache, the despair and the pain never leaves.

Monday, 31 May, 1999: Nothing, not a damn thing we are hearing. I think of all the good times and the best things the family was involved in. Then my mind will take me to the moment of Jane's death and I will be filled with revulsion for the two individuals who took Jane's death. Who gave them the right to make that decision? I will never give up thinking the police will get whoever is responsible. We gave Jane life, what gave them the right to give her death?

6 November, 1999: Two years to date and still no further ahead, no substantial news to get our hopes up. We patiently wait with utter frustration, meanwhile the pain goes on.

Ron Iddles and his team have had to investigate many murders since Oaks Day, 1997, but they keep coming back to the Thurgood-Dove case, refusing to believe it is unsolvable.

They have had other detectives to review the case to see if they have missed anything. They have travelled around Australia, interviewed more than a thousand people and chased down nine hundred tips. They believe the answer is somewhere in the material they have gathered.

Now the polygraph test has added some hope. It is not a breakthrough; it is just a lead, and there have been leads before that petered out to nothing. But it is a hope.

Ever polite, the Magills show you past the front door and out through the covered porch. Helen points to a new shrub still in its black, plastic pot, a camellia they will plant later that week.

'We had to get that one,' she says with a tired smile. 'It's a Sweet Jane.'

Jockey Smith's Last Stand

Peter Haddow

Creswick is a town where not a lot happens but when something does it's headline-grabbing stuff, such as on 12 December 1882 when the town made front page news around the world. Twenty-two miners were killed when a worked-out shaft was mistakenly bored and water flooded the new shaft. Five other miners waited two days underground before their rescue. It was Australia's biggest gold-mining disaster.

Squatters Charles, John and Henry Creswick had settled the Creswick area in 1842. When alluvial gold was discovered in 1852, sheep became an afterthought to the precious metal. By 1861 the town had 5,000 residents, a third of whom lived in tents. Peter Lalor, of Eureka Stockade fame, was a mine director there and tried to break a strike by employing Chinese miners. In the 1870s, when gold was running out in Ballarat, 4,000 diggers still worked the Creswick mines. Diggers also found the fossilised remains of crocodiles, evidence of a different, warmer climate millennia earlier.

By the turn of the century, much of the forests around Creswick had been laid bare, its timber having provided the roofing and lining for the underground mine shafts some of which still exist today. When the gold ran out, butter, cream and corn became the town's main products and in 1910 Australia's first forestry school was established.

There is not a lot of crime in Creswick but it's like anything else that happens in the town. When it's big, it's BIG. On one Saturday in December 1992 the town made national news. Headline-grabbing stuff. It was when James Edward 'Jockey' Smith, former Public Enemy Number One, made his last stand.

*

On Saturday 5 December 1992 the two-man police station of Creswick was closed. Gary Chandler, the sergeant, was on sick leave and Russell Cook, the senior constable, was on holidays. They were good country coppers, entrenched in the local community through their involvement in committees, who knew just about every one of the 3,000 residents. Even off duty, their presence was felt everywhere – in the streets, the football club, the bandstand, bowling club, the hospital, the bed and breakfast, the caravan parks, the lakes and in the three hotels. People did the right thing.

Police officer Ian Harris, thirty-one, had been seconded to Creswick from Ballarat. (Creswick is located nineteen kilometres from Ballarat and ninety minutes from Melbourne.) Harris had worked a few shifts with Russell Cook to help familiarise him with the area but now he was on his own. In ten days at Creswick he had made no arrests nor had he charged anyone.

Harris started work that day at 1.00 p.m. Driving into Creswick he stumbled across a fire at the Robin Hood Hotel and assisted in directing traffic. Youths were reported to be causing trouble at St George's Lake, Creswick. The closest backup was at Ballarat, a good ten minutes away, but he was confident he could handle anything that came his way.

In his eleven years as a police officer Harris had encountered almost everything that a police officer could expect to encounter. Before his transfer to Ballarat in 1991 he had worked at some of the busiest police stations in the State such as Preston, Reservoir and Collingwood and served a term with the Protective Security Group. None of them was a place for the faint-hearted and Ballarat itself was no rest home.

*

That same afternoon Darren Neil came out into the sunshine, wet and muddy from exploring an old Creswick mine shaft with his sons Jarrod, eight, and Travis, six. Neil and his wife Sharon had been separated for three months and he was enjoying this time with them. Both he and Sharon had been born and raised in Creswick. Coming out of the mine shaft and into the hot afternoon sun, Neil shared a stubby with his business partner and they talked about what they had seen.

*

It was 'all quiet' at the Lake. The youths had gone and Ian Harris reported to Ballarat D24 that it was an 'N.O.D. G.O.A.' meaning that there was no offence detected and the offenders had already left. He continued driving around the Creswick area and doing hotel walk-throughs. At one point, he answered the radio in the police car. There was another call to the Creswick Caravan Park – a domestic. He notified D24 that he was 'on the way'.

*

Two days earlier a Holden Commodore had pulled into the driveway of a forty-hectare property on the Glenlyon-Malmsbury Road some forty kilometres east of Creswick. Guiseppe Corso, fifty-nine, the caretaker, watched as three people came to the front door.

Christopher Binse – who called himself Bob – was an armed robber and prison escapee wanted in two States. His girlfriend Lorna Skellington called herself Candy. These two were accompanied by a third man who called himself Tom. The trio asked about a holiday farm to rent for two weeks. Corso was short of money and offered them his spare back room. They said they were from Tasmania and over the next few days nothing they did aroused any suspicion. They were quiet and generally kept to themselves.

Corso knew Tom as a short, fat man who wore glasses and had an obvious liking for gold. He wore a gold watch, a black belt with a gold buckle, two gold rings on his left ring finger and another gold ring on his left middle finger. On his right middle finger, though, he wore a silver ring – in the shape of a horseshoe. His left little finger was bent at the last joint, like an old footballer's who had tried to take one too many marks. He also wore a tight-fitting stomach brace.

*

In fact, Tom was better known as Edward James Smith, or Jockey Smith, once dubbed by police and the media as Public Enemy Number One.

Born in Colac (Victoria) on 3 October 1942, Smith had always been interested in horses. He bought his first in 1958 for twenty-eight pounds and earned the nickname he grew to hate – Jockey – while an apprentice jockey at Caulfield. His riding career did not last long as in 1961 he was caught breaking into garages and shops and sentenced to eighteen months imprisonment. It was the first of more than twenty-five convictions.

Soon after his release he and Ronald Ryan were caught committing a shop burglary. Smith tried to shoot his way out but the revolver jammed. (And Ryan went on to achieve greater infamy when he was executed in 1967 for the murder of a prison officer while escaping from Pentridge prison.)

Then in 1973 Russell Cook, then at St Kilda Crime Cars but coincidentally based at Creswick in 1992, escaped with his life while searching Smith's car. Smith came from the back seat squeezing the trigger of a firearm which fortunately failed to discharge.

In 1974 Smith moved to Sydney where he was soon arrested and charged with conspiracy to commit armed robbery. Skipping bail he returned to Melbourne where seven weeks later, after a tip off, he was arrested while sunbaking on a Sandringham beach. Two days later he escaped from Pentridge after scaling a two-metre interior fence and using a visitor's pass to exit the prison.

As Tom Cummings he lived in Nowra, New South Wales for three relatively peaceful years, racing his own horses at Sydney and provincial meetings. In 1976, however, he shot and wounded Constable Jerry Ambrose after a car chase in Kensington (NSW). Then in 1977 Smith and two others broke into the home of Sydney bookmaker Lloyd Tidmarsh and during the robbery shot him dead. His daughter Michelle witnessed her father being murdered and identified Smith as the main offender.

When confronted by Detective Bob Godden making a call from a Nowra telephone box, Smith stuck a .38 revolver into the stomach of the detective. The detective saved himself by jamming his thumb between the firing pin and the hammer as Smith pulled back the trigger.

The convictions for the shooting of Constable Ambrose and the murder of Tidmarsh were later quashed on appeal. Smith accused detectives of verballing him and maintained that he had made no admissions. His life sentence for the attempted murder of Detective Godden was reduced to fourteen years.

In February 1992, Smith was released on parole. He had spent almost twenty-five of the previous thirty years in prison. The day after his release from Long Bay gaol, he was shot in the chest, stomach and thigh by a gunman as he walked with his wife, Valerie

Hill, into the foyer of their Bondi flat. After a month in hospital, where he lapsed in and out of consciousness, Smith checked out. He refused to co-operate with police whose intelligence suggested the would-be assassin was someone close to his wife. Further information indicated that Smith was heavily armed and intent on exacting revenge. Occasionally he was seen drinking in a Bondi Junction hotel but otherwise police thought he was trying to keep a low profile and living somewhere in Terrigal. It was not to last long.

Between 16 November and 28 November 1992 the North Drug Unit of the Major Crime Squad photographed Smith and his wife with Julie Anne Cashman and Carrick Norman Joseph at 63 Mirreen Avenue, Davistown on the New South Wales Central Coast. The Unit was investigating drug dealing, and Smith was recorded offering amphetamines and marijuana to Cashman and Joseph.

On 29 November Smith drove his white 1987 Ford Fairmont to Erina shopping centre. Store detectives from Grace Brothers apprehended him for shoplifting a steam iron, kitchen knives and a plastic drinks tray. While escorting him back to their office he threatened to shoot them with a small revolver.

One of the store detectives, Delia O'Hara, made to grab the weapon but stopped when she saw it was not a toy. Smith then ran through the car park and got in the back seat of a parked Fairlane. Continuing to point the revolver, he ordered the driver Trevor Rose and his wife Beryl to drive out of the car park.

'Faster, come on, drive faster,' Smith said, while holding his collar up with his right hand.

Trevor Rose was concerned about the traffic in the shopping centre and refused to go as fast as Smith wanted, or to take the risks that he demanded. At the roundabout at Terrigal Drive and Erina Fair, Rose told Smith to, 'Take the bloody thing,' and got out taking the keys with him. Traffic banked up. Smith went after Rose wanting the keys while Beryl fled from her side of the car. Told the keys were still in the car Smith returned to the Fairlane. When the keys could not be found he rushed to a second car trying the doors but they were locked. Smith went to a third, a Nissan Pulsar.

Kristine Riley and her friend Lucia Ziolo were returning from the Gosford Leagues Club when Smith indicated for her to stay where she was and went to her door.

'Wind your window up, don't open it!' yelled Trevor Rose, but Riley did not hear him.

'Would you please get out of your car?' said Smith in a calm but urgent tone of voice.

'Pardon?' asked Riley.

Smith already had the door open. He withdrew his hand slowly from the pocket of his bomber jacket and pointed the revolver directly at Riley. She grabbed her handbag and with Ziolo left the car. Smith got in and accelerated away and was last seen in Kincumber, where roadblocks and a large police search failed to locate him. When he finally returned to 63 Mirreen Avenue he mentioned leaving the area by train and wearing a disguise. That night Cashman, Smith and Joseph left the house and checked into a motel.

The following day, 30 November, they returned to the house and discovered a listening device. It was all the warning Smith needed and he left quickly taking with him a mobile phone and a police scanner. It was a warning Cashman and Joseph did not heed and they were subsequently arrested and charged with serious drug offences. The arrests attracted wide publicity and it is unlikely that Smith did not learn of their fate.

*

Christopher Dale Binse was also being pursued by the police, in an operation code-named Operation Farnsy. On 8 September 1992 he had escaped at gunpoint from the prison security wing of Melbourne's St Vincent's Hospital only to be recaptured in New South Wales following an armed robbery.

On 24 October Binse once again escaped, this time from Parramatta Gaol. On 23 November, wearing a false moustache, sunglasses and a peaked cap, he held up the Doncaster (Victoria) branch of the Commonwealth Bank. He had followed a bank officer on his way to work and tried to force him to open the bank door. When the bank officer refused, Binse blasted the glass door with a single shot from a sawn-off shotgun. He then ran into the bank, mounted the counter and threatened staff while they filled his bag with $160,000. Binse fled from the bank to a waiting car believed to have been driven by Lorna Skellington.

Further inquiries led police from the Victorian Armed Robbery Squad to believe that Binse and two others intended to rob an

Armaguard security truck somewhere in the northern suburbs of Melbourne.

Detective Sergeant Steve Curnow of the Armed Robbery Squad sought approval for the use of the Special Operations Group when he learned that Binse and his associates might be at the Corso farm. From 5.00 a.m. on Saturday 5 December, members of the Special Operations Group and the Protective Security Group placed the property under surveillance. From their embankment, hidden amongst the trees and grass, they could not see the farmhouse but were able to observe the comings and goings of various vehicles along the driveway of the property. Early that morning they saw a man walk around the vicinity of the house, but they could not identify him. He was not their target. In fact none of their observations indicated that Binse or his girlfriend Skellington were present until about 4.10 p.m. when they were seen coming into the driveway.

In his office in Melbourne, Curnow was advised of the sighting and arranged for all members of the Armed Robbery Squad to meet at Daylesford for a briefing.

At 4.45 p.m. Skellington and Binse drove out of the property but the 'dogs' lost them. Fortunately for Operation Farnsy, they returned to the property at 6.20 p.m. with Binse now wearing a dark wig.

*

While this occurred, Senior Constable Ian Harris was settling the dispute between the drinkers at the caravan park. The proprietor wanted them to leave if their behaviour continued to be disruptive and Harris gave them a chance. If he had to return, he would lock them up. D24 called him to the radio. There was a domestic in Clunes Road, Creswick and at 4.50 p.m. he drove out of the caravan park.

*

Guiseppe Corso cooked spaghetti for his guests and discussed with them farm life and food. When the evening meal was over, Corso went to bed. Skellington watched the start of the movie *The Day of The Jackal* while 'Tom' and Binse talked in the lounge room. At the same time, Senior Constable Harris returned to the Creswick police station where he had something to eat. In another two hours he would be off duty.

*

The telephone was being monitored at the Corso farm and the police knew that 'Tom' was going to leave the property and go to Daylesford, then return. He drove out of the property in a white Ford panel van, stopping to close the gates. A Special Operations Group officer recorded the time at 8.20 p.m.

*

Ian Harris had been back on patrol for about an hour, visiting hotels in the Smeaton, Kingston and Newlyn area. He was travelling along the Midland Highway intending to check again on the Creswick hotels when he saw the white Ford panel van in front of him travelling at eighty kilometres per hour, twenty kilometres under the speed limit. Occasionally the panel van moved laterally across its lane. Having breath-tested 1,700 drivers over three years while in the Traffic Alcohol Section, Harris knew what signs indicated a person driving under the influence of alcohol. It was either a driver who had had too much to drink or just as likely a tired farmer going home after working a tractor all day.

He decided to follow the Ford panel van and gave the registration details to the D24 operator at Ballarat, Sergeant Greg Davies, who checked it on the computer.

'That vehicle on the move? It comes up as a stolen serial …'

Ian Harris did not want to intercept the vehicle straight away. It was getting dark and being in isolated bush he had few safe options should anything happen. His headlights followed the Ford into Creswick.

'I'm about fifty yards behind it coming from Newlyn into Creswick, just past the 60k sign,' Harris told D24.

Ian Harris was not concerned but he was cautious. It would not be the first time a stolen car had been recovered but not removed from the stolen car list. He felt reassured that Sergeant Tony Miller, of Ballarat traffic operations, was about ten minutes away in Warrenheip. Perhaps five in an emergency.

The stolen car turned left into Albert Street, the main street of Creswick. It then turned right into the driveway of the Farmers Arms Hotel, a watering hole for the town since about 1880. Its windows fronted the main road and the driveway through to the bottle shop. The stolen car pulled into the empty bottle shop lane while the attendant Craig Clarke was in the cool room. There were about fifteen drinkers in the public bar, some watching TV or playing pool. Another eighty people were in the lounge, including a group of women celebrating a hen's night.

'Creswick 202, the vehicle has just pulled up outside the Farmers Arms Hotel. I'm going to have to intercept it,' said Harris.

He slowly turned into the hotel apron, the headlights illuminating the driver's side of the stolen car like a searchlight as it entered the driveway of the bottle shop. Sergeant Greg Davies of D24 requested Sergeant Tony Miller to 'head in that direction at light speed.'

Miller was already accelerating rapidly along the dark Daylesford Road when he acknowledged Davies' message with the single word, 'Copied.' At the same time the Ballarat divisional van, 303, left its area quickly. The driver, Senior Constable Malcolm Scott, radioed, 'Heading there.'

Ian Harris gently tooted the horn of the police car.

Smith shielded his eyes momentarily from the headlights as he looked towards the police officer. The door opened wide as Smith made his way towards Harris. Remaining seated in the police car Harris could see keys in the ignition and felt that it was another sign that everything was in order, although he was not yet getting relaxed. He thought the owner could be taking his car back to Northcote where it had been stolen the previous day.

As the driver walked towards Harris, Greg Davies asked, 'Creswick 202, are you still with me?'

'Affirmative, mate. I'm speaking to the driver. The keys are in the ignition so it may not be a stolen vehicle as yet.'

'... it's stolen on the terminal. It states here stolen 4 of 12, '92 between 1255 and 1305 from Northcote. How many heads you got on board?' asked Greg Davies.

Ian Harris opened the door of the police car and got out to meet Smith. At 180 cm to Smith's 167 cm, he towered over him.

'Whose car is that?' Harris asked nodding towards the panel van.

'My mate who lives up the Newell Highway.'

'Have you got any identification on you?'

'Yes.'

Smith then turned and walked back to the panel van and searched the glove box while Harris sat back listening to the police radio.

Smith came back carrying something low in his left hand, a Ford owner's manual, as Harris got out to meet him. He couldn't see what it was in Smith's hidden right hand, but he thought nothing of it. It was going to be a simple car check and then they would go their separate ways and he would clear the stolen car from the terminal.

Ian Harris suddenly froze. Smith held a .38 Taurus five-shot double-action revolver at his stomach. Harris had a million thoughts running through his mind in that second and all of them centred on how to avoid being killed.

'Don't touch the gun,' Smith said.

'No, don't, don't,' Harris said as he moved his right hand towards the .38 Smith & Wesson on his gun belt.

'Don't touch the gun.'

'I'm not,' Harris said, taking his hand away as Smith raised the revolver from the police officer's stomach to his chest.

Harris raised both his hands above his head while at the same time trying to edge away. With his free hand Smith reached for the police officer's revolver but Harris edged away. Harris kept moving sideways and away so that Smith's hand was always just out of reach of his revolver. The 13 cm height difference was the only advantage he had and he intended to use it as much as he could. Each time Smith reached for his revolver, Harris felt the barrel end of the Taurus press against his stomach. He considered kicking or punching Smith, even knocking the revolver from his hand but each plan of action was deterred by the weapon itself. It was closer to a cannon than a small hand gun.

Mark Byrnes, a storeman, was gathered at the window of the hotel with other onlookers when he heard Smith say, 'Don't go for the gun or I'll kill you, I'll do you in!'

'I'm not going for it. I'm not doing nothing. Cool down. Let's try and settle this,' said Harris, equally insistent.

Jason Francis, a local panel beater, was sitting inside with his back to the window while events unfolded outside. Suddenly his friends yelled out, 'Shit, they're bluin'.' Francis turned around and saw Harris reassuring Smith. 'Settle down, calm down,' then, 'Someone help!' as he went towards the back of the police sedan with his hands in the air.

Francis and others from within the hotel went outside and watched. Smith had his back to them and was yelling, 'I'll give you ten seconds to get your gun out of your pocket and get on the bonnet or I'll blow you away!'

While this occurred, Craig Clarke, the bottle shop attendant, had come out of the cool room and walked to within three metres of the pair. Harris called to him: 'Get away, he's got a gun! Get help!'

Clarke raced back to the bottle shop and picked up the phone and rang Ballarat D24 while watching Harris, almost a rubber man, bent backwards across the boot side of the police car, his hands up in the air. A cloud of dust formed above the ground as Smith fired a shot at the feet of Harris. Where was his backup? Police sirens – the best music a police officer can hear when in trouble – could not be heard.

'What do you want? What do you want?' Harris asked.

'Lay down over your bonnet. Keep your hands away from your gun.'

*

The headlights of a maroon HJ Holden station wagon led the way into the driveway of the bottle shop. With his two boys in the front with him Darren Neil was looking forward to going home and having a few more stubbies before calling it a night. He came east along Victoria Street and turned left for the hotel bottle shop driveway. As his station wagon approached the driveway he tensed as he spotted the police car. After exploring the mine shafts he'd had more to drink at his business partner's house and couldn't afford to lose his licence.

Neil quickly reversed his wagon back into Victoria Street then drove forward, making sure he flicked the left turn indicator. He didn't want to give the police any reason to pull him over. He accelerated quietly along the road, keeping his eyes on the police car and looking out for any more police.

Then he saw Smith aim a revolver at the head of the police officer. He kept looking into the rear vision mirror watching Harris back away from Smith. The more he thought about it, the more he felt something wasn't right. He had to do something.

'We'd better go back, kids.'

Neil was 150 metres past the hotel when he turned around. Smith was still pursuing Harris around the police car. As he turned into the apron of the hotel he heard a shot as Smith fired again at the feet of the police officer.

Harris yelled out, 'Run him over, run him over!'

Neil pushed his sons under the dash but didn't feel right about them being there. They were screaming and resisted his efforts to hide them. He stopped, his vehicle facing the driver's side of the police car and quickly went to the front of his station wagon. Smith turned and pointed his revolver towards Neil saying, 'Don't.'

Neil walked towards Smith and Harris who were near the passenger-side door of the police car. He thought Smith had a starter's pistol and had drunk a few too many beers. He was wrong on both counts. Neil walked straight up to Smith, asking Harris, 'Are you alright? Are you alright?'

Then to Smith he said, 'Settle down a bit,' and pushed him hard with both hands directly on the chest propelling him backwards as Smith continued waving the revolver around. Smith fired a third shot into the ground about 150 cm away from the feet of Ian Harris. Jarrod and Travis screamed.

'I'm going to kill you,' Smith said, pointing the revolver at Harris's head.

Neil rushed back to the station wagon and drove past the police car then turned towards the main bar, almost completing a U-turn. He then opened the door for his terrified children and guided them towards the main bar. Someone opened a door and pulled them inside. Meanwhile Harris continued to back away with his hands raised in the air. He was at the front bonnet of the police car when Smith reached for his shirt collar. Harris resisted, causing two buttons to pop from the shirt.

Neil raced back to the idling station wagon while Smith swept his revolver from one to the other. Back inside the station wagon Neil reversed, then momentarily stopped. Engaging first gear he then leaned across the passenger seat and accelerated, kangaroo hopping, towards Smith and Harris.

'Run him over, run him over!' yelled the police officer.

As the car got closer, for reasons unknown to him even today, Darren Neil braked. He could have pinned Smith against the side of the police car but stopped short. Smith fired a fourth shot. Adam Francis saw the station wagon brake to avoid Harris who stepped aside at the last moment.

At the same time Smith turned and aimed his revolver at Neil, frozen in his seat, and fired a fifth shot. Harris, seizing the opportunity, drew his revolver and squeezed the trigger three times.

Licensee Christopher Frankel, twenty-nine, ordered everyone in the hotel to 'duck for cover'.

Bullets struck Smith once in the upper right side of the chest and once in the upper right side of the stomach. Smith then reared backwards over the passenger-side bonnet of the police car and fell out of sight on the driver's side. Harris and Neil rushed to the tail-gate area of the station wagon and took cover.

Harris then crept back over to the police car edging along the driver's side of the boot and peeked around the corner. Smith was lying on the ground with blood flowing freely around him. It was obvious he was dead.

Harris went to the driver's door and reached in for the transmitter where he updated D24. From the moment of his first radio contact regarding the white panel van to now, four minutes had passed.

Davies requested all other police to stand by while he picked up Harris's transmission. It was muffled and he asked Harris to repeat: 'Three shots have been fired outside the Farmers Arms hotel and I shot him. Can you get an ambulance, please?'

The transmission was poor and Davies took Harris to be saying that three shots had been fired from a shotgun. Harris gasped for breath as he spoke, as if he had just finished a run up the Rialto tower.

People from inside the hotel came outside to check on Smith and as a precaution Darren Neil picked up Smith's revolver lying near his body and placed it on the boot of the police car. Harris put it inside the boot for safekeeping and when other police arrived he replaced it where it had originally fallen.

'Yeah, Roger. You have units on the way to assist you now. Are you all right yourself?'

'I've got no damage to me …' gasped Harris.

Licensee Chris Owens was later to describe him as being 'terrified – all pumped up like he couldn't believe what had happened'. Darren Neil went over to the obviously distressed police officer. It seemed to Neil that Harris was concerned he would be seen as a murderer, acting without justification, rather than someone who had acted to save lives, including his own.

'You did the right thing,' Neil reassured the police officer.

Together they put up crime scene tape then Neil went to his children, who were crying. He told them it was all over, the bad man couldn't hurt them any more. He hugged them to him and showed them his shirt and arms. 'See I'm alright,' he said and stayed with them until other police arrived. Later he was taken to the Creswick police station while a family friend looked after his boys. While he waited to be interviewed he worried about being asked to blow into a breathalyser – it was his only concern.

When the police had finished with him he returned to the Farmers Arms Hotel which was closed but he was able to get a coffee. He wanted to get his station wagon but wasn't allowed as it was still part of the crime scene, so he walked the 1.25 km home.

*

Outside the hotel Sergeant Tony Miller watched as Detective Senior Constable Doug Mathers of Ballarat CIB pulled on surgical gloves and checked Smith's revolver. In Smith's back pocket was a wallet containing $4,118.75 and a NSW driver's licence in the name of James E. Smith, born 3.10.1942.

Looking over his shoulder at the licence, Miller said, 'It's Jockey Smith.'

'Jockey Smith?' said Mathers.

Miller repeated again who he thought it was but Mathers still doubted him, saying, 'You've got to be joking!' Mathers believed that Smith was in New South Wales, an opinion shared by even the most experienced police until fingerprints and a positive identification from the deceased's brother Ron confirmed that Miller was right.

*

Detective Sergeant Steve Curnow of the Armed Robbery Squad moved fast when he heard the news of the shooting. So fast that at 11.17 p.m. that night he and other members of the Armed Robbery Squad reached the Glenlyon farmhouse where the Special Operations Group was holding Binse, Skellington and Corso in various rooms. The three were taken to Melbourne for interviewing while crime scene officers searched the property and found a mobile phone, two portable radios, two Realistic radio scanners, a shotgun cleaning kit, seven wigs, two false moustaches and sideburns, a Gregory's Sydney street directory and a Melways street directory opened at page 30 (the northern suburbs of the Northcote/Preston area). Various locations on this page had been highlighted. It was obvious something more than a holiday was being planned by Binse, Skellington and Smith.

*

On 7 December 1992 a post-mortem was conducted on the body of Smith. During the post-mortem Smith was found to be wearing a black holster and in it was a plastic bag containing nine .38 hollow point cartridges. In the left pocket of his jeans was a canister of mace.

Smith's solicitor Chris Murphy was reported in the *Sydney Morning Herald* as saying that Smith had come '… out of jail on the run, was shot within two days of getting out and then led a life in hiding. He was marked for death by his enemies and I know that he considered the worst of those were in the police force. I know that he believed he was on hit lists because of enemies he made in the police force.'

Inmates from Long Bay jail had a large wreath delivered to Smith's funeral in Geelong East. Those family and friends present listened as Reverend Paul Downie spoke for Smith's wheelchair-bound mother Jean. He recounted how Smith never asked her for help despite his troubles, saying on her behalf that, 'Son, you worried me lots but you was mine and I loved you lots. So did many others.'

Earlier in the week Smith's mother told journalists that he had always kept in touch and sent her cards for Mothers Day and at Christmas, but 'like most boys' forgot her birthday.

'He was always kind and gentle,' she said.

*

Immediately following the shooting, Ian Harris phoned his wife Jacinta and told her what had happened. She had been visiting her parents, and Harris asked her to stay with them for the time being. Jacinta was relieved to know he was unhurt and reluctantly agreed. After being interviewed by Homicide he went home to find the phone ringing. It was his Ballarat colleagues about to finish night shift. It was 6.30 a.m. and they brought some beer with them. The police psychologist came up from Melbourne but Ian was in no condition to speak to her. When Jacinta came home she found him asleep in a chair surrounded by a sea of workmates and empty stubbies.

Two days later Harris travelled to Melbourne where he saw the police psychologist, then a doctor who gave him a week off. Someone had threatened to kill him and he was offered 24-hour protection in Ballarat. He was already hyper-vigilant and continually looking for possible escape routes even before he knew of this threat. His feelings of personal safety would never be the same again. As a compromise he agreed to random patrols past his house but did not want to feel a prisoner in his own home. Having been involved in Witness Protection, it was the last thing he wanted for his family.

Everywhere he turned there was mention of the shooting and people wanting to talk about it. He couldn't escape for a moment. Even with the aid of sleeping tablets he slept poorly, experiencing wild dreams of fighting – always violence, of being in high-speed chases and serious car accidents. Almost six years later, he still has trouble sleeping.

Jacinta took a week off from her job to be with him and returned to work exhausted. People asked her how it felt 'to be married to a hero' but she knew nothing more than what she read in the newspapers or saw on TV. Like many police officers Ian kept what happened at work in his locker at Ballarat, to protect his family. But Jacinta wanted to know and his inability to open up to her was a weight on her mind. During the inquest he finally discussed with her what had happened. Jacinta felt she couldn't cope and went to work an emotional wreck. She later saw a psychologist who helped her to recover.

The next year was a difficult one. Harris seemed to withdraw into himself. He needed to escape from the dark humour and the relentless interest of his well-meaning colleagues. One remarked that he didn't have to do firearm training any more as he had already passed. Harris found such comments upsetting rather than helpful.

Jacinta was concerned to see him lounging about the house drinking beer and watching TV all day. The happy-go-lucky person she married was missing. Away from work for three months, he returned as a D24 operator, then towards the end of 1993 felt able to return to section. In a short period of time he had two accidents driving the Ballarat divisional van. His concentration had deteriorated and he was extreme in his attitudes towards anyone who was a possible threat to his and his partner's personal safety, particularly during the period of the inquest.

After more time off work he resumed duty, ironically as an assistant to the District Firearm Officer. While he doesn't feel up to resuming operational duties he enjoys working at Ballarat D24, particularly during 'hot incidents'. He is comforted by the fact that he is locked inside the control room so that nobody can get at him. Before the shooting incident Jacinta never worried for his safety whereas now she does and is glad he is not operational.

Even today there are only two places where Ian Harris feels safe. Inside his home and inside the police station where he works.

*

After walking home from the Farmers Arms Hotel, Darren Neil was in bed for only a short time before the telephone rang. It was 5.30 a.m. and the media wanted an interview. Soon afterwards he could hear a news helicopter overhead. It was all too much so he went fishing. When he got home a photographer and journalist were in his backyard. To get rid of them he gave an interview, the first of many. To get some peace he got a silent number, but the media rang him at work and visited him there as well as at home. Some offered money while others aggressively pushed for another interview. He went bush for a few days hoping it would all be over when he came home. Apart from complimenting him on his actions, the Creswick locals generally respected his privacy.

For a while he and his family were wary of any strange cars that passed by their home and particularly so when relatives of Smith visited the Farmers Arms where someone had painted JS LIVES on the driveway.

Darren and his wife reunited after the shooting. Jarrod, now thirteen, has frequent nightmares and does not like being left alone in a room at night. News of prison escapes concern him – he thinks what he saw in 1992 will happen again. Travis has shown no effects from what he witnessed. Unlike the support offered Ian Harris there has been none for the Neil family.

'We just want to get on with our lives,' said Sharon.

*

On 2 March 1994 Darren Neil was presented with the Star of Courage by Governor General Bill Hayden at a bravery award ceremony at Government House.

On 26 May 1995, during a graduation parade at the Glen Waverley police academy, Deputy Commissioner Brian Church presented Ian Harris with the Valour Award.

Ian Harris and Darren Neil have seen each other from time to time and promised to get together for a beer. They have yet to keep their promise and maybe they never will, but there is a bond between them that few friends will ever share.

The Triggerman

Pippa Kay

THE DATE, 29-5-88, is written in tidy rounded numbers by an officer in the Witness Protection Unit, Long Bay on the top right-hand corner of Bill Vandenberg's suicide note. It contrasts with Bill Vandenberg's handwriting, which is untidy but generally legible. The entire seven-page suicide note is written in angular capital letters. It starts with a message to 'G' [name suppressed] and the kids:

> Please remember something I said and sung many years ago on my escape to Melbourne.
>
> We'll meet again I don't [know] where I don't know when but I know we'll meet again some sonny [*sic*] day.

Vandenberg had confessed to being the 'triggerman', the hitman who shot Megan Kalajzich, and had recently given evidence against her husband, Andrew Kalajzich, at the trial. His dilemma had been that while testifying against Kalajzich, he was also digging a hole for his best friend, Kerry Orrock.

'G' and 'the kids' are Kerry Orrock's family. The day before Vandenberg's suicide, Orrock had been sentenced to life imprisonment for supplying the murder weapon used for the murder of Megan Kalajzich.

*

I had been following the case since Megan Kalajzich was shot as she slept beside her husband, Andrew, on 27 January 1986. Part of my interest stems from the fact that I am distantly related to

Andrew and Megan (though I had never met Megan) and know many of their friends and relatives. Andrew Kalajzich was a mover and shaker in the early 1980s and built the very successful Manly Pacific International Hotel on Manly beach.

When he was charged and eventually convicted of his wife's murder, I began assembling information on the case with the intention of writing a book.

*

The Crown presented a case against Kalajzich that centred on Vandenberg's confession to the hitman-style murder. It involved the following cast of characters:

- Warren Elkins, the disk jockey/manager of Dalleys Disco on the ground floor of the Manly Pacific International Hotel, who asked Vandenberg to find a hitman for his boss. Elkins was a snappy dresser who adorned himself with gold jewellery. Girls were impressed. At the time of Megan's murder he was living with two girls, a Monday-to-Thursday girl, and a Friday-to-Sunday girl, and neither knew about the other. He was suspected of sabotaging the hotel's security with a number of expensive pranks, such as the theft of the hotel's keys.
- George Canellis (another self-confessed hitman – now retired) was originally asked to do the job, by Vandenberg. He is a tough-looking character, an expert in firearms and breeder of Rottweilers. He claims he followed Megan while she was shopping but when she smiled at him, his hitman's heart melted and he refused to do the job, claiming he 'didn't do domestics'. He also refused to return the $5,000 deposit he had been given. So it seemed to Vandenberg that he had no choice but to do the job himself.
- Kerry Orrock, a gaunt man with serious health problems. He had owned a fuel transporting business (occasionally employing Canellis as a truck driver) as well as a service station in Kurri Kurri. Orrock was convicted for supplying the murder weapon to Vandenberg, who was a close friend.

Many people believe that *both* Megan and Andrew were the hitman's targets, and that Andrew was lucky to escape – if you can call anyone convicted for murder 'lucky'. And many people also believe that Vandenberg was not capable of doing the murder.

Four bullets were fired that night: two bullets into Megan's cheek and two bullets into Andrew's pillow. Did the hitman miss his target? Was Andrew Kalajzich then framed for his wife's murder? Kalajzich's solicitor told me he believed the answers to these and many other questions surrounding the case were lost with Vandenberg's suicide on 29 May 1988.

After an inquiry under Justice Slattery AO QC failed to cast doubt on Kalajzich's conviction, I was given access to documents and photographs and began my search for the truth.

*

A suicide note, I suspected, would be the most honest, heartfelt statement a man could make. Would this be a good place to start? Vandenberg had made many statements to the police, but he changed his story often, and it was difficult to know which version of the 'truth' would be the most reliable.

Bill Vandenberg was arrested on 14 February 1986 when Detective Inkster and other police knocked on his door and asked if he knew anything about the murder of Megan Kalajzich. Inkster claims he was not expecting a confession and so was surprised when Vandenberg told him to look no further: 'You don't have to worry about losing him,' he said, 'because you have got him now. It was me who pulled the trigger.'

In a statement written in April 1986, Vandenberg recalls Inkster coming to his Elizabeth Bay flat:

> [O]ne of the questions they asked was 'we want to know the name of the trigger man and the name of the person that paid to get the job done.' All of a sudden I then realised they had no idea that I was the triggerman. So I said to them 'Hang on a minute with your questions and let me talk.' They stopped to listen (and I might add that they were never rude). I said 'you have gone this far with your investigating and have done well so now I don't see any reason to make things harder for you so to help the situation I will now tell you that I am the triggerman so that should make it easier for you.'

He was driven to Manly Police Station. On the way he pointed to the spot where he had thrown the murder weapon and the police took a photo of him.

It was a busy day at the Manly Police Station. Three interview rooms were being used in connection with the case. Elkins, who had been arrested while duty-free shopping with one of his girlfriends, and Orrock, who had been arrested at his home in Kurri Kurri, were each being interviewed. Their records of interview were typed (this was before compulsory tape-recording of interviews), a tedious process by modern standards. Carbon copies were made, which were slid under the door of each room to be picked up by police in a central area who could assemble the information.

During his first interview, Vandenberg told police that 'two Yugoslav types' were behind the murder and he was supposed to murder both Megan and Andrew. The best way to get Andrew, he had been told, was from a public car park at the rear of the Manly Pacific, which looked down on to the exit ramp to the hotel car park.

Vandenberg had a break for dinner between five and seven, and it was during this break that Andrew Kalajzich was arrested. On his solicitor's advice, Kalajzich said nothing.

Vandenberg changed his story after this and again over the next two days. Now it was Andrew Kalajzich who wanted his wife murdered because she was selling shares in the hotel.

*

Vandenberg's suicide note continues:

> To J and M [Vandenberg's brother and sister-in-law]
> I have gone in search of my greatest love I had in Life 'Anthony' and I'll pray and hope I do meet him there.

Anthony was Vandenberg's young nephew (J and M's son) who had died a few months before Megan's murder after a long illness with muscular dystrophy. Vandenberg and Anthony were very close and Vandenberg slept in the same room with his young nephew whenever he visited his brother. It appears that he hoped to meet Anthony again after death.

*

Another six pages of suicide note were found in his cell, still attached to a lined A4-sized writing pad. They were examined by an expert who confirmed that the handwriting was Vandenberg's.

Photographs of Vandenberg's cell, taken shortly after he was found dead, show him on the floor against the far wall, his head near a toilet and hand basin. He had hanged himself from a high cupboard door, using torn-up and knotted green fabric removed from the workshop area of the prison. On top of his bunk bed (on the other side of the cell) is a white plastic chair. Beside the bed is a small triangular table. He probably used the television off this table and used it and the chair to elevate himself somehow before slipping the noose around his neck. It would have been difficult to do this from the bed, since the distance between the chair and the cupboard from which he hanged himself looks to be at least ten feet.

A desk or bench unit abuts the cupboard. Vandenberg's glasses are next to the cupboard. He would have needed them to write his final message, removing them before slipping the noose over his head. Under the desk is an Adler electric typewriter, connected to a power point by an extension power cord. Why did he not use this cord instead of the green fabric?

The typewriter is interesting. In it is a sheet of ruled A4 paper and unreadable words to 'Max' [a fellow inmate] written in large print in red texta. Also in red texta on the case of the typewriter is a further message to Max, telling him to 'please take this.'

Vandenberg's body was photographed from a number of positions. His neck has striped welts from the noose. In one photo the eyes and mouth are open, as if he were speaking. Although his face is pale, the skin on his scalp, ears and back is purple, as if bruised. It is not bruising, however – it is peripheral cyanosis, the blueness of the skin caused by lack of oxygen. He wears a towel under his trousers, like a nappy.

On the third page of his suicide note Vandenberg apologised to the officer who would find his body:

> … as this is the second time in two weeks he's had to put up with the shit I left him but please be assured I didn't plan this for when you were on as I have a higher regard for you …
>
> [B]ecause of what I know about dying this way I

> wanted to make it as clean as possible for the people finng [*sic*] me up. I hope that little part might be appreciated.

I have no doubt that Vandenberg wanted to kill himself.

*

Although once married, Vandenberg was homosexual. Paul Blake, an attractive red-headed young man, was his 'special' friend at the time of Megan's murder (though Blake was married and denies having had sexual relations with Vandenberg). Shortly after the murder, Blake received $10,000 from Vandenberg which he used to pay off his bankcard. He did not give evidence at the trial. Police claimed he couldn't be found, but eight years later, during the Slattery Inquiry, he told the court that he'd been living in Adelaide and had received a subpoena from South Australian police. However, he did not feel inclined to travel to Sydney to appear at the trial, and no one seemed to insist.

In 1985, the year before Megan was murdered, Vandenberg was the manager of the Sea Galleon restaurant in the Rex Hotel in Kings Cross and did his drinking at the 'Bottoms Up Bar', a bar described by John Bracey, a private investigator hired by the Kalajzich legal team, as:

> ... possibly the most sleaziest bar in Sydney. The clientele varies from numerous farely [*sic*] assorted criminals the bottom end for want of a better term of the homosexual community ... and probably New Zealand-based transvestites. Prostitution both male and female would seem to be a popular vocation to a number of the members of the clientele. We find it quite likely that should one wish to find some unsavoury person on the Sydney scene at the Bottoms Up Bar would certainly be the most appropriate place to attempt to locate such persons …

In late 1985 and early 1986, Bill Vandenberg was drinking heavily. Friends, including Kerry Orrock, described him as frightened and confused. His drunken confabulations included plots involving gold shipments, the Philippines and prominent politicians. No one believed him. On New Years Eve, 1985, he quit his job at the Sea Galleon and went on a drinking binge.

A few days later he was staying at the Crest Hotel in Kings Cross, too frightened to go back to his flat in nearby Elizabeth Bay. Kerry Orrock had travelled down to Sydney to rescue him from this situation by taking him back to Kurri Kurri.

There, Vandenberg was given lessons in firing a gun. Both Orrock and Canellis described him trying to hit an aviary in Orrock's backyard. Canellis, who was prone to using colourful language, told the court that Bill 'couldn't hit a bull in the arse with a shovel full of wheat'. When he aimed at the aviary and missed, they 'shit-split outta there'.

Yet the bullet holes in Megan's cheek, were one centimetre apart – a sign of a marksman with a steady hand.

Vandenberg told the police he had never met Kalajzich. There is hearsay evidence from his friend Paul Blake that he spoke to someone who claimed to be Andrew Kalajzich on the phone.

Eight years after the event, during the Slattery Inquiry, Blake gave the following evidence to Michael Finnane QC (now Judge) of this overheard telephone conversation.

'What had he said about Mr Kalajzich before this?' Finnane asked.

'Well, of course, when he mentioned about the proposed murder, he had said to me that – I asked who the lady was, he said it was a lady.' Blake hesitated under the influence of apparently strong emotion. 'He said it was a lady that he had to –'

'Murder?' Finnane helped him find the word that seemed to be stuck.

'Yes, murder, and he mentioned the name Megan Kalajzich and Andrew Kalajzich, Andrew Kalajzich owning the hotel over in Manly.'

'So he gets the phone call, he puts his index finger up to his lips, he mouths the word Kalajzich to you?' Finnane prompted.

'That's correct,' Blake nodded.

'You then walk over to him; you sit next to him and you listen to the conversation and you could tell the person speaking was a male, it was a male voice?'

'Yes.'

Hearsay evidence like this would not normally be permitted during a trial in front of a jury, but this was an inquiry, with no jury, and the rules of evidence were stretched at Justice Slattery's discretion.

According to Blake, the conversation Blake overheard went like this:

Kalajzich: 'How come it didn't happen?' (referring to a failed attempt at the murder of Megan)

Vandenberg: 'Because your son was there.'

Kalajzich: 'Fuck my son, I want her dead.'

Vandenberg: 'I'm not going to kill your son. It's bad enough I've got to kill one person. I'm not going to kill an innocent boy.'

Kalajzich: 'I don't care who's in the fucking house, my son, my mother-in-law, I want her fucking dead, do you understand me, fucking dead.'

Finnane asked Blake how it was that his memory for this overheard telephone conversation was so good after eight years, to which Blake replied: 'Well, if you think about it, what kind of a person would say something like that about their own family? It is something you would etch in your mind for the rest of your life, believe me.'

I sat next to an elderly friend of the Kalajzich family who had known Andrew since he was in short pants. She gasped every time the 'f' word was said and seemed upset. Later she told me she couldn't believe Andrew would ever say such a thing, and I'm not sure which worried her most – the 'f' word or the allegation that he had also wanted his son and mother-in-law killed, as well as his wife.

In none of his statements did Vandenberg mention this telephone conversation that occurred with Paul Blake within earshot, though in a hand-written statement he describes an occasion when Warren Elkins (allegedly Kalajzich's agent) came to his flat in Elizabeth Bay:

> [After a failed attempt Warren Elkins] said he would ring his boss but he would not be very pleased with the whole matter so he rang back to his boss … after a while he stopped talking to whoever and addressed me saying he wants to talk to you and I said 'OK.'
>
> [T]he voice at the other end said, and he sounded a very arrogant man, 'You have really made a mess of it.' I explained that I never really intended to get involved with it but I had and the situation had gone wrong and there wasn't much I could do about it.

*

About midnight of 10/11 January 1986, a couple of weeks before Megan was shot, she was attacked in the carport of their Fairlight home. She described this attack in a letter to a friend:

> If you have any spare bodyguards I could do with one. The other night I came out of the garage to find some 'jerk' waiting for me with a black balaclava & a batton [*sic*] in his hand he managed to hit me on the head but my scream scared him off. He knocked me off balance so [I] came down the stairs like the flying Nun. So I'm covered in bruises and the nerves are shot to pieces.

Vandenberg was a short, slightly built man who wore glasses. He admitted to this assault as well as the murder, but stressed that he wore 'a green army hat' pulled down low, and that he carried a cut-down rifle with a silencer on the end. When he aimed to shoot her, he said, the weapon didn't fire, so he tapped her on the head with it instead and she fell down some stairs and screamed. He is adamant in a number of records of interview and court transcripts that he did *not* wear a balaclava.

So did Megan make a mistake in her description? It seems unlikely that she would imagine a balaclava, even in the semi-darkness of an unlit carport.

Bill Vandenberg would turn in his grave if he saw the way this scene was depicted in the telemovie *My Husband, My Killer.* He is a bumbling clown, wearing a balaclava over a pair of glasses that kept fogging up, and therefore unable to see what he is doing.

Megan reported hearing a car start, followed by a car door slamming, and felt that the man who had attacked her had an accomplice in a car nearby. She assumed she had sprung a would-be thief, but was puzzled because he didn't grab her handbag.

Earlier that night she'd had dinner with Andrew and some friends. The day before the assault she had taken Andrew's car to be serviced while he had driven hers to the hotel. They had swapped cars at the end of the evening in the hotel car park, and she drove home in her own car while Andrew spent a little more time at the hotel doing his routine checks before returning home. It is likely that whoever assaulted Megan was confused by the car swapping.

Megan was assisted into her house that night by a neighbour who had heard her screaming. Police were called. She suffered a few bruises to her legs and a small abrasion behind her ear where someone had hit her but, as her letter suggests, she did not take the episode very seriously.

*

When Kerry Orrock heard the news of Vandenberg's suicide, he refused to believe it. He was convinced that his friend had been murdered in his cell and was upset that he was not permitted to give evidence at the Coroner's Inquest into Vandenberg's death. In a handwritten letter dated 24 May 1988, Vandenberg complained to Kerry:

> I am having trouble sleeping tonight and I can't get a sleeping tablet as the doctor took me off them due to an accidental overdose of them. So now on a night like tonight I'm in trouble and there is not a damned thing I can do about it.

Five days later, in his suicide note, he states:

> My pills are now starting to work on me and I'm just waiting for [officer] to make his hourly check then I will wish you good luck in the future …

What pills? Where did he get them? asked Orrock, now panic-stricken. If Vandenberg had been murdered, he thought, he was also a likely candidate.

Despite apparently rigid controls within our correctional institutions, drugs of all kinds seem to be available to inmates, even illegal ones, even to 'at risk' and suicidal inmates, even in the high security, Witness Protection Unit at Long Bay. The coroner did not question the fact that Vandenberg had somehow got hold of some 'pills'.

The doctor who performed the physical examination of Vandenberg's body commented that he looked older than his forty-six years. X-rays of the larynx showed a linear fracture in the right greater horn of the hyoid bone that is typical of death by hanging. Routine screening tests for poisons and alcohol returned a negative result, but no specific tests were done to determine what type of 'pills' he had taken.

Four days before his suicide, Vandenberg had a brief appointment with a psychiatrist. He had been prescribed anti-depressant medication previously but had stopped taking the tablets. This psychiatrist did not believe the earlier accidental overdose was a suicide attempt, accepting Vandenberg's explanation that he had merely taken the tablets he had been hoarding to get rid of them because of a spot search of his cell. They had only made him sleepy.

*

The psychiatric report from the inquest makes interesting reading. Vandenberg was the sixth of eight children. His mother had divorced his father and emigrated to Australia when he was fourteen. Vandenberg had a poor relationship with the significant women in his life and blamed his mother because she had not taken proper care of her family. He also blamed his ex-wife for having an affair with a policeman before their divorce, and blamed his daughter for only ringing him when she needed money. Given this, the psychiatrist could understand why he was willing to murder Megan Kalajzich, particularly when he believed that she had been losing a million dollars a day gambling on the stock market. Unfortunately, when he later learned that this was not true, and that in fact she was a nice woman, it led him to feelings of remorse and depression.

The psychiatric report failed to mention that Vandenberg was homosexual or anything about his love for his nephew Anthony.

What drove Vandenberg over the edge was learning that his friend Kerry Orrock had received a life sentence for his involvement in the murder of Megan. This remorse and depression is supported by his suicide note:

> My actions are done with a heavy heart but find myself incapable of living with myself. The sentence given to Kerry is in my opinion the unfairest sentence I have yet heard of and has put me in the position of having distroyed [*sic*] his life as well as [G] and the kids and that is unbearable.
>
> I hope the appeals court will make good that injustice to Kerry. His part was so minor compared to Warren [Elkins] …

> I didn't want to die but I also can't live with the shame of my doing to Kerry's kids whom I regarded as my very own …

Vandenberg does not dwell on the murder. I assume he is referring to Megan and her family when he writes:

> I distroyed [*sic*] the life not only of the woman but just as much her daughter and son as well as her mother. All of them are the innocent victims of my terrible crime.
>
> What I have done tonight should still be lawful as I think I've taken a life and deserve to lose mine.

He does not refer to the shooting at all.

When he adds, 'I think I've taken a life,' I wonder if perhaps he is unsure, but I have no doubt that he feels responsible for Megan's death, in the same way that he feels responsible for the other lives he has 'distroyed', that is, members of her family, Orrock and Orrock's family.

*

The Coroner needed to be certain that Vandenberg's death was suicide and not murder because of an alleged murder plot that had been uncovered in the Long Bay Programmes Unit in late 1986. This alleged plot became the focus of an ICAC Inquiry into the Use of Informers, and received considerable media attention.

Many prisons have Programmes Units. In theory these are small units wherein prisoners may undertake courses or programmes of training aimed at improving their socialisation both within the prison system and outside in society. But the Programmes Unit at Long Bay in 1986 was a euphemism. Staff and prisoners more appropriately called it 'The Dog Box'. It occupied two levels, ground and first floor (called 'middle landing') and was physically separated from the Metropolitan Remand Centre by an iron-barred gate covered with toughened perspex.

Most prisons also have a Protection Area for prisoners who are considered at risk within the main prison. The Programmes Unit at Long Bay contained up to fifty 'dogs' – informers or witnesses against other criminals. It also housed 'rock spiders' – persons accused of sexually assaulting children. Mainstream prisoners tended to exact their own brand of justice within the prison system and thus 'dogs' and 'rock spiders' needed protection.

Bill Vandenberg was housed in the Programmes Unit at Long Bay because he was giving evidence against Andrew Kalajzich, and perhaps also because of rumours that he was a 'rock spider'. He preferred his own company and made himself useful by painting the cells and hallways when he wasn't working as 'sweeper' in the visiting area.

The alleged plot to murder Vandenberg was another complex conspiracy to murder, involving particularly 'heavy' criminals including Peter Drummond, Fred Many and Tom Domican.

Peter Drummond, on his own application, entered the Programmes Unit in September 1986. He was on remand for murder, and did not fit the usual profile of a prisoner needing protection. It was alleged that he had gained entry to the Programmes Unit specifically for the purpose of murdering Vandenberg.

Fred Many was also in the Programmes Unit in late 1986. Earlier that year, while on parole, he had raped a fifteen-year-old girl and left her for dead. Because this brutal crime provoked much media questioning about the advisability of releasing prisoners like Many on parole, he was vulnerable to attack if housed within the main prison.

According to Fred Many, one day in late September or early October 1986, Peter Drummond told him, 'The old dog has got to go,' meaning Vandenberg. Drummond asked Many for help.

The alleged murder plot came unstuck, however, when Drummond was transferred away from the Programmes Unit a month later. According to Many, Tom Domican now entered the plot, though he was not held in the Programmes Unit.

Meanwhile, on 2 December 1986 Bill Vandenberg was moved to Parklea. It was claimed to be for his own safety, but the prison van did a considerable detour via Castle Hill police station where Vandenberg signed a statement for Detective Inkster and agreed to give evidence for the Crown against Andrew Kalajzich.

I wondered why it was necessary to use Castle Hill police station for this. Did the knowledge of a murder plot brewing within the prison motivate Vandenberg to put pen to paper? On his website, Tom Domican claims this was the case. He asserts that there was no plot to murder Vandenberg, rather that it was a scare campaign devised by Detective Inkster, whom he described as 'an ambitious man'. He claims that:

> [I]n transit to Parklea prison, Vandenberg was taken to Castle Hill police station where Det. Sgt Bob Inkster was waiting, the ground work already done by Many [and others] … he had little trouble convincing Vandenberg that Kalajzich and Elkins was [*sic*] out to poison him …
>
> [Vandenberg] provided Inkster with statements which implicated Andrew Kalajzich, Warren Elkins and Kerry Orrock in the murder of Megan Kalajzic [*sic*]. This raises the serious question, what weight can be given to statements obtained in this manner, where the coercion and inducements are so blatantly obvious?

Domican and Drummond, the two remaining alleged conspirators in this alleged plot to murder Vandenberg, were tried and found guilty. They were sentenced to fourteen years each in March 1987. A new Witness Protection Unit (WPU) was established at Long Bay to replace the old Programmes Unit. Detective Inkster had been instrumental in forming this unit and Vandenberg was one of its first inmates. He was transferred to the WPU from Parklea.

This apparent resolution came undone, though, when Leigh Johnson, a solicitor visiting another prisoner, claimed Fred Many had spoken to her within the visiting area and had told her that the evidence he had given implicating Domican and Drummond in the plot to murder Vandenberg was untrue. When Drummond and Domican then appealed their convictions, the Court of Criminal Appeal ordered that they be retried. In view of Leigh Johnson's statement casting doubt on Many's original evidence, the Director of Public Prosecutions declined to proceed further against them.

If we believe what Fred Many told Leigh Johnson – that there was never a plot to murder Vandenberg – then we should also be aware that he was rewarded for giving this original (false) evidence against Drummond and Domican with the promise of an early release – a promise that prison authorities fulfilled.

In its chapter on the plot to murder Vandenberg, the Independent Commission Against Corruption Report concludes, under the subheading 'Happy Ending', with this:

> In the circumstances there is no reason why the two prisoners should not have received some rewards for their assistance. It cannot be right that assistance will be recognised and rewarded only if it results in convictions, because that would inevitably lead to perjured evidence as desperate prisoners sought to buttress their testimony so as to secure a conviction.

But this ending was not so happy for Kirstyn Austin, who had been raped by Fred Many and left for dead in September 1986. She was then fifteen years old. When Fred Many was released early as his 'reward', in spite of the threats he had made against her while in prison, she was forced to assume a new identity and enter the witness protection program. Fred Many's early release received considerable media attention in New South Wales. Not long after his release he was found dead in his girlfriend's flat from a drug overdose.

*

In March 1988 Andrew Kalajzich and Kerry Orrock were tried for conspiring to murder Megan Kalajzich.

Warren Elkins, having been offered an immunity from prosecution if he pleaded guilty to the charge of conspiracy to murder, gave evidence for the Crown against Andrew Kalajzich. He was sentenced to ten years. Vandenberg had been sentenced to life. Orrock was expecting an immunity from prosecution similar to Elkins, but did not get it and was charged and tried with Andrew Kalajzich.

Kalajzich's trial barrister expressed his doubts that Vandenberg was the hitman who killed Megan, telling the Slattery Inquiry that he believed it more likely that Vandenberg was the 'wheels'.

During the 1988 trial, Vandenberg's knowledge of guns was tested when he was asked to hold the murder weapon – a rusty cut-down rifle threaded to take a silencer, with no stock or trigger guard. He held it out in front of him as one might hold a pistol. There were titters and giggles from the jury and court watchers at the back of the courtroom.

When asked how he held the gun on the night he murdered Megan, he said, 'I don't really know.' Nor did he know what a cocking mechanism was, and he seemed confused about the functions of other parts of the weapon.

In his address to the jury, the prosecution predicted jury concern about whether or not Vandenberg had committed the murder. He reminded them that Vandenberg was not on trial, and had already been sentenced. The jury's duty was to determine whether Andrew Kalajzich had been the person who had instructed a hitman to murder his wife.

Justice is blind, I thought, but I could not turn a blind eye to this absurdity. Vandenberg's 'confession' was the foundation of the case against Kalajzich, and yet it had not been challenged in a court of law, apart from a hearing for sentencing. How could a jury arrive at a valid verdict on Kalajzich's guilt or innocence under these circumstances? Perhaps they could not understand why a man might confess to a murder if he hadn't done it. I recalled Evan Whitton's observation in *Trial by Voodoo*:

> [P]ersons with even modest experience know that an innocent person may falsely plead guilty to a crime for any number of reasons, including that he is mentally disturbed, that he is shielding someone else, or most usually, because unscrupulous police have told him he is 'down' for it and that if he pleads guilty they will put a word in for him, but if he does not they will 'load' (fabricate evidence against) him with other more serious crimes. But even in the face of such experience, English law, unlike European law, does not require the Crown to actually prove the case against a man who pleads guilty; it proceeds straight to sentence.

Kalajzich's trial barrister believed Vandenberg enjoyed the publicity and notoriety he received as a result of this confession. He reminded the Slattery Inquiry that every high-profile murder brings some crazies out of the woodwork.

Was Vandenberg mentally disturbed? Certainly he was depressed and drinking heavily in the weeks before Megan was murdered. Was he protecting someone? It is possible he was protecting Paul Blake, who received $10,000 shortly after the murder but has an alibi for the night of the murder.

Vandenberg was terrified of George Canellis, the man who claims he was originally asked to do the murder but didn't. Canellis does not have an alibi for the night of the murder, something the police neglected to check, until it was revealed by the Kalajzich legal team at the Slattery Inquiry.

Andrew Kalajzich believes Canellis was the man who entered his house, shot his wife and fired two bullets at him but missed. On his website he says: 'I allege that Canellis had the gun, the silencer, the contract for murder plus the experience and skill to carry it out. Canellis was confident enough to state "I am serious in telling the jury I am prepared to murder but not to lie to protect myself."'

*

In April or May 1988 (some time during the trial) Vandenberg was interviewed for a television special by Steve Barratt of Channel 9. In an unprecedented move, a television crew entered the Witness Protection Unit where they filmed an hour-long interview. Because of his suicide a few days later, it was never broadcast. I viewed it at the Slattery Inquiry.

Alive, Vandenberg reminded me of a mouse – a timid, tidy little man with big ears, who twitched and blinked and spoke rapidly when he was excited. When Steve Barratt asked him about the actual shooting he looked down at the floor shrugged his shoulders and said 'I can't talk about that.'

Was this because he had had difficulty in coming to terms with it, or because he wasn't there?

Towards the end of his long suicide note, he becomes less coherent. Here he mentions killing a cat and sending a dog to the RSPCA:

> Do you know that I ran over a cat and killed maybe [in the] early sixties and that took me days to get over.
>
> I once lived in Gladesville and had a mongrel dog but I loved it and sent it to the RSPCA because my little nephew kept picking up and eating the shit and that took me a long time to get over.

*

I was looking for the truth – some sort of confession in Vandenberg's suicide note. It is apparent that the truth has not been told from the following cryptic message:

> I saw a priest for the first time in this unit about last September and have not seen once since. Tonight Brother John promised to send one, Father Terry McDonald, to see me but unfortunately that's too late I felt I could have poured by complete heart out to him without restricting the man so the final pieces would have fallen in place for Bob [Inkster] as to why a respectable man came to get himself involved in such a disastrous mess. I often hoped [J] might have come on his own but never had the heart to tell [M] not to come as I had too much feeling for her as my sister-in-law to say I couldn't talk in front of her.

Is this not a cry from a man who wants to unburden himself and tell someone – a priest or his brother – the whole story? I was fascinated by the phrase: 'I could have poured *my* complete heart out to him.' It looked like a Freudian slip, and I had to check it against photographs of the original letter to be sure this was what he wrote. 'By heart' suggests something learned by rote, not necessarily the truth, so that the 'pieces would have fallen in place for Bob' (Detective Inkster).

Vandenberg has nothing but praise for the man who arrested him, Detective Inkster. He thanks Inkster and another detective for their honesty in this whole matter' and says that:

> [N]othing was based on verbals … They had every right to treat me with contempt but always acted the thorough gentlemen and if this case does not give them the credit they deserve then the police force would need to be disband[ed] and restructured as they have proven to be the most honest people I have had the great pleasure (unfortunately under terrible) circumstances. They never once suggested any threat nor did they ever offer me inducements they only ever asked me to search my conscience for the truth so as to make it easier to live with myself.

He also sings the praises of various other officers within the corrective services department: 'They have generally done more than should ever be asked. I do hope that some of this letter will sometime be produced …'

*

Vandenberg concludes his suicide note with a further message to his brother and his sister-in-law:

> I should mention as it's unfortunately a very big part in my last few years and that I'm now crying over and that was the loss of my very special nephew Anthony who as a person meant more to me in my life than anything else had and when his end came that was the beginning of my end.
>
> I hope it's not looked down on by his father but I have to say I've missed you I am now so totally worn out I can hardly see the letters so I have to finish this off so …
>
> Please don't let them treat me as a crim if I'm dead I should return to the bosom of my family as I serve my time very hard but unable to go any further.
>
> For the family my appreciation would be that I've shamed you while I lived please don't allow that to happen while I'm dead. I hope to take my last breaths with Anthony if you don't mind [J] and [M] and kids.
>
> PS
>
> I intendent [*sic*] leaving no note at all but felt I couldn't leave the family as well as WPU and Bob Inkster with some explanation because guessing and knowing is a different matter.

The primary message conveyed to me by the note is that Bill Vandenberg was a heartbroken man, grieving for the love of his life, his young nephew Anthony. I can't help but be moved by this. After Anthony's death, Vandenberg began drinking heavily. He was vulnerable. It was important to him to apologise to everyone concerned for the 'mess' he had left them to deal with – in fact, he seems obsessively concerned about this (for example, the nappy, the dog shit his nephew ate, as well as the more relevant concerns for Orrock's and Megan's family). His involvement in the murder of Megan (and I have no doubt he was involved) helped make his suicide inevitable.

In his confessions he called himself the 'triggerman' (not the shooter or the murderer). According to the Macquarie Dictionary the word 'trigger' means 'to start or precipitate something, as in a chain of events or scientific reaction'. He knew little about guns. I cannot imagine him holding a rifle with a silencer attached to Megan's head and firing two bullets into her brain, then calmly aiming at Andrew (or his pillow) and firing two more bullets. Perhaps he felt responsible for initiating the chain of events that led to Megan's murder and the 'mess' he created afterwards.

I hope the truth did not die with Vandenberg. If there is reasonable doubt about the role Vandenberg played in this murder, we must ask: Who was he protecting, and why?

Sources

Austin, K., & Fife-Yeomans, J., *Injustice*, Random House, 1998.

Whitton, E., *Trial by Voodoo*, Random House, 1994.

I.C.A.C. Report on The Use of Informers, January, 1993.

Report of the Inquiry into the conviction of Andrew Kalajzich, Hon. John Slattery AO QC, 30 May 1995.

Andrew Kalajzich's website: www.kalajzich.com

Tom Domican's website: www.tomdomican.com.au

Atonement
The Mystery of Constance Kent

Lucy Sussex

I. Teaching French to a Murderess

Oh give attention, you maidens dear
My dying moments are drawing near
When I am sentenced alas to die
Upon a gallows gloomy and high.
Oh what a sight it will be to see
A maiden die on the fatal tree

My father belongs to the quiet older Australian type, but he has encountered some interesting people, from Edith Sitwell to Eddie Mabo. He doesn't say much about them, but what he does is pithy and apposite. Take the one murderer he met (as far as I know): Pauline Parker, best known from the film *Heavenly Creatures*. In 1954, when she and Juliet Hulme murdered Pauline's mother, it was quite the most notorious crime ever to hit the quiet city of Christchurch, New Zealand and somehow worse because Juliet's father was Rector of Canterbury University. Hence my family connection: because Pauline and Juliet were very bright, there was concern about their education, post-conviction. Various professors at Canterbury would periodically visit Paparua Prison, where Pauline was held, carrying textbooks.

Said John Garrett, Professor of English: 'If you're an ordinary student, you get an ordinary tutor. Kill someone, and you get the professor.'

So Dad taught a murderess French. 'She was a very nice young woman,' he recalls.

I wonder if anyone ever said the same about Constance Kent. She and Pauline Parker are linked by the act of murder, for which both were convicted, though nearly a century and a hemisphere apart. Both were aged sixteen at the time, and both were charged with killing family members. They served prison sentences, and were then released, apparently successfully rehabilitated. Although Juliet Hulme was revealed in the 1990s to have a new identity as the best-selling historical crime author Ann Perry, the media firestorm which accompanied this revelation quite failed to locate Pauline Parker. There were rumours that she had become a nun, that she worked in a bookshop, but nothing definite. Unless Pauline Parker re-emerges, then she has another point of comparison with Constance Kent: a vanishing act. Constance Kent, upon her release, migrated from her native England to Australia and a successful new life. Not even when she was 100, and being photographed for the occasion by the Sydney daily papers, did anyone make the comparison between the sweet old lady and the Victorian murderess so notorious she was modelled in wax for Tussaud's Chamber of Horrors.

There is, though, one marked point of difference between the Misses Kent and Parker, and it has to do with the nature of their victim. Pauline committed matricide, killing her mother; Constance Kent fratricide, killing her three-year-old stepbrother. Killing within the family is associated with primal taboos; killing a child is popularly regarded as the most heinous of crimes. Powerful and irrational notions of defencelessness or innocence are involved, with murdered children idealised as angelic, even in this secular age. These attitudes are thoroughly complicated when the killer is also a child or little more than one. Consider the killers of James Bulger, for instance. Their post-prison prognosis is unknown, but they could do worse than emulate Constance Kent, of whom one biography was entitled *Saint – With Red Hands?* After her release from prison she spent the rest of her long life alleviating the sufferings of others.

Atonement? Surely. Yet was it for her crime she atoned, or for someone else's? There was no doubt whodunnit in the Bulger case, nor with Parker and Hulme. But the circumstances surrounding the 1860 death of three-year-old (Francis) Savill Kent remain singularly murky, the investigation being either deliberately obstructed, or bungled by police. Two individuals were brought before the magistrates, Constance and the Kent family nursemaid, Elizabeth Gough, but evidence proved insufficient for either to be charged. Five years later Constance admitted to the murder, but her confession was dubious: at the very least, the child did not die in the manner she described. The confession precluded a full and adversarial trial, but her account of the murder could (and should) have been demolished by any competent legal or forensic authority. That it was allowed to stand, that she then was sentenced to twenty years in jail, was due to a general unwillingness to address the question: why would she lie in her confession? To this date, the murder has never been reconstructed satisfactorily, though many have tried.

It remains, like Constance herself, a mystery. The whole affair is obscure and utterly gross. About the only facts not in dispute are that, early one morning in the English summer of 1860, little Savill Kent was found crammed down a privy outside his family's rented house in the small village of Road, near Bath. He had a stab wound in one side and his throat had been cut – neither injury being the cause of death.

II. The Facts of the Road Murder

To the dirty closet I did him take,
The deed I done caused my heart to ache,
Into the soil I did him thrust down,
Where asleep in death he was quickly found

The privy was a usual destination during the Victorian era for unwanted, illegitimate babies, given the lack of reliable contraception and the premium on female virtue. However Savill was legitimate, a wanted, much loved, indeed spoilt child, and nearly four years of age. It was other children in the large Kent family who were unloved, neglected, even by our standards abused. The household comprised various servants; paterfamilias Samuel Savill Kent, an Inspector of Factories, aged fifty-nine; his second wife Mary, over twenty years his junior and eight months pregnant; and their three children, Mary Amelia, aged nearly five, Savill and the baby Eveline. Also present were the four surviving children from Samuel Kent's first marriage: Mary Ann, Elizabeth (both in their late twenties), Constance and her brother William, fifteen.

Those who advocate a return to Victorian values may be well advised to examine the Kents. Samuel Kent was a man aspiring upwards in class, notably expressed in the country houses he rented, which were imposing and rather beyond his means. He was proud of the maternal family name of Savill, which was associated with property, although he came from a manufacturing and trade background. The father of his first wife, Mary Ann Windus, was both a merchant and a member of the Royal Society of Antiquaries. Kent married Mary Ann in 1829, and they had ten children in sixteen years. By the time of Constance's birth in 1844, Mary Ann had become an invalid, and Kent hired a nursemaid-cum-governess, Mary Drewe Pratt, a grocer's daughter, to assist in the house. The following year, William was born, and Kent assumed an unusual living arrangement: he and his wife occupied bedrooms at opposite ends of the house. Constance, it was recalled, 'slept in a room inside of the governess, who always locked the door between when she came to bed. Mr Kents bed & dressing room were on the other side & when he was away the governess said she was frightened to be alone & Constance had to sleep with her.' (1929 letter)

The home life of the Kents did not escape the attention of neighbours and Samuel Kent's employers, both being censorious. Nonetheless Kent would not give up Miss Pratt. For some years the curious and tense *ménage à trois* continued, the wife withdrawn in her rooms, the children sent to boarding schools (when Kent could pay the bills), the governess mistress of the house and of Kent as well. Then, in 1852, Mary Ann Kent died. After the conventional period of mourning, Kent and Mary Pratt married and soon began a new family.

Mary Pratt had been an affectionate and fond governess to Constance and even, it was claimed in a 1929 letter, estranged her from her 'poor mamma' as part of the family power game. Yet when her own children were born, the situation changed. The second family were preferred, the older children slighted. Mary Ann junior and Elizabeth were too meek to protest, but Constance had more spirit and was consequently frequently chastised: '2 days were spent shut up in a room with dry bread & milk & water for tea, at other times she would be stood up in a corner in the hall

In the magistrate's court, Peter Edlin, Constance's lawyer, had told Whicher that, 'The steps you have taken will be such as to ruin her life' – a prophetic statement, as five years later Constance admitted her guilt. She had undergone a religious conversion, the result of living in an Anglo-Catholic convent, whose priest, the Reverend Arthur Wagner, was an enthusiast for the confessional. What she actually said to him in the sanctity of the confession box is unknown; Wagner refused to reveal it. Nonetheless, he carried a letter by Constance to the authorities that made her confession public. The motive was given as hatred for her stepmother although, perversely, Constance stated that both Mary Kent and her father 'had always been kind to [me] personally'.

Because Constance pleaded guilty, she avoided a full trial, which might have subjected her confession to scrutiny. Moreover, she refrained from pleading insanity, which in many observers' minds was the only possible explanation for her behaviour. Weeping, the judge sentenced her to death, and in anticipation of a hanging, a last testament broadside ballad, in dreadful doggerel, was composed and circulated. It is quoted throughout this essay. However, given Constance's youth at the time of the offence, the penalty was commuted to life imprisonment. She spent twenty years in jail, despite several appeals for clemency.

III. WHODUNNIT: THE EXPLANATIONS

My own dear father they did suspect
That he would suffer they did expect,
I was apprehended, but I got clear
Tho' I was the murderess of my brother dear

A number of writers have tried to explain the mystery of Road House, of whom perhaps the most famous were Charles Dickens and Wilkie Collins. Wrote Dickens to Collins, privately and salaciously:

> Mr. Kent intriguing with the nursemaid, poor little child awakes in crib and sits up contemplating blissful proceedings. Nursemaid strangles him then and there. Mr. Kent gashes body to mystify discoverers and disposes of same.

Both the *Times* and the *Bath Chronicle* published articles that, without naming Kent, contained the same implication. Indeed, the local papers were a mine of tabloid gossip and speculation on the case. True crime writer Bernard Taylor, who has examined British Government files on the case, notes that the Home Secretary, Sir George Lewis, received a letter making the same accusation and wrote on it: 'This anonymous writer is not far off the mark.'

Kerry Greenwood, editor of this book, also concurs with the theory, stating: 'It would not be the first or last time that a child was killed for that reason.' So do Yseult Bridges, author of *Saint – With Red Hands?* (1954), and Mary Hartman, who discusses the case in *Victorian Murderesses* (1977). There is much, indeed, to support it. Kent was applying at the time for a much needed promotion which, given his reputation, a further scandal could have scuttled. The fact that the child was suffocated, apparently with a flannel found in the privy, suggests an attempt to keep him quiet that went too far. It was recalled that little Savill was a tattle-tale to his Mamma. Samuel Kent's own sexual history shows that he was not averse to affairs under his roof. Indeed the household had an unusually high turnover of female servants, due – it was gossiped – to Kent's sexual harassment of them.

Moreover, both Kent and Elizabeth Gough acted suspiciously after the child was missed. They both made comments, later reported to police, that the child's blanket was missing. Yet this was not apparent at the time: the bed was as neat as if the child had been drawn out from under the covers, with the counterpane on top concealing the lack of blanket. In fact, the blanket was found thrown over the body. It would seem that the bed had been re-made, most likely to conceal the struggle that would have occurred if Savill was smothered there.

The accounts of the Road murder show that Kent resisted attempts by the police to invade or impugn his domestic sanctum. Class factors were involved here: police tended to come from the lower social strata and their attentions provoked anxiety – they were powerful, yet 'other'. Dickens' magazine *Household Words* praised Whicher and his ilk, yet also commented in 1859: 'It is never a wise or safe proceeding to put arbitrary authority and power in the hands of the lower classes [...] we shall never have a well-administered police system till gentlemen hold commissions in the police as they do in the army.' The writer of this article was

Charles Allston Collins, brother of Wilkie and Dickens' son-in-law. However, even allowing for class bias, and grief, Kent's behaviour towards the police was odd – as if he were systematically impeding or interfering with the investigation

Kent was able to pull his Inspector's rank (equal to that of magistrate) when dealing with the local police, convincing them that outsiders had killed his child. He even locked two constables 'below stairs' in Road House for several hours which, as several commentators have noted, would have given him the opportunity to destroy evidence. At the (unsatisfactory) inquest, only two members of the household were questioned, Constance and William Kent. As for Sergeant Whicher, Kent briefed him about his family, selectively volunteering or withholding information. Whicher learnt that Constance's mother had suffered from insanity, with the implication that it had been transmitted to her daughter; he learnt about her interest in Madeline Smith; and her unfeminine behaviour in running away. He clearly was not told that the Kents were in the habit of locking Constance up or else he would not have tried to force a confession by incarceration. Constance had learnt to deal with such treatment imaginatively: when 'the governess put her down in a dark wine cellar, she fell on a heap of straw and fancied herself in the dungeon of a great castle, a prisoner taken in battle fighting for Bonnie Prince Charlie & to be taken to the block next morning.' (1929 letter)

It is possible that Samuel Kent killed his child and tried first to cover up by accusing an outsider, even going so far as to name various of the local villagers (with whom he enjoyed unfriendly relations) as responsible for the crime. Then, when it could no longer be denied that the killer was a member of his own household, he threw suspicion on his daughter Constance, whom he attempted to portray as mad. From this reading he emerges as a truly monstrous paterfamilias. The difficulty with it is that Constance confessed to the murder, and continued to maintain her guilt, even sixty years after the events.

Kent was the first to voice suspicions of Constance, yet evidence of animosity between her and Savill seemed minor. She teased but also romped with him; he in turn made her simple bead jewellery.

In *The Great Crime of 1860*, an account of the case written by a family friend, Dr Joseph Stapleton, Mary Ann Kent's madness was discussed, with the claim being made that she had gone insane in 1835, nine years before Constance's birth. The implications of this assertion were appalling – as the Victorianist Richard Altick has noted, 'her loss of mind did not deter her husband from begetting six more [children] on her body.' Later writers on the case have dismissed claims of Mary Ann Kent's madness. She appears most likely to have been depressed, hardly surprising given her ill-health, seclusion and the affair her husband was blatantly conducting with the family governess, the real power in the household.

The most likely reason why Mary Ann was labelled as insane was that this gave credence to the idea of Constance as a mad murderess. It also exonerated Samuel and his second Mary of the charge of driving their daughter to the desperate act. Had she not tried to run away four years previously? What she was fleeing would be, by our standards, abusive. Even Dr Bucknill, who examined her for signs of insanity and found none, noted the Kent family's 'depths of household misery'.

Kent's liaison with Mary Pratt meant isolation for the family before his first wife's death, which blighted the social lives and marriage prospects of the two eldest daughters. Only men would visit, for conventional Victorian women could be tainted by association with an infamous house:

> The two eldest girls made friends with some young people … but as they would not call at the house they were forbidden to meet them, the same ban was placed on the younger children. One day Constance and her brother were supposed to be attending to their little gardens … they heard some merry laughter from a neighbouring garden, they went to the hedge & looked over longingly at the children playing … they were invited to join but were afraid, they were seen and their disobedience punished, the little gardens were uprooted and trampled down, Constance made some futile events to revive hers. No pets were allowed, two little tropical birds sent by the eldest son [who died before the murder] to his sisters were consigned to a cold back room & died. The few relatives who visited got into disgrace over the governess & their stay was brief. (1929 letter)

After Kent married Pratt, the household was no longer the object of censure, but it was nonetheless an unpleasant place. When the twelve-year-old Constance ran away with her brother William, it was because her life was 'dull and monotonous, she was not wanted, everyone was against her'. (1929 letter) It is hard not to regard Samuel and Mary Kent as physically and mentally cruel to Constance. That she should come to hate her stepmother is not unusual for a teenager in a blended family, even without the considerable provocations detailed. But did she hate her enough to kill Savill? Such was her private motive, confessed to Bucknill. The public motive, as reported in newspapers, was to avenge the wrongs done to her mother, wrongs for which her father was at least as guilty as her stepmother.

Bernard Taylor, re-examining the evidence in the 1980s, came up with a novel explanation for the murder. Samuel Kent and Elizabeth Gough had indeed been 'intriguing', not in a nursery but in a spare room. While they were absent, Constance took Savill, with the intent of murder, but accidentally smothered him as she carried him downstairs in the blanket. She stabbed the child in the privy, chosen because of her act of defiance four years previously, then returned to her room up the back, using the servants' stairs. In the meantime, Kent and Gough returned to the nursery and found Savill missing. Kent immediately guessed that Constance was responsible and went to the privy, where he found the body. In a futile attempt to direct the murder enquiry elsewhere, he cut his own child's throat.

The major difficulty with this explanation is that it requires incredible presence of mind of Kent. After what must have been a considerable shock, he had both to intuit his daughter's guilt and find the body. It should be remembered that when Savill was discovered missing, nobody in the household immediately accused Constance. The idea that Kent was able to conduct a search, even with his dark lantern (the Victorian version of a torch), which was later missed from the house, without waking a household full of sleepers, seems unbelievable. That two people should, quite independently, mutilate the same corpse also beggars disbelief.

Here is an explanation that is both clear and likely. Something took place in the nursery which woke a frightened Savill Kent. He was accidentally smothered in an attempt to shut him up. A panic ensued, a desire to get the body out of the house, out of sight and away from immediate detection. The body was carried downstairs in the blanket and when the kitchen door was opened it revealed the knives. The child was taken to the privy, either to suggest an outsider was involved (who would not have known about the splashboard) or, if we assume Samuel Kent was involved, to incriminate Constance. There the body was mutilated in a kind of killing frenzy. In the nursery, Savill's bed was re-made to conceal the signs of a struggle.

Yet none of the explanations I have outlined address the question: if you are guilty, why lie in your confession? And if you are innocent, why confess? The study of criminal behaviour has considerably advanced since the Victorian era, yet an examination of the literature concerning adolescents killing within the family does not yield ready answers. It is very rare for girls to kill, and thus difficult to generalise from other cases. However, when murder occurs it is generally the result of parental abuse, the exceptions being when the killer is mentally ill or a psychopath. A fourth exception might be made for cases of *folie à deux*, where two children appear to have egged each other on to kill, as with the Bulger case, Parker-Hulme, and Mary Bell (although this case also involved parental sexual abuse). If Constance acted alone, as she claimed, then the most persuasive reason would be her abusive family background. Certainly, her father and stepmother were physically and mentally cruel to her. However, the crucial trigger event – something occurring immediately before the crime, escalating tension to the point where the only way out is murder – is missing. In fact, all reports had the Kent household in an unusual state of serenity. Something may have driven Constance Kent to murder, yet we do not know what it was.

IV. The Confession

Long, long I pined in deep distress
At length the murder I did confess,
The Vile Road murder, as you may see,
Committed was by no one but me

Four versions, some fragmentary, exist of Constance's confession. One was a letter she wrote to Sir John Eardley Wilmot, who had been active in her defence. It contained an account of how the crime was committed, but unfortunately the relevant pages from this letter are missing. The other versions are a police report by Inspector Frederick Williamson, which discusses the Wilmot confession, and a letter by Bucknill, written at Constance's request, which was widely reprinted in the press. Some details were also repeated in court by Miss Gream, Lady Superior of Wagner's Brighton convent.

The gist of the Bucknill letter, the most extensive account, is as follows. Constance declared she stole her father's razor, the sole instrument used, and waited until the household was asleep. She went into the nursery without waking anyone there, withdrew Savill's blanket from between sheet and counterpane, and removed the child from his bed. She carried him downstairs, wrapped in the blanket, and out the living-room window. Savill was still asleep. In the privy she lighted a candle she had previously secreted and 'inflicted the wound in the throat. She said she thought the blood would never come, and that the child was not killed, so she thrust the razor into the left side and put the body with the blanket round it into the vault [of the privy].' That done, she returned to her room, washed two spots of blood off her nightdress and went to bed. The razor she cleaned and returned to her father's wardrobe, burning her nightdress some days afterwards when she discovered the blood was still visible. She stated that nobody had assisted her in the crime nor after the fact. Williamson's report adds the detail that she stabbed Savill twice, but otherwise agrees with Bucknill's.

It cannot be known how much white noise is contained in these accounts, nor what (in the case of Bucknill or Gream) leading questions were asked. As various modern commentators have noted, the howdunnit is ridiculous. Taylor, although believing Constance guilty, notes a number of discrepancies. If the razor was, as claimed, the only instrument used, then she was lying: it is impossible to stab with such a weapon, and the more likely implement was a sharp knife, such as the ones left so conveniently outside the kitchen door. It is difficult to believe that she got the large child downstairs and out the window (which was heavy and had a tendency to stick at the 6-inch mark) without waking him. Furthermore, to kill a child in the manner described – inflicting a clean and deep ear-to-ear cut – required some expertise with the razor. Blood would come immediately, and in drenching arterial spurts that would cause far more than two bloodspots. If

Williamson's report was correct, she claimed to have stabbed the child twice, not once as was the case. Moreover, the blanket was found not wrapped around the body but on top of it.

The tragedy is that this unreliable and fantastic account went unquestioned, particularly by Dr Joshua Parsons, who had performed the original autopsy. Faced with the confession, he withdrew from his contention that Savill had been suffocated. Bucknill certainly knew that Constance was lying about her motive, at least in her public statements. She did this, he later stated, from 'regard for the feelings and interests of her father and brother'. Yet he seems not to have drawn from this little white lie the inference that the rest of the confession might also have been dubious.

Why, if you admit to a murder, lie in its details if your confession is genuine? It is possible that Constance was so traumatised by the event that she blotted it from her memory (in the way that Ann Perry/Juliet Hulme now claims she did). At the time, however, Constance showed no sign of trauma, appearing stolid, mousy and teenaged. Yet how could she not have been in a state of distress at the time of her confession? She had spent the five years since the death shut out of her home, as if she were indeed the guilty party. Residing at a succession of schools, she was constantly pointed out as the girl suspected of an appalling murder.

Finally, seeking refuge, Constance enrolled as 'Emilie' Kent in a genteel nursing course at the High Anglican convent of St Mary's in Brighton. On her twenty-first birthday she achieved adult status, and also inherited £800 from her mother. She tried to give the money to charity, via Wagner, founder of the convent (who knew her real identity) but he refused. She then took to leaving smaller amounts of the inheritance in the church alms-boxes, which Wagner quietly retrieved and put aside. Wagner's other, more significant refusal was to her request for confirmation in the Anglican church. Confirmation can be refused if the applicant has not been baptised or is not a churchgoer. We do not know Wagner's reasons, but it would seem most likely that he considered her to be guilty of murder, and thus not in a state of grace. Without confirmation Constance could not receive communion. Although surrounded by the religious, she was excluded from their rite of fellowship.

Wagner and Miss Gream have both been accused of pressuring Constance to confess, although a sacramental confession by its nature should be free and voluntary, not extracted under duress. Certainly, the psychological pressure of refusing confirmation/communion to a religious convert would have been powerful: Wagner was effectively performing an act of religious blackmail. In any event, Constance confessed, and even at the age of eighty-five (according to an anonymous letter from Sydney thought to be written by Constance), maintained her guilt, albeit in the third person:

> ... she planned and carried out her most callous and brutal crime, one so vile & unnatural that people could not believe it possible for a young girl, in fact she failed to realise till she came under religious influence 5 years later when filled with deep sorrow and remorse she told the clergyman of the place that in order to free others of any suspicion cast on them, it was a duty to make a public confession of her guilt.

What if Constance's confession was false? The wording of the Sydney letter is curious, particularly the use of the word 'realise': 'she planned and carried out her most callous and brutal crime, one so vile & unnatural that people could not believe it possible for a young girl, in fact she failed to realise till she came under religious influence 5 years later.' She failed to realise what? That her crime was appalling, or that she had committed it?

It also should be noted that the details of the crime, the how as well as the whodunnit, were much canvassed in the media and in several books. Indeed, one website argues that Constance's wording in her account of the murder would appear to derive in part from Stapleton's *The Great Crime of 1860*. Little in the confession, in fact, could not have been drawn from such sources, and the confirmation of a second- rather than a first-hand account, would support the case for her innocence or amnesia. It is just possible, however, that Constance, having implicated herself following leading questions from Wagner and Gream, deliberately made an inaccurate confession. She may have thought its flaws would prevent its acceptance, but was tragically caught out when nobody queried the errors.

Another reason for a false confession might have been to protect someone. Constance did admit in her confessional statements that she had 'regard for the feelings and interests of her father and brother'. It has been argued that her reason for not pleading insanity was William, whose prospects could have been blighted by evidence of hereditary insanity in the Kent family. Moreover, Constance declared that she confessed 'in order to free others of any suspicion'. It had been initially suspected that Constance and William might have been joint killers, which is why they were the only members of the household questioned at the inquest. Had they not run away together, something in which Constance had been the instigator? William did indeed have reason for detesting Savill, as he (the eldest surviving son and heir) was effectively being displaced by the younger boy. Witnesses attested that the Kents had disparaged William and praised Savill to their faces, declaring that William would never amount to anything. Moreover, Mary Kent, on the pretext of William's muddy boots, had banned him from using the front staircase; he had to use the back, the servant's stair, as if he indeed were no more than a menial. If Constance had opportunity, then so too did he, and a stronger motive. Yet it was widely felt that William was too timid to be a killer. He was too much of a girl, said Elizabeth Gough.

It is clear that Constance went through some kind of crisis at St Mary's, which Yseult Bridges believes was a crisis of faith. Given her behaviour at the time, a breakdown seems likely, the symptoms being cloaked by her religious conversion. Yet she had stoically survived a most unhappy childhood, and it must be wondered what could have triggered such a collapse. Her confessor, Wagner, was in his late thirties and on the photographic evidence quite personable. Constance might have been in love with him. Perhaps she confessed as the ultimate attention-getter?

Or did she perhaps 'realise' that something was 'vile & unnatural' about her, something directly attributable to her family background? In the Sydney letter, she made an extraordinary admission: she and William showed physiological signs of congenital syphilis (inherited from the parent). '[H]e had very pronounced Hutchinsonian teeth, the youngest daughter's teeth were also slightly so affected, may not the fact that five children pined (merasmus) [*sic*] in infancy, have been owing to the same causes'. Part of this diagnosis is wrong: Marasmus, a gradual wasting (as in malnutrition), is not normally associated with disease. Infant mortality was high in the Victorian era, and the loss of five infants would not have been excessive. However, Hutchinson's teeth, in which the incisors are narrow, notched and sometimes appear striped 'as humbugs', is hard to mistake. If only Constance and William were affected, it would suggest an *in utero* transmission, with Mary Ann Kent becoming infected late in her married life, most probably via her husband.

In the Sydney letter, Constance writes as the professional nurse, clinical, remote, detached. Yet a terrible stigma was attached to the disease, which she would have felt personally. Had Constance also possessed 'very pronounced Hutchinsonian teeth', it could have prevented her from training as a nurse. In popular belief, syphilis was a sentence of death or insanity. The stress of living with and concealing the affliction would have been considerable. She must have become aware of the diagnosis at some stage in her hospital work, but when? And what was her reaction?

What if Constance Kent learnt at St Mary's that she (and to a greater extent her brother) were visibly affected by, and possibly carriers of, one of the most feared and incurable of all diseases, made worse because (like AIDS) it was transmitted by venery? She showed signs of shame and guilt and tried to give away her mother's money – as if by doing this she could escape an even nastier inheritance. Such a discovery would have been devastating; and given the other pressures she was under, strong cause for a breakdown.

There may, of course, have been a much simpler explanation. False confessors usually fall into four categories: attention-seeking; pathologically obsessed with a particular crime (usually of a sexual nature; the largest group of confessors falsely claim to be rapists); sufferers from Munchausen's Syndrome, who cannot tell the difference between fantasy and reality; and the insane. None of these seems to fit Constance Kent. Psychologist Frank Payne, however, notes a fifth category of false confessor. He says that if we discount attention-seekers, most false confessions are

> driven by depression. People who are depressed feel very negative about themselves and the world. Some feel a need to punish themselves (hence slashing yourself up, making decisions that you know you will regret, etc.). Sometimes the guilt feelings become so bad that actual delusions develop – untrue and sometimes bizarre ideas.

> People can believe they are demonic, or rotting inside. So someone suffering from serious depression can actually come to believe they are guilty of a crime, and confess in the context of this delusion. Others would know they aren't guilty, but come to the conclusion that they should confess anyway, just in order to be punished. (A bit like flagellating yourself – often done by depressive religious types to 'purge' themselves, but driven by intense guilt feelings).

He adds that Constance Kent 'sounds like a prime candidate for depression and could fit either model'. Of all the possible explanations I have canvassed for her extraordinary confession, this one is perhaps the saddest.

V. The Aftermath

Farewell my father, my father dear,
I know for me you will shed a tear,
Yes, your wicked daughter in shame must die,
For that cruel murder on a gallows high

I see the hangman before me stand
Ready to seize me by the law's command
When my life is ended on the fatal tree
Then will be clear'd up all mystery

Constance Kent was released in 1885, with the now middle-aged Wagner present to escort her into a new life. Her stepmother had died in 1866, her father in 1872, leaving William Kent head of the family. His biographer, A.J. Harrison, notes that he had reconciled with his father and sincerely grieved for him. William studied at King's College, London and began to make a name for himself as a naturalist. When his father died, he gained the responsibility of his step-siblings who, besides Mary Amelia and Eveline, comprised Acland, born a month after the murder, and Florence, born the following year. In 1884, William, who had informally changed his surname to Saville-Kent, his wife (another Mary Ann) and Mary Amelia emigrated to Australia. The two eldest Kent daughters were settled and middle-aged in England, but Acland,

Florence and Eveline followed William to Australia the year after. With them went Constance, now known as Ruth Emilie (or Emilia) Kaye. Of the many curious things about the Road Murder, one of the oddest is that a convicted murderess should, so soon after her release, chaperone her victim's siblings on a voyage across the world. They must have been singularly forgiving, feeling her to be no threat.

Acland died young in 1887, with William getting special leave to attend his deathbed, and the other Kent children settled uneventfully in Australia. William became a noted marine biologist, working in various Australian colonies, with Constance generally accompanying him. She was in Melbourne in 1890 when an outbreak of typhoid epidemic led to a call for volunteer nurses. In volunteering she rediscovered her old calling and began formal nurse training at the Alfred Hospital, graduating in 1892. She worked in a variety of senior and responsible positions, becoming matron of a private hospital in Perth, matron also at Prince Henry Hospital in Sydney, the Leprosarium in Long Bay and the Industrial School of Girls in Parramatta. As she wrote in the Sydney letter, she 'single handed fought her way to a good position and made a home for herself where she was well liked and respected …'

Constance Kent celebrated her centenary in 1944, for which she received a telegram from the King and a visit from the Anglican Archbishop of Sydney, bearing flowers. She died not long after and was cremated at Rookwood Cemetery in Sydney. It can only be stated that the jury remains out on her case. She was either murderess or martyr; perpetrator of an appalling crime or victim of an equally appalling miscarriage of justice. Yet there can be no doubt that she made something positive of her subsequent life. Her last letter, although written just before her hundredth birthday, is nevertheless concerned with others, notably the difficulty of buying good Christmas presents for children during wartime. Whatever Constance Kent may have been, Emilie Kent emerges as an admirable, yes, even very nice woman.

Sources

Richard Altick, *Victorian Studies in Scarlet*, London, Dent, 1972.

Yseult Bridges, *Saint – With Red Hands?* The Chronicle of a Great Crime, London, Macmillan, 1954.

[Charles Allston Collins], 'Some Wild Ideas', *Household Words*, 30 April 1859, 505–10.

'The Dreadful Murder at Frome', http://www.askwhy.co.uk/awfrome/09/rodemurder/html

A.J. Harrison, *Savant of the Australian Seas: William Saville-Kent (1845–1908) and Australian Fisheries*, Hobart, Tasmanian Historical Research Association, 1997.

Mary S. Hartman, *Victorian Murderesses: A True History of Thirteen Respectable French and English Women Accused of Unspeakable Crimes*, New York, Schocken, 1977.

Judith Knelman, *Twisting in the Wind: The Murderess and the English Press*, University of Toronto Press, Toronto, 1998.

Ann Mitchell, *The Hospital South of the Yarra*, Melbourne, Alfred Hospital, 1977.

Francis Payne, email to Lucy Sussex, 19 October 2001.

John Rhode [Cecil Street], 'Constance Kent', in *Anatomy of Murder*, London, John Lane, 1936, 43–86.

Bernard Taylor, Cruelly Murdered: *Constance Kent and the Killing at Road Hill House*, London, Grafton, 1989.

'Trial and Sentence of Constance Kent', London, Disley [n. d.].

Notes on contributors

TOM AUSTEN is an author and historian. His recent work includes *Country Images, Western Australia* and *A Cry in the Wind.*

RICHARD BOURKE is a Melbourne barrister practising in the area of criminal law.

LINDY CAMERON, a convenor of Sisters in Crime Australia, is the author of *Golden Relic, Blood Guilt* and *Bleeding Hearts*. The latter won the Crime Readers' Vote award at the 2001 Ned Kelly Awards. Her essay 'Meaner than Fiction' appeared in the first volume of *On Murder*.

JOHN R. CARROLL'S titles include *No Way Back, The Clan, Cheaters* and *Hard Yards*. He currently resides with his wife in New York City.

NICK CAVE moved from Melbourne to London with his band The Birthday Party in 1990, and four years later he formed The Bad Seeds, with whom he has made eleven studio albums. He is author of the novel *And the Ass Saw the Angel*, and his *Complete Lyrics* was published last year by Penguin.

STEVE DOW is an author and journalist. His most recent title is *Gay*.

RICHARD EVANS is a lecturer in journalism at RMIT. He is currently writing a history of the Pyjama Girl murder mystery.

PIPPA KAY'S award-winning short stories have been published in anthologies, and she expects her book *Doubt and Conviction: The Kalajzich Inquiry* will be published in 2002.

PETER HADDOW works as a lecturer, script advisor for film and television, and private investigator. He is the author of *Hoddle Street: The Ambush and the Tragedy*. His story 'The Murder of Jessica Lang' appeared in the first volume of *On Murder*.

RICHARD HALL has written a number of books, including *Tiger General* and *Black Armband Days*. He recently edited *Sydney: An Oxford Anthology.*

ASHLEY HALPERN, a Melbourne barrister, began his legal life with Legal Aid and now deals with complex criminal cases in higher courts.

SHIRLEY HARDY-RIX has been a crime and court reporter on television and radio. She now lives in Melbourne with her husband, Brian Rix, a detective inspector with the Victoria Police.

TERRENCE GARDINER, with Vikki Petraitis, co-authors a true-crime column in the magazine *Crime Factory*. He has also written for the *Australian Police Journal*.

SHELLEY ROBERTSON is a specialist forensic pathologist based in Melbourne with over 14 years experience in murder investigations. She also has a law degree and frequently gives evidence in court.

VIKKI PETRAITIS is the bestselling author of *The Frankston Murders*. Her other titles include *The Phillip Island Murder, Rockspider*, and *Victims, Crimes and Investigators*. Vikki also writes for *Crime Factory* and the *Australian Police Journal*.

ANDREW RULE is a senior writer for the *Age*. With John Silvester, he has edited and published a series of 13 bestselling crime books. In 2000 he wrote and narrated a television documentary on the Jennifer Tanner case, a story he broke for the *Sunday Age* in 1996 and for which he won the Graham Perkin Australian Journalist of the Year Award. His story 'Presumed Dead', co-authored with John Silvester, appeared in the first volume of *On Murder*.

CRAIG SHERBORNE is a Melbourne journalist.

JOHN SILVESTER is an author and Crime Editor at the *Age*. He received the Quill Award for investigative reporting in 2000 and jointly won the Ned Kelly Award for true crime writing for his book *Underbelly 3* in the same year.

LUCY SUSSEX is currently writing *Cherchez les Femmes* about the first women writers of crime fiction.

RACHAEL WEAVER is completing a PhD on Frederick Bailey Deeming and the culture of late nineteenth-century Australia.

MARK WHITTAKER has co-authored, with Les Kennedy, *Sins of the Brother: The Definitive Story of Ivan Milat and the Backpacker Murders* and *Granny Killer: The Story of John Wayne Glover*. He and his wife, Amy Willesee, are currently writing a book on the royal family massacre in Nepal.

MARTIN WIENER is Jones Professor of History at Rice University, Houston, Texas. His essay on Annette Myers arises from research for a book on intersexual murder in Victorian England.

Publication details

Stories by Kerry Greenwood & Ashley Halpern, Richard Bourke, Rachael Weaver, John R. Carroll, Vikki Petraitis & Terrence Gardiner, Pippa Kay, Lucy Sussex, Shelley Robertson, Lindy Cameron, Shirley Hardy-Rix and Richard Evans appear for the first time in this anthology.

Tom Austen's 'Go Hang Yourself' is an extract from *The Stranger: Crime and Prejudice in Australia*, St George Books, 1992 © Tom Austen.

Nick Cave's Murder Ballads were published in *Complete Lyrics*, © Penguin (UK) 2001.

A longer version of Steve Dow's 'Keitho and Davo' appears in his book *Gay*, available at www.worldwriting.com. It was also extracted in *HQ* and the *Age*.

Peter Haddow's 'Jockey Smith's Last Stand' first appeared in the *Australian Police Journal* as 'Jockey Falls at Last' and was judged Best Crime Story of 1999.

Richard Hall's '"He Wasn't Afraid of Death": The Killing of Victor Chang' is an extract from *Tiger General: The Killing of Victor Chang*, © Pan Macmillan 1995.

Craig Sherborne's 'No Ordinary Neighbourhood' first appeared in the *Sunday Herald Sun*, October 2000.

'Lady's Day' and 'Pure Evil', by Andrew Rule and John Silvester, were published in *Underbelly 4*, Floradale Productions and Sly Ink, November 2000, © John Silvester and Andrew Rule.

A version of Mark Whittaker's 'Room For Disquiet' first appeared in the *Weekend Australian Magazine* as 'Bad Blood'.

A version of Martin Wiener's 'The Trial of Annette Myers' was delivered as a paper at AVSA, Ballarat, February 2001.